LIVING IN HOUSES

For my mother, Dru, for sharing her many stories of
Yearnor Cottage with me during lockdown.

RUTH DALTON

LIVING IN HOUSES

A Personal History of
English Domestic
Architecture

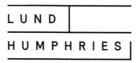

First published in 2022 by Lund Humphries

Lund Humphries
Huckletree Shoreditch
Alphabeta Building
18 Finsbury Square
London, EC2A 1AH
UK

www.lundhumphries.com

Living in Houses: A Personal History of English Domestic Architecture
© Ruth Dalton, 2022

ISBN (hardback): 978-1-84822-495-7
ISBN (eBook PDF): 978-1-84822-605-0
ISBN (eBook Mobi): 978-1-84822-607-4
ISBN (eBook ePub): 978-1-84822-606-7

A Cataloguing-in-Publication record for this book is available from the British Library.

All rights reserved. No part of this publication may be reproduced, stored in a retrieval system or transmitted in any form or by any means, electrical, mechanical or otherwise, without first seeking the permission of the copyright owners and publishers. Every effort has been made to seek permission to reproduce the images in this book. Any omissions are entirely unintentional, and details should be addressed to the publishers.

Ruth Dalton has asserted her right under the Copyright, Designs and Patent Act, 1988, to be identified as the Author of this Work.

Cover illustrations from top to bottom: extended elevations showing 93–97 Gower Street; Wharf Place (canal side); Haberdasher Street terraces; Gloucester Grove block and lift/stair tower; part of an Elm Village terrace.

All elevations © Ruth Dalton.

Copy edited by Pamela Bertram
Designed by Jacqui Cornish
Proofread by Patrick Cole
Cover designed by Mark Thomson
Set in Arnhem Pro and Supreme LL
Printed in Estonia

Contents

Acknowledgements	6
Introduction	9
1 Yearnor Cottage (1651): The Story of the Rural Vernacular Tradition	14
2 Priestpopple (*c*.1700): The Story of a Small-town Brewery Continuously Reinvented for its Time	38
3 Gower Street (1789): The Story of the Growth of Georgian London	58
4 Orchard Place (1824): The Story of a Regency Villa Fallen on Hard Times	76
5 Wharf Place (*c*.1902): The Story of Warehouse Loft-living and Yuppies	94
6 Bradwell Road (1902): The Story of an Edwardian Semi-detached House Absorbed into a New Town	120
7 Haberdasher Street (1912): The Story of Model Dwellings for Workers	136
8 The Gloucester Grove (1977) and North Peckham Estates: The Story of a London 'Sink Estate'	156
9 Elm Village (1984): The Story of the First Mixed Tenure (Fair Rent, Shared Ownership and Cost Sale) Estate	182
Epilogue	207
Notes	208
Bibliography	226
Index	234
Illustration Credits	240

Acknowledgements

Overall, Valerie Rose, my editor, for being so encouraging and enthusiastic about my 'lockdown project' idea; Andrew Stone, for taking photographs of Elm Village, Haberdasher Street, the remains of the Gloucester Grove Estate, London Wharf and Gower Street when my plans to visit and photograph them were stymied by various COVID-19 lockdowns; Igor Olszewski for his wonderful sketch illustrations at the beginning of each chapter; Marie Castro for undertaking some of the archival work, on my behalf, in London when COVID-19 restrictions prevented travel; Jane Quinn for her administrative assistance; The Lancaster Institute for the Contemporary Arts (LICA) at Lancaster University and the Beyond Imagination project (funded by Research England) for their financial support for this project.

Chapter 1: My mother, Drusilla Ellis, for sharing her stories about, and many old family photographs of, Yearnor Cottage; Bill Foster, the current owner of Yearnor Cottage, for his generosity in letting me look around again; Michael Hammett and Michael Chapman of the British Brick Society for their assistance and lengthy discussions on the origins of the bricks of Yearnor Cottage.

Chapter 2: Roger Higgins, who first converted the Priestpopple buildings into a house, for sharing his memories of this process with me and for giving me permission to use his original photographs; Neil Wilkinson and Mitch Forster, the current owners of Priestpopple, for lending me 'the yellow folder' of information about the house; Paul R. Ternent of the Northumberland Archives for his assistance in copying archival material when the archives were closed to the general public due to lockdown; Kate St Clair Gibson, Local Studies Librarian, at the Northumberland Archives for her help in tracking down the origins of the 1863–5 map of Hexham.

Chapter 3: Professor Sandra Kemp, Director of The Ruskin Library, Museum and Research Centre, for her assistance in tracking down the origins of Ruskin's quote about Gower Street (and generally all things 'Ruskin').

ACKNOWLEDGEMENTS

Chapter 4: David France of D. France Masonry Ltd, for reminding me of the process by which Orchard Place's column capital was replaced, and permission to use the photograph of the new column capital.

Chapter 5: Professor Laura Vaughan of University College London for helping me decipher George H. Duckworth's Booth notebook entry (being an expert on the Booth Maps); Paul Wood and Mike Brooke for helping to solve the mystery of the two London Wharf fire photographs; Debbie Smith, Heritage Coordinator, Tower Hamlets Local History Library and Archives, for her help on the origins and history of London Wharf.

Chapter 6: Roberta and Mark Musson, the present owners of the Bradwell Road house, for sharing the architect's original specification and their photographs of the house with me; Professor Julienne Hanson, former colleague and former neighbour in Loughton and always an inspiration; David Thom for speaking to Peggy Bodley, on my behalf, about her memories of the house when it was a post office, and to Peggy for sharing them; Barry Corbett and Hans van Lemmen (President of the Tiles and Architectural Ceramic Society) for their help in tracking down the manufacturers of the terracotta commemorative plaque; Barry Attoe of the Postal Museum for his assistance in trying to work out whether the rumours about the house being a post office during the war were correct (prior to Peggy's confirmation); and Dr Paul Cureton of Lancaster University for his assistance with scanning the original architect's specification.

Chapter 7: David Bartle, archivist of the Worshipful Company of Haberdashers; John Fowler of Stock Page Stock for his correspondence and generally for letting me pick his brains about Stock Page & Stock and Haberdasher Street; Steven Smith, architect and current resident of Haberdasher Street, for sharing his material and photographs of Haberdasher Street; Christopher Maunder Taylor, surveyor and former employee of Stock Page & Stock, for his memories of serving on the Haberdashers Property Committee during the period when the flats were being sold off; Tamara Atkin, the present owner of my Haberdasher Street flat, and her brother, the current inhabitant, in particular for their photographs of the interior and their permission to reproduce the photograph of the roof terrace garden.

LIVING IN HOUSES

Chapter 8: Christine Camplin, from The Peckham Society, for copying an archive newsletter article on the North Peckham Estate; Stephen Moss, journalist, for sharing information with me about the architect Timothy Tinker, as well as for his interesting article about the nearby Heygate Estate; Timothy Tinker, an architect who worked on the adjacent North Peckham Estate; all the members of the Facebook group 'Who used to live on the Gloucester Grove Estate in Peckham' for sharing their memories of the estate and flats, and also, for their invaluable help in recalling what had been the names of the (now demolished) original blocks; Dr Phil Jones for sending me a copy of his unpublished working paper; Professor Deyan Sudjic, Dr Ruth Lang, Professor Sarah Wigglesworth, Stefi Orazi, John Boughton, Thaddeus Zupančič and Dr Elain Harwood for their thoughts and advice (and commiserations) on the knotty problem of identifying individual architects from the GLC's housing department; a special thank you to Dr Elain Harwood for her support in finding some articles on the Gloucester Grove Estate that I had been unable to otherwise find; Serge Lourie for his recollections of chairing the internal inquiry into Gloucester Grove's mismanagement; Emad Alyedreessy for his assistance with drawing the perspective diagram of the estate.

Chapter 9: Sandra Dystant, our former next-door-neighbour in Elm Village, for taking some photographs for me at the beginning of the first COVID-19 lockdown and for sharing some of her memories of the estate; Peter Mishcon, the architect of Elm Village, for spending time to talk to me about the scheme and for the use of some of his photographs/drawings (this was for the second time, and so this is also a belated thank you, only 26 years too late, for his help with my master's project as well); Michael Brookes, another of the architects who worked on Elm Village, for his comments and observations on my first draft of this chapter.

And, finally, to my family – Sheep, Aidan and Amelia – for their enduring patience with my latest writing obsession. As always.

Introduction

What makes an architect? As someone with a responsibility for educating architects, it is clear to me that schools of architecture play a fundamental role in shaping the architects of the future, and there is indeed a niche area of research into how this process of inculturation takes place in universities and in the architecture profession. And yet we all come to schools of architecture with a lifetime's experience (albeit maybe one of only 18 years or so) of having lived in buildings with which we have an intimate acquaintance – our homes – and this is the springboard from which we launch ourselves into our architectural careers. Of course, from this point onwards, once we start on that journey towards becoming architects, we all continue to live in buildings, namely, the houses that become our homes.

Some architects will eventually go on to design and live in houses that they have built for themselves, but even for architects, this is a rare thing; it is like the old adage, 'cobbler's children always go barefoot'. The vast majority of architects will spend their lives living in houses that they have *not* designed. Just like everyone else, these houses are ones that just happened to be available at the right time, in the right place, for the right amount of money (purchase or rental) and, if fortunate, may have some architectural character of their own. Do architects choose their houses in a different way or for different reasons than non-architects? What effect do the houses that we live in have upon how we develop and grow as architects, and eventually on our own practice? And what of the stories that those buildings themselves have to tell us?

And so, this book is a story, or two stories intertwined: it is certainly a history of English domestic architecture, but it is told through a handful of examples known intimately to the author and to the architect (the author) whose life is the thread that connects them all. The architectural story spans approximately 370 years via settings that range from village and town to 'New Town' and city. The buildings in this book include: purpose-built and/or architect-designed houses;

LIVING IN HOUSES

converted buildings with numerous former uses; ideal dwellings (from the Hoxton artisan-dwellings to the co-ownership/timber built experiment which was Elm Village); 'accidental' homes (from a former brewery to a former warehouse); every social class/status, and covering a large variety of building materials (wood, brick, stone, steel frame and concrete) and styles (vernacular, Georgian, Regency, Victorian, Edwardian, post-Second World War modernist/Brutalist and postmodern (PoMo)). Please refer to Tables I.1 to I.5 for a summary of the different characteristics of the houses featured in this book.

I would like to stress that this book is not an architect's self-aggrandising book showcasing their own, impossibly aspirational, home/s. If you look at Table I.5, you will see that the houses described in this book cover a range of residential tenures, ranging from private rentals to local authority tenancy, as well as shared ownership with a housing association and finally owner occupation. In fact, there is an interesting sub-narrative that runs through the latter part of this book, and it is the story of English social housing as told through Chapter 7, on Haberdasher Street, which illustrates, wonderfully, the transition period between the model dwellings movement and the beginning of council houses, through to Chapter 8, on the Gloucester Grove and North Peckham Estates, which represent the high point of council house construction – or, as John Boughton refers to it in his excellent book on the rise and fall of council housing, its 'swansong'. The book ends with a chapter on Elm Village, an example of what was to follow: mixed tenure, social housing provided by a housing association. In many respects, the chapter on housing associations takes us back full circle to the roots of the model dwellings companies. Indeed, had I deliberately set out, at the age of 18, to experience as wide a variety of houses as possible, I could not have made a better selection. What does this very personal collection of houses tell us about the history of housing in England and of the importance of place and the meaning of home through these buildings? And what are the lessons that I, as an architect, have learnt from a lifetime of living in each of them?

There are two timelines in this story: the chronology of the buildings themselves, the earliest being built in 1651 and the most recent in 1984; and the timeline of when I lived in them, spanning a period of over 50 years. For the nine buildings in this book, their story could be told using

INTRODUCTION

either of these two timelines, but I have chosen to use the sequence of time in which *they were built*, rather than when *I lived in* them, since it feels that the focus should primarily be on the houses rather than the inhabitant – they are permanent while I have been only a very transitory figure in their various histories.

As I recite their names – Yearnor Cottage, Gower Street, Haberdasher Street, Wharf Place, Blakeney Close (Elm Village), Bradwell Road, Priestpopple and Orchard Place (this is the order I lived in them) – it feels far more akin to speaking aloud the names of old friends or past loves than of inanimate buildings. And through the writing of this book, through the process of physically – and in some cases only virtually – re-visiting them all, I have fallen in love, all over again. During the writing of each and every chapter, I have felt as if I could move back again, in a heartbeat, given half a chance. Is this the same for everyone? For me, even these names resonate with feelings, experiences, a sense of light and shadow, of materiality, of small intimate details that were so familiar at the time, of sounds and smells, of a life fully lived in, and shaped by, these places. And so, this is a history of housing unlike any other, since each example is as dear to me, and intimately known, as an old friend.

Table I.1   A summary of the houses' locations, original functions and original social class

HOUSE	LOCATION	ORIGINAL FUNCTION	SOCIAL CLASS
Yearnor Cottage	Village (hamlet)	House and smithy	Artisan/skilled working
Priestpopple	Market Town	Brewery	n/a
Gower Street	City	House	Upper middle
Orchard Place	Market Town	House	Upper middle
Wharf Place	City	Warehouse	n/a
Bradwell Road	Village / 'New Town'	House	Lower middle/working
Haberdasher Street	City	House	Artisan/working
Gloucester Grove Estate	City	House	Working/lower
Blakeney Close	City	House	Mixed

LIVING IN HOUSES

Table I.2 Date of construction, age at time of writing and architectural styles of the houses

HOUSE	DATE	AGE	ARCHITECTURAL STYLE/ERA
Yearnor Cottage	1651	371	Rural Vernacular
Priestpopple	c.1700	322	Vernacular Industrial
Gower Street	1789	233	Georgian
Orchard Place	1824	198	Regency
Wharf Place	c.1902	120	Victorian Industrial
Bradwell Road	1902	120	Edwardian
Haberdasher Street	1912	110	Edwardian/Pre-First World War
Gloucester Grove Estate	1977	45	Post-Second World War Modernist/Brutalist
Blakeney Close	1984	38	Post-modern (PoMo)

Table I.3 Architect/builder

HOUSE	ARCHITECT/BUILDER
Yearnor Cottage	Vernacular
Priestpopple	Vernacular
Gower Street	Georgian 'master builder' and subcontractors, unknown
Orchard Place	Architect, unknown
Wharf Place	Probably no architect, industrial vernacular
Bradwell Road	Architect, unknown
Haberdasher Street	Robert Page, Stock Page & Stock
Gloucester Grove Estate	Housing Branch of the GLC Department of Architecture and Civic Design, K.J. Campbell, Principal Housing Architect. Architects: Oatley, Jackson & Elson
Blakeney Close	Peter Mishcon & Associates

INTRODUCTION

Table I.4   The construction materials used for the houses

HOUSE	CONSTRUCTION MATERIALS
Yearnor Cottage	Handmade brick, some stone, wattle and daub internal walls
Priestpopple	Sandstone (and some brick)
Gower Street	London stock brick and stucco
Orchard Place	Sandstone ashlar, lath and plaster internal walls
Wharf Place	London stock brick, steel frame
Bradwell Road	Red Bedford brick, decorative terracotta mouldings
Haberdasher Street	Polychromatic brick (London stock and red)
Gloucester Grove Estate	System-built concrete panels with brick cladding
Blakeney Close	Timber construction, brick cladding and pre-cast concrete details

Table I.5   Tenure

HOUSE	TENURE
Yearnor Cottage	Freehold, owner occupier
Priestpopple	Freehold, owner occupier
Gower Street	Private rental (university)
Orchard Place	Freehold, owner occupier
Wharf Place	Leasehold, owner occupier
Bradwell Road	Freehold, owner occupier
Haberdasher Street	Private rental
Gloucester Grove Estate	Local authority (council) tenancy
Blakeney Close	Shared ownership with housing association

1

Yearnor Cottage (1651)

The Story of the Rural Vernacular Tradition

1.1 Sketch drawing of Yearnor Cottage

YEARNOR COTTAGE (1651)

Introduction: My Lived Experience of this Home

The house that I grew up in had been bought by my grandparents (an insurance broker and housewife) shortly before Christmas 1952 when my mother was 12 years old. It lay at the heart of the small Leicestershire village of Burton Overy and consisted, at that time, of a number of separate buildings: two labourers' cottages (of a standard 'two-up, two-down' layout), a forge (formerly used by the village blacksmith), stabling for the horses (presumably while waiting to be shod) and some ramshackle pigsties, along with a pair of dubious outdoor toilets in the garden. Christmas 1952 stands out as being particularly memorable for my mother due to the fact that initially only a single room was habitable (the roof leaked badly and she recalls dripping water everywhere). There was neither heating nor hot water and so all three of them huddled together in one room while trying to make the miserable, cold and damp experience as festive as possible. In the New Year, my mother escaped, appreciatively, to boarding school and thus missed the inconvenience of the vast amount of building work required to render the place liveable.

One notable discovery, upon moving in, was an abandoned, Victorian lacemaking pillow on a yew stand found in the storeroom above the forge. Given the Eastern Counties' traditions of lacemaking, it was possible that at some point the blacksmith's income had been supplemented by his wife's or daughter's lacemaking. Indeed, it is not improbable that the room above the forge could have been used for lacemaking, since it would always have been warm from the heat of the forge below, cold fingers being less than ideal for the nimble activity that is lacemaking.

My grandfather began an extensive programme of building work in order to transform this motley collection of vernacular buildings into a post-war family home. First, he merged the two cottages into one, removing one of the two staircases, creating new internal connections and bricking up one of the two front doors, as well as demolishing the pigsties and outhouses. When they first moved in, the roof had still been partially thatched, this being the infamous, leaky roof of Christmas 1952, and today the neighbouring cottage still serves as a much-lauded, splendid example of how Yearnor Cottage might have

LIVING IN HOUSES

originally appeared. But being in insurance, my grandfather had a deep-set abhorrence of what he judged to be *highly flammable* thatch, and so wasted little time in replacing the roof entirely, banishing the romantic thatch forever into history. When, finally, the home was finished, it acquired a name (historically it had none, being merely an accretion of different buildings). It was duly named after the small Somerset cottage in which my grandparents had spent many happy holidays, Yearnor Cottage (pronounced 'Yarn-er').

Through a quirk of circumstances, I also came to grow up in Yearnor Cottage. My grandfather, being tempted into one final architectural project, decided to build a more modern, compact and more easily manageable house for my grandmother, who had been finding that Yearnor Cottage was becoming too large and cumbersome as they

1.2   Garden elevation of Yearnor Cottage, *c.*1954

approached retirement. The new building project occupied the site of the original forge and extended into the rear garden (more or less where the pigsties and outdoor toilets had been). But sadly, my grandmother died of a sudden heart attack just weeks before the new house was completed, and so, somewhat on the spur of the moment, my mother, sister and I (I was aged four) moved into Yearnor Cottage, while my grandfather moved next door into Forge Mews (as he eventually came to name it). My bedroom became the room above what had been the forge's stables (most likely a former storeroom). This room had been modernised during the building of Forge Mews and so was probably the only room in the whole cottage with a level floor, vertical walls and more than one right angle.

My recollection of the house is that the bedrooms were bitterly cold in winter since we had no heating upstairs; on winter mornings, I would have to scrape the ice from the inside of the window, just to look outside. The cottage was, however, undeniably warm and snug downstairs when the living room fire was lit and uniformly cool in the heat of the summer. The house always felt dark, with uneven, creaky floors. I recall the beams being so extraordinarily low that even at my eventual adult height of 5'2", I habitually had to duck to enter my bedroom (and woe betide the unwary, tall visitor!). As a family, we mostly lived in one room (a living room/dining room combined), a north-facing, low-ceilinged room with a multitude of dark beams, with a large Parkray woodburning stove in the fireplace, which felt romantic. I was certainly conscious of the age and endurance of the house and it felt as if it had a character of its own. This precocious, architectural sensitivity may be nothing more than the influence of my favourite childhood book, Alison Uttley's *A Traveller in Time*, vividly set in an old Elizabethan farmhouse. In this, the narrator imagines the past lives of former inhabitants who have lived in the house and, eventually, is able to slip into the past to experience it directly, something I longed, with a passion, to emulate. Every time we dug our garden, we found traces of past inhabitants, fragments of pottery, glass bottles and clay pipes, even (something I treasure today) a tiny porcelain figure of a girl, less than an inch tall, and I kept these things, imagining who had owned them before; I might just as easily have become an archaeologist as an architect.

LIVING IN HOUSES

1.3   Aerial photograph of Yearnor Cottage, *c.*1978

The History of Rural Vernacular Housing

The history of rural vernacular housing in England truly begins in the 17th century, since although a smattering of medieval houses survives, earlier houses tended to be of the grander sort: manor houses and the country estates of the landed gentry or the townhouses of wealthy merchants. The first, substantive evidence of how *ordinary people* lived

YEARNOR COTTAGE (1651)

dates back to the 17th century. One of the reasons why so few houses survive from this earlier period is simply that the majority of workers' homes (serfs, peasants, villeins) were built using poor quality, and less durable, materials. They mostly used wood as their primary structural building material, with infill walls of wattle (woven panels of twigs called withies or thin pliable strips known as laths) and daub (earth, dung and fibres), and often with thatch roofs (even less durable than wood) – hence, they were simply never going to have a long lifespan.

What is particularly interesting about the 16th–17th centuries is that there occurred an explosion in house building, almost entirely replacing the older medieval housing stock. This occurred at the same time that the use of longer-lasting materials became commonplace for the middle and working classes – for example, the use of stone and brick became far more typical (although still often used in conjunction with a timber, primary structure). For this reason, it can be considered that the history of *ordinary houses* essentially begins at this time. This period is known as the Great Rebuilding, a term first coined by the historian W.G. Hoskins,[1] and is generally thought to have taken place between the late 16th and late 17th centuries. The Great Rebuilding is somewhat disputed now, since it is thought to be far more nuanced, with more regional variation and less strictly temporally bounded than Hoskins first assumed; but, nevertheless, it is a useful historical concept, and if we adopt Hoskins' definition of the Great Rebuilding, we can see that Yearnor Cottage was built right at the very end of this period. Beginning this book, therefore, with a house built in 1651[2] is an extremely good place to start any history of English housing.

Why did the Great Rebuilding occur? Hoskins suggests that we can look to the labour market at the time to explain this. He describes how, from the 1540s, anyone working on the land (which was most people) had a previously non-existent security of tenure for which their rents had also been fixed, at exactly the same time that prices of agricultural products had been rising steadily. In 'The Rebuilding of Rural England, 1570–1640', Hoskins observes that 'It is enough to say that the gap between costs and selling-prices widened with increasing speed after the middle of the sixteenth century and persisted down to the Civil War. No yeoman with his wits about him could fail to accumulate money-savings on a scale hitherto unknown.'[3] It is

LIVING IN HOUSES

Hoskins' view that the availability of more durable building materials coinciding with a novel, widespread, disposable household income was one reason that led to the growth in house building.

In many respects the Great Rebuilding can be considered not only a brief period in British history (although it was), but also, perhaps more interestingly, a pivot point between the ancient and modern cultures of domestic housing, the point at which everything changed in the home and set us on the path towards what we would recognise clearly as being the house of today. Prior to the Great Rebuilding there were two parallel traditions of house-form, each with a different origin.[4] One vernacular type was the *long house*, of which there are variants to be found all over Europe (in Britain, surviving long houses have been found predominantly in Devon, Wales, Cumbria and Scotland). The long house was essentially a long (hence the name) and proportionally narrow, low, single-roomed building, of which people typically occupied one end and farm animals the other. The second, and more dominant, tradition was the *hall*, also typically a single-storey, single-roomed building, but proportionally of a squarer shape compared to the long house. The most important feature of this room was a central fire around which all household members could sit and with an opening in the roof for smoke to vent (if you were lucky). Unlike the long house, farm animals were typically housed in separate barns.

Let us now focus on the hall, the dominant house type in medieval England (and certainly the dominant house type in the Midlands and South-East), rather than the long house. This single space was where everybody gathered and engaged in the entire range of activities that might conceivably have taken place indoors: cooking, eating, sleeping and all types of social interaction. This single space was open to the roof, and as a consequence, there were rarely upper floors. Smoke was intended to escape through a hole in the roof or, somewhat inefficiently, at the top of a gable wall just below the roof ridge, so that the single space would have been extremely smoky, as well as being dark due to narrow, glassless, window-openings. The key invention, therefore, that began to alter domestic space irrevocably was the chimney, a device for simultaneously channelling smoke out of the building while also preventing water from entering the same way.

YEARNOR COTTAGE (1651)

It is unclear when chimneys were invented but it was probably around the 14th century. They became more common during the Tudor and Elizabethan eras, and by the time of the Great Rebuilding chimneys had become more or less ubiquitous. The consequences of houses having chimneys were numerous. First, rather than needing to have a single room open to the roof, multiple storeys could be stacked on top of one another, since the presence of a ceiling above a room would no longer trap smoke beneath it – any smoke could simply bypass upper levels through the chimney. Second, it was apparent that fireplaces could also be stacked vertically above one another, with parallel flues occupying the same chimney space. Third, once the technological refinements of these new, innovative chimneys had been ironed out, it was clear that more than one chimney could be incorporated into a house – for example, one at each gable end or back-to-back against an interior wall. This meant that rooms were not reliant on each other for a single source of heat; a house could be sub-divided into multiple rooms, each with its own, independent, heat source. This resulted in a gradual specialisation of activities in different rooms: rather than having a single room in which everything had to happen, rooms could be allocated a specific purpose: a kitchen, a bedroom, a parlour, and so on. Fourth, the concept of privacy began to develop, although it is not clear whether this was a cause or effect of the sub-division of rooms, or the fact that rooms were no longer dark and smoky (and intimate activities that might have previously been rather surreptitious or covert became more obvious and visible). Did we become more private because the proliferation of rooms permitted us to be so, or did we embrace the ability to sub-divide our houses into numerous rooms because of our newfound sense of the private self? Most likely the two (a sense of privacy and the sub-division of spaces) developed in parallel.

This leads us to another possible reason for the Great Rebuilding: this period in time also coincided with a population explosion which, it could be argued, necessitated the building of more houses, the extension of smaller ones, or their demolition and replacement by larger ones. However, Hoskins suggests that growth in population around this period was less the cause of the Great Rebuilding but rather an effect of it, since with better housing conditions, comes

LIVING IN HOUSES

better health and a reduced infant mortality rate. He attributes the Great Rebuilding to two causes: greater affluence and disposable income (as discussed at the beginning of this section), as well as a developing sense of the importance of privacy.[5] It does not need a lot of imagination to connect the concept of increased privacy and the development of dedicated rooms for 'sleeping' with an increase in the number of children being born.

And so, we arrive at the 17th century. The long house is all but forgotten (or has been adapted and altered gradually, and thus is no longer recognisable as being a different type to the hall), and the hall has morphed into a house that we would *almost* recognise today. Often it comprised of two storeys, each containing a number of specialised rooms such as the hall, passage, kitchen, pantry, buttery and parlour on the ground floor, with additional spaces for sleeping and storage above. In a paper by the building historian Maurice Willmore Barley on the use of upper floors in rural houses, he observes that the upper floors of houses of the 16th and 17th centuries have a number of different names, for example, 'chamber and solar; vance roof, loft, cockloft and garret (never attic)';[6] he later concludes that the word 'chamber' tended to be used more often when there was a bed in the room, and that the other terms were used when the upper floor was predominantly used for storage. In the next section, I will describe what I presume to have been the original layout of Yearnor Cottage, if compared to plans of contemporaneous cottages (for example, in Raymond Wood-Jones' excellent book, *Traditional Domestic Architecture of the Banbury Region*).[7]

Yearnor Cottage is a good example of what would have been a typical yeoman's house of the mid-17th century. But who would have lived in Yearnor Cottage? The earliest maps of Burton Overy clearly indicate the site of the village smithy right in the centre of the village where Yearnor Cottage still stands. We also know that there was still a forge in the property when my grandparents moved in in 1952 (my mother can recall it quite vividly), and so it is probable that the village blacksmith had always been in this approximate location. And this location is a particularly advantageous one, as it lies in the very middle of the village, on a through-road connecting the village to its two neighbouring villages to the east and the west. It also happens to

YEARNOR COTTAGE (1651)

be situated directly opposite the village pub, meaning that customers of the blacksmith could leave their horses to be shod, while they had a quick, refreshing drink at the public house.

There is some confusion as to whether the blacksmith lived in Yearnor Cottage, since the thatched cottage next door to Yearnor Cottage is known as 'Smith's Cottage'. However, indisputably, the two cottages forming Yearnor Cottage and its forge appear to have always been part of the same property. It is possible that the collection of buildings, as built in 1651, were originally constructed to house the blacksmith and his forge, but he later came to reside in the larger Smith's Cottage, next door, while the two smaller cottages could have been occupied by his extended family/apprentices. Both Wood-Jones and Hoskins comment on the fact that multiple generations within a single household were common, with the idea of a 'house within a house', or self-contained households within a larger building footprint, being a convenient way to accommodate different generations.

In a previous paragraph, I mention that Yearnor Cottage is a good example of a yeoman's house, but what was the class structure in the 17th century, and where would a blacksmith have fitted into it? We must first note the significance of when Yearnor Cottage was built: 1651 was a turbulent year, being the final year of the English Civil War – the year that began with Charles II being crowned King of Scotland in Scone, and which ended in the autumn of the same year, with his escape to France. The English Civil War was a time of great upheaval and social change in Britain. The feudal system had entirely come to an end by the late 16th century and the Civil War served to lay the foundations of a new and emerging middle class.

The class structure, below the level of the monarchy and nobility, in the late 17th century would have comprised of wealthy landowners and high church officials at the top, followed by gentry (gentlemen and merchants/tradesmen), yeoman (those who owned and worked their own land) and the newly formed middle class, which included artisans, shopkeepers and tradesmen, as well as navy and military officers. Finally, at the bottom would have been the labouring poor, servants and eventually cottagers and paupers. In 17th-century society, a blacksmith would have been considered to be firmly middle

LIVING IN HOUSES

class, along with other artisans (who were often members of guilds); he would have been considered neither rich nor poor, but would have been comfortably well-off and certainly able to build and live in his own house and raise a family. He would have also played an important role in the village.

The population of Burton Overy was approximately 155[8] people in 1651[9] and consisted of about 62 houses (records from 1670). Each village would have had its own blacksmith, since it was almost impossible to manage without one. The 17th-century blacksmith did far more than just make and fit horseshoes; they made any and all things that could be manufactured from iron: craftsmen's tools such as hammers, files, chisels, iron nails and axes, as well as farming implements such as scythes, knives and sickles. They helped produce many of the necessary components for horses and wagons, such as bits, horseshoes and carriage bolts, and undertook the fitting and repairing of wagon wheels, and so on. They even produced/repaired household objects such as pots and pans, and could even be called upon to act as locksmith or armourer if the need arose. So not only were blacksmiths an essential part of village life, respected and valued for their skills, but the smithy, as described in *The Sociology of an English Village*, was 'known locally as "t' gossip shop" . . . the blacksmith performs the function of a "clearing house" for parish gossip and distribution centre for messages between households situated far apart'.[10] In other words, the blacksmith is firmly situated at the heart of village life.

To summarise, Yearnor Cottage is an excellent example of an early modern house, built by a member of the newly emerging middle class at the very end of the Civil War and towards the end of the Great Rebuilding; only a small number of such houses still exist today.[11]

Layout: The Cottage Plan

These plans show how the cottage was arranged when I came to live in it in 1974 (as altered by my grandfather in the 1950s) and a second set of plans, overleaf, showing a reconstruction of how the cottage/s might have originally been laid out (using other 17th-century house plans as a guide).

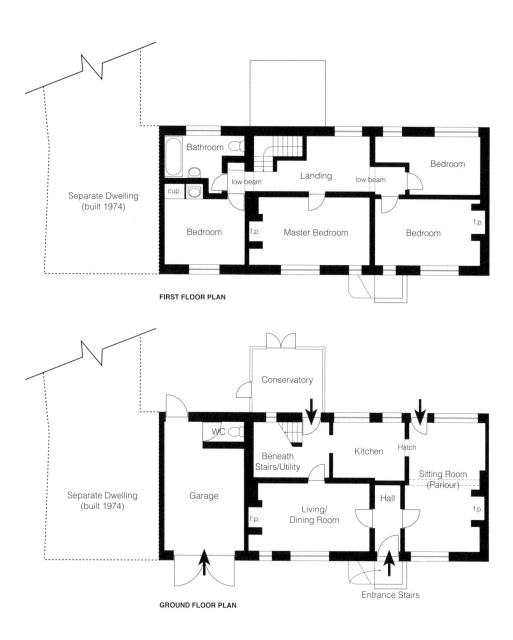
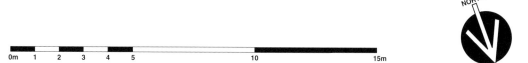

1.4 Yearnor Cottage plans, *c.*1974

LIVING IN HOUSES

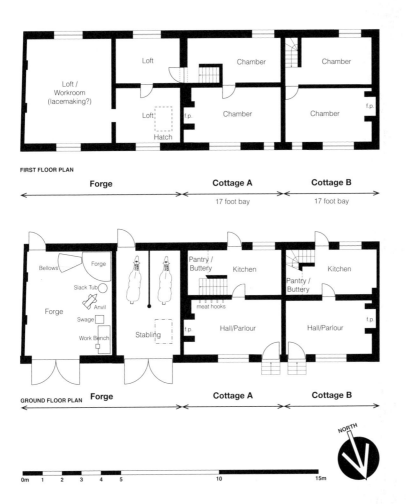

(left)

1.5 Reconstructed plans of Yearnor Cottage, probable 1651 layout

(right)

1.6 Location of the original back door to Cottage B showing part of the timber post and truss construction (note also the horse shoe on the door lintel, found in the garden and placed here by my grandfather)

Originally, the two cottages (I will call them Cottage A and Cottage B), together with the stables, formed part of a standard, rectangular, three-bay building of post and truss construction, with the forge occupying an additional, slightly larger bay at one end. The cottages occupied a single bay each and comprised two rooms on the ground floor and two upper-level rooms. Wood-Jones suggests that 'In Leicestershire . . . the bay spacing is . . . seventeen feet'[12] and it is interesting to note that the bay spacing of the two cottages appears to be exactly 17 feet. Today the timber-framing of the bays is less visible from the front, but is much more obvious from the garden (Fig.1.6).

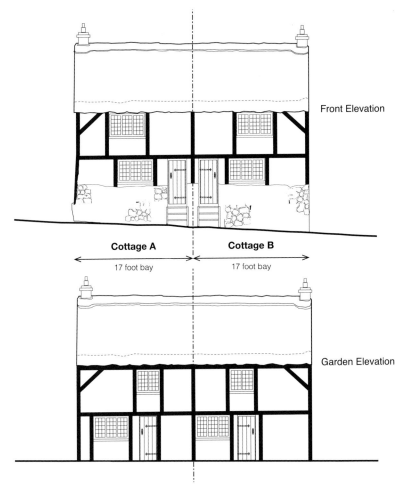

1.7 One possible interpretation of how Yearnor Cottage may have looked when first built, showing the stone plinth, presumed exposed timber frame with wattle and daub infills, thatch and the double entrance to the two cottages

Originally the two front doors were located side by side (the outline of the original door can still be seen in a photograph in my possession, from the 1960s, but the mis-matched brick-infill has recently been rendered to conceal all traces of this). The front doors were accessed via a few steps (Yearnor Cottage sits on a raised rubble stone plinth) and these are in a different configuration from the modern entry steps, as can be seen in another photograph, *c*.1900.

In each of the two cottages you would have been able to enter directly into a room without first passing through any entrance space, and on the drawings I have labelled these rooms as the Hall/Parlour (Fig.1.5). This room would have been the main living space, a room for dining, conversation and entertainment (and is essentially the room into which the medieval hall evolved). During the 17th century it became typical to place services at the rear of the house; therefore, I suggest that in each cottage the kitchen would have probably occupied the room to the back of the house, connecting each cottage to its garden. I have also indicated the possible presence of a pantry/buttery as well; the pantry was a small room/area for the storage of dry goods and bread, and the buttery was for the storage of bottles (from the French word *bouteillerie*), which in the case of Yearnor Cottage was more likely to have been ale rather than wine, given the social class of the occupants.

With two downstairs rooms connected by a single internal doorway and each room also connected to the outside, the cottages can be considered a variant of the through-passage plan, which Wood-Jones noted was 'characteristic of the regional yeoman house in the first part of the 17th century'.[13] A through-passage plan simply means that there were opposing front and back doors in alignment, connected by a nominal 'passage' passing through all inner room/s. However, I can see no evidence that the back doors of the two cottages were ever in a different location to where they are today, and so the two cottages should be considered an *offset*, rather than a *typical*, through-passage plan.

In both cottages, the stairs lead directly from the kitchen to the upper floors. These have been drawn according to my mother's memories of the layout in 1952, prior to my grandfather's alterations. In particular, she recalls vividly the narrow, winding stair to the rear of Cottage B, which she describes as being almost like a spiral staircase. In contrast, the stair in Cottage A was originally a straight flight of stairs running up through the middle of the house. She remembers this stair as being far steeper and narrower than any modern staircase, almost halfway between a stair and a ladder (for reasons of safety, my grandfather removed this stair and built a new one, with a quarter-landing, moved back against the cottage's rear wall). There was no upper landing, as we would expect today; rather you emerged directly into the first chamber at the top of the stair and would have had to pass through one sleeping chamber to access the other, an arrangement which we would find most peculiar in a modern house. The stair in Cottage A also accessed the upper-level storage lofts and the possible workshop (where the lacemaking stand was found) above the stables and forge respectively.

LIVING IN HOUSES

Materials

There are so many aspects of Yearnor Cottage's building materials that are worthy of discussion here, being so very different to the house-building materials we commonly use today, namely its form of timber construction, handmade bricks, horizontal sliding sash windows (also known as 'Yorkshire sash' windows), original thatch roof and interior wattle and daub walls. But in this next section, I would like to focus on just one aspect of the cottage: its bricks.

As mentioned previously, Yearnor Cottage is a timber-framed building, resting upon a low stone wall. The brick panels are used merely to *fill in* the gaps left between the timber structure. It should be noted, however, that the brickwork might not have been the original 1651 infill material (which may easily have been wattle and daub), but could have been added later as brick became more readily available since it was both more durable and far more desirable (one way of showing off a homeowner's increasing affluence was to replace exterior wattle and daub walls with bricks). This kind of brick-infill panel goes by the truly delightful name 'nogging' (Fig.1.8). Today, Yearnor Cottage's nogging is only visible on the rear elevation as the front elevation has been fully replaced by structural brick between the primary bay timbers.

What intrigued me, when I started to think about the brick nogging of Yearnor Cottage, was wondering where the brick might have come from in the late 17th century, since industrialised brick factories (and there was a local brick factory[14] in the nearby town of Market Harborough) had yet to exist at this time. We do know, however, that there had been brickmaking in Leicestershire since the late 15th century, but at that early date, bricks were only used for the houses of wealthy landowners. When Yearnor Cottage was built (or possibly had its original wattle and daub infill panels replaced by brick), the brickmakers would have used traditional, pre-industrial methods: hand-moulding and firing in clamps or simple up-draft kilns.

It is most likely that the bricks for Yearnor Cottage were made locally. Indeed, a map of the traditional field names of the parish indicates one field called Brick Kiln Close, and according to a history of the village written by the Burton Overy History Group, this kiln is believed to have ceased working in the 18th century. In the 17th

(right)

1.8 An example of brick nogging showing the infill panel of bricks within the timber frame and brace. This is from the rear of Yearnor Cottage

(below)

1.9 From left to right, Smith's Cottage, Forge Mews and Yearnor Cottage

century, the transportation of bricks was difficult since bricks were heavy and bulky, roads were poor, and a horse-drawn cart could only carry a maximum of 300 bricks; therefore, the distance from where bricks were *made* to where they needed to be *used* had to be kept as short as possible. The distance from Yearnor Cottage to Brick Kiln Close was just over a third of a mile, and so it is feasible that this is where its bricks might have been made.

The question of *what* material was used to make the bricks is essentially a question of what was locally available at the time. Early brickmakers sought out the more accessible, surface deposits of clay, which could be easily extracted with basic hand tools. Clays from such surface deposits, particularly when associated with gravel (and there were multiple gravel pits in the village), would have included pebbles which often survived the firing process and are sometimes visible on the surface of the bricks. Such pebbles can clearly be seen on some of the oldest bricks of Yearnor Cottage, which would, most likely, have been made from local Charmouth Mudstone.

In 'Brickmaking in Leicestershire before 1710', Alan McWhirr states that 'The earliest surviving dated example of a brick frontage to a small house . . . carries a date stone of 1686.'[15] If Yearnor Cottage was originally built of brick, or even if the brick nogging was used to replace earlier wattle and daub infill panels and this 'refurbishment' was carried out within 35 years of it being first built, then Yearnor Cottage could potentially be one of the oldest brick houses, of a middle income, ordinary household, in the county of Leicestershire.

The Influence and Inspiration of Rural Cottages

Without doubt, the romantic image of the thatched cottage still exerts a powerful cultural influence even today, not least for the tourist industry for whom villages retaining high numbers of thatched cottages are considered and promoted as being some of the most beautiful tourist destinations, as well as being quintessentially English. There is something about inglenook fireplaces, original beams and uneven floors and walls that seems to capture our imagination. The thatched cottage represents, for many people,

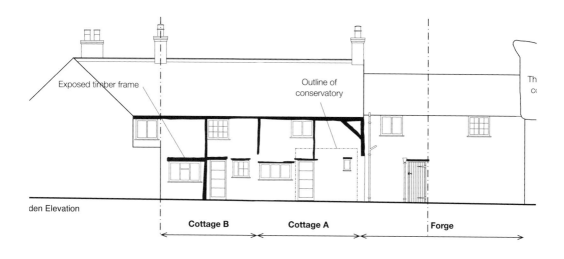

1.10 Elevations of Yearnor Cottage and Forge Mews, c.1974

the perfect 'rural retreat' for a holiday, with such cottages being consistently in high demand as holiday homes. Conversely, for the home owner, a thatched cottage is now a status symbol (rather than a symbol of rural poverty, as it might once have been), so much so that former thatched cottages that have been subsequently re-roofed with tiles are occasionally converted back to their original thatch by some owners. One reason that they are now status symbols is simply due to the fact that thatched roofs need to be rethatched every few decades, meaning that they can be quite costly to maintain, as well as the fact that they incur higher insurance costs due to an increased fire risk; only someone with the means to afford such ongoing costs would commit to owning such a property, however great its rustic appeal.

1.11 The current interior of Yearnor Cottage

So, what is the influence of the romanticised rural cottage today? It would be easy to say that regional vernacular houses exert little or no influence on contemporary architecture apart from an occasional 'nod' to the local context for the sake of pleasing planning departments; or, as in the case of the town of Poundbury in Dorset, a more deliberate attempt to try to recreate a vernacular village 'feel'. But there is another way in which vernacular architecture, in all its regional variations, is seeing a resurgence and is exerting a powerful influence over modern architecture, and that is due to the need for the building industry to become more sustainable. This manifests itself in two ways: one is looking to former solutions, such as thatch, for materials that are inherently 'green' and can provide renewable, sustainable solutions to a range of building needs such as heating, lighting, insulation and ventilation. The other is a renewed desire to minimise the distance that building materials must be transported to building sites, the architectural equivalent of 'food miles'.[16]

Focusing on the sustainability of building materials, straw and thatch, for example, are excellent insulating materials. Straw first came to architectural prominence via Sarah Wigglesworth and Jeremy Till's

YEARNOR COTTAGE (1651)

Straw Bale House in London (coincidentally, also located on the site of a former forge), which recently celebrated its 20th anniversary. This house was very much ahead of its time in terms of its use of straw, as well as other innovative, environmentally friendly materials, so much so that in 2015, the *Architects' Journal* asked: 'Is this the most influential house in a generation?'[17] The Straw Bale House did not use thatch for its roof but did use straw for some of its walls, providing a thick layer of insulation on its coldest, north-facing elevation.

Wigglesworth and Till certainly brought the potential of straw as a modern building material to the attention of the architectural community, and it is interesting to note that straw bales need not be just a solution for small-scale house building. In 2011, Make Architects built what was, at the time, the largest straw bale building in the country for the University of Nottingham, known as the Gateway Building, a 3,100 m^2 home for the School of Biosciences and School of Veterinary and Medical Sciences. Unlike the Straw Bale House, this does not look at all like an eco-building; at first glance, it would not look out of place on any contemporary university campus. However, its walls were built using prefabricated modular straw bale panels, consisting of a timber frame filled with compacted straw and externally finished with render – in many respects not so far removed from the wattle and daub infill panels in the timber structure that may have formed Yearnor Cottage's original walls. The importance of the Gateway Building's render – not unlike Yearnor Cottage's 'daub' – is that it provides a breathable outer layer that serves to both protect the straw from the weather while also preventing the build-up of moisture inside the panel, which would eventually lead to the straw becoming mouldy or rotting. Another factor that is particularly interesting about this building is that, wherever possible, materials such as the straw were sourced locally, reducing the distance from production to site. Again, parallels can be drawn between this and the locally made bricks of Yearnor Cottage being transported less than a mile from the kiln to the building.

If we consider straw not as a wall insulating material, but as an external material – that is, thatch[18] – we can also find examples of modern architects experimenting with thatch. For example, the University of East Anglia's Enterprise Centre by Architype Architects, built in 2015, is essentially a modern office building that also happens to be thatched,

LIVING IN HOUSES

although in this case it is some of its walls that are thatched, rather than its roof. And returning to the domestic scale again, there is the wonderfully quirky Jeffry's House, designed by Emily Mannion and Thomas O'Brien, which is more of a folly or shelter, but has both a thatched roof and thatched walls covering an irregular, angular form that is anything but traditional in appearance.

It could be argued that the modern equivalent of wattle and daub walls manifests itself in the growing interest in using hempcrete. Daub, pressed into and around the wattle, was a mixture of clay, earth and sometimes dung, aggregates, such as sand or crushed stone, reinforced with natural fibres such as straw, hair, flax or hay. Similarly, hempcrete is an alternative to concrete in which hemp fibres are mixed with a lime-based binder. It is less dense than concrete and the inclusion of the hemp fibres makes it a far better insulator than concrete, so architects are beginning to recognise its unique properties. It was most recently used to construct the Flat House in Cambridgeshire by Practice Architecture, where they employed a system of pre-fabricated hempcrete panels. All of these examples serve to demonstrate that perhaps the time has come to re-evaluate former building materials, especially given the current need for more sustainable construction practices, and perhaps we can still learn something from the humble, vernacular cottage.

Personal Lessons Learnt for Architectural Practice

Can I look back on my childhood growing up in Yearnor Cottage and see the beginnings of lessons learnt for my own practice as an architect? I think there are a few things that have influenced my own architectural practice, aside from knowing the meaning of the phrase 'wattle and daub' from an early age. I think the first lesson I internalised was the importance of warmth – my memories of getting dressed beneath the bedclothes to avoid the arctic temperatures of my bedroom are ones I can still recall in an instant. As a consequence, I have always placed a huge importance on insulation, double-glazing and avoiding cold bridges (weak points in the design of a building envelope where a thermally conductive material can allow heat to 'leak' out through conduction). As it becomes ever more imperative to

YEARNOR COTTAGE (1651)

design buildings that are both sustainable to build and do not require large amounts of heating/energy to run, understanding how to design for thermal comfort is an increasingly valuable skill for architects. Perhaps all architects should be forced to spend a winter living in a poorly insulated, cold building.

Another lesson I may have learnt from Yearnor Cottage is a sensitivity to scale. I am certainly smaller than average in height but in Yearnor Cottage I was forced to duck to pass through doorways. I therefore know not only what it is like to be made to feel small in a space, but I also know what it is like to feel over-sized (rather like Alice in *Through the Looking Glass*, rapidly changing her size when she drinks a potion to make her small, then eating a cake that makes her larger than life). This ability to think at different scales and to play with a sense of scale is important for architects, as is the ability to design for a range of different occupants of all shapes and sizes. Saying that, I do have rather a penchant today for high ceilings, which perhaps I can also attribute to a childhood spent regularly ducking my head.

But most of all, I think a childhood spent in Yearnor Cottage gave me a delight in the quirkiness of buildings, a love of a building's own idiosyncrasies and peculiarities, such as the complete lack of level floors and walls that were part of Yearnor Cottage's personality. If every building has its own unique character, then the skill of the architect is to discern that character – even if a building is yet to exist – and help to tease it out.

2

Priestpopple (*c.*1700)

The Story of a Small-town Brewery Continuously Reinvented for its Time

2.1   Sketch drawing of the Priestpopple house

PRIESTPOPPLE (*c.1700*)

Introduction: My Lived Experience of this Home

We went to view the house at Priestpopple,[1] not with a view to buying it, but rather to settle a bet. We had recently moved to Northumberland for work, to be closer to our children's grandparents and because we thought it would be a good place to raise our family. We had been living, temporarily, in a tiny rental house in Corbridge while we searched for a permanent home. I found myself, quite accidentally, looking through a listing for a large, and quite intriguing, house in Hexham. When I remarked, in passing, to my husband that there was a five-bedroom townhouse for sale in Priestpopple in Hexham, he, with his superior Northumbrian knowledge, replied, 'Don't be daft, there are no townhouses in Priestpopple', and so the dispute, and subsequent bet, ensued.

He was *almost* correct in his statement, as Priestpopple is the main high street and one of the ancient thoroughfares running through the town, full of pubs, restaurants and the usual shops found in any market town: there really *are* no large townhouses on this street – with one exception and it is remarkably hard to find. It is practically a *stealth house*. When we went to view it, we found ourselves standing in front of an opening,[2] squashed between a newsagent's shop and a pub on one side and what was, at the time, a hotel on the other. Two, heavy wooden doors barred the way and within these was set a small 'door-inside-a-door', or a wicket, that even I, at 5'2", had to duck to climb through. The wicket led to a courtyard, and right at the very back of the courtyard lay the house.

The rather surreal, magical nature of the house did not stop there; instead it became quirkier and quirkier, from trapdoors to strange wooden ramps and yet more secret doors. I recall, during our viewing, being shown around one of the top floor rooms and remarking on the utility of a small built-in cupboard; the owner chuckled, 'You think this is a cupboard? Go ahead, open it!' It turned out to be a tiny, 4½-foot-high door leading to a ramp, which in turn connected the room to the master bedroom. Later this became our daughter's room and she loved this little 'secret passage' that connected her room to ours. The pièce de resistance, however, was the master bedroom itself, almost 10 metres long, with exposed roof beams and trusses (the aforementioned

2.2 The 'stealth house', as seen through the archway, at the back of the courtyard

PRIESTPOPPLE (c.1700)

2.3 The master bedroom of the Priestpopple house, showing the exposed roof trusses containing the 'marriage marks'

trapdoor connected the master bedroom to the living room below). Indeed, the bedroom alone was bigger than my entire two-storey house in Camden had been (see Chapter 9). The biggest surprise of all, however, was its surprisingly large garden, somehow inserted into the midst of this central town site. We were instantly smitten, and we made an offer on the spot.

Our familiarity with the house, once we had moved in, did nothing to dull our delight in it. It was undoubtedly the funniest, quirkiest, weirdest (in the best possible way) place we have ever lived, and it was with such a wrench that we eventually left it. As with many of the houses I have lived in, it was the little things I loved. I discovered that the beams in the master bedroom contained carvings. First, there were the 'marriage marks' – these are Roman numerals carved into the beams by the joiners showing which pieces fitted together, but these had been added to by later graffiti, 'Will + Ann', so the carvings progressed from marriage marks to marks of romance. As well as our room, both our children had exposed trusses in their rooms.

41

Front Elevation

Garden Elevation

Side Elevation

PRIESTPOPPLE (c.1700)

(left)

2.4 Priestpopple elevations

(below)

2.5 The view from the garden showing clearly the three separate buildings: the oldest stone part, to the left, the later stone/brick part to the right (which share a valley gutter down the middle, where the two roofs meet), and the 'workshop' at the back

The house had originally been two buildings, with the eastern building being the older of the two; this meant that the 30-inches thick, internal wall running through the middle of the house had once been an external wall and so contained window openings. These old windows, which probably never held glass (this was reserved for the rich), had shutters instead, one pair wooden and one pair metal, and so these shuttered windows provided unexpected visual 'connections' between rooms, connecting a bedroom to the living room and the master bathroom to a WC. (It was possible, if one of you was in the bathroom, to open the wooden shutters and have a conversation with someone else sitting on the toilet next door!)

I began this story with the tale of finding the house, for the first time, through the little wicket door. The strangeness of the reverse route – walking out of the house, through the quiet courtyard and then opening a little door and stepping out into a suddenly busy and bustling town high street – never lost its magical appeal. It always felt rather like stepping through the back of the wardrobe door into Narnia: beyond the wicket door lay another world.

History of the Priestpopple Brewery

The Priestpopple house is really three buildings combined into one: the oldest, the east building; the west building, which is the same size and sits alongside the earlier building; and the workshop, oriented at 90 degrees to the other two buildings and located behind them. It is unclear when the separate Priestpopple buildings were constructed. This is far less easy to determine where a building was not originally a house, as houses are strongly connected with people's lives through censuses and voting lists. At best, a functional building may be alluded to, indirectly, via trade directories. Trade directories were first produced in the 18th century and typically provided a short history of a town, parish or village, and then went on to list all the farmers and tradespeople. For example, in *Pigot's Trade Directory* of 1834[3] for Hexham, a blacksmith, a brewer (John Armstrong), two cartwrights, two gardeners and seedsmen, a gun maker, two joiners and cabinet makers, one millwright, one rope and twine maker, a slater, a plumber and brass

LIVING IN HOUSES

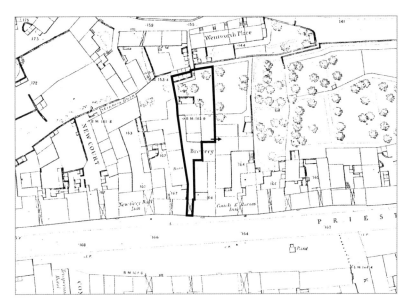

2.6 Extract from Ordnance Survey map '25 inch to the mile' (c.1863–5) showing the site being partially used as a brewery. The arrow indicates the possible connection to the Coach and Horses Inn

founder and one stonemason[4] are all located in Priestpopple. There are also five shopkeepers (or 'dealers in groceries and other sundries') listed as having their premises in Priestpopple, along with two taverns and public houses, one of which is the Coach and Horses (this was owned by a James Turnbull and is next door to the Priestpopple house, a fact which becomes relevant later).

Despite scrutinising the early maps, it is infuriatingly difficult to discern the stage at which the Priestpopple house first appears. This is because its location, set in the middle of a parcel of land bordered by Priestpopple to the south, Wentworth Place to the north and Fore Street to the east, was (and is) such a densely packed jumble of different buildings, sitting cheek by jowl, that it is almost impossible to determine, on small-scale maps, where one building ends and another begins. However, the two or three buildings that later merged to become the Priestpopple house do *seem* to feature on John Wood's 1826 *Plan of Hexham*, which would make the building at least as old as the Orchard Place house (Chapter 4), if not older. There is no question that it appears on the 1863–5 large-scale Ordnance Survey map of Hexham, where one of the buildings, at least, is clearly marked as being a brewery (Fig.2.6).

PRIESTPOPPLE (c.1700)

Another way to date a house is by considering aspects of its structure and materials. The person who was responsible for converting the buildings into a house, Roger Higgins, invited some local historians[5] to visit and give their opinion on the building's age. They noted that 'The [floor]boards on the first floor seem original timbers, [and] look to be before 1700.'[6] They also observed that 'The bathroom has an original window, with two old timber shutters and vertical metal bars, in what was the west outside wall before the later build to the west [and] the sitting room has c. 1700 bricks in the east wall and a window with two opening metal shutters.' They were clearly of the opinion that the east building was the oldest part, and dated from before 1700. Judging by the building fabric and maps, the west side, built alongside the first building, was possibly built in the early 1800s.

If we have, more or less, established the house's approximate age, the next question must surely be, what was it used for? As already mentioned, part of the building is certainly shown as being a brewery on the 1863–5 Ordnance Survey map, and in Marjorie Dallison's article on Priestpopple she describes how a 'brewery existed behind the late 18th-century inn and coaching house, appropriately named the Coach and Horses Inn, on the north side of [Priestpopple]'.[7] What other evidence is there that this was a brewery, and if so, who might have owned it?

To enter the Priestpopple house from the courtyard, you must walk down a cobbled alley running alongside the house, which leads to the front door and to a separate, large workshop (also part of the house). The outline of a former well can be clearly seen in the pattern of the cobbles as a ring of circular stones (see the photograph overleaf). A well, or another source of fresh water, would have been essential to any brewery, and so the presence of a nearby well supports the theory that the house was once a brewery. Furthermore, in Brian Bennison's doctoral thesis on the brewing trade in the North-East, he describes the layout of another brewery in Hexham, the Hexham Old Brewery (built in 1773, closed in 1857 and re-opened in 1866): 'The malting portion of the building was of three storeys in height but most of the premises were of two storeys . . . Malt was stored and ground in the basement[8] and lifted by chain and bucket elevators to hoppers directly above the brewery's two mash tuns.'[9] Bennison adds that an important feature of breweries, at this time, was their reliance on processes that took advantage of

(overleaf)

2.7 View towards the front door of the Priestpopple house; note the circular arrangement of stones within the cobbles in the foreground, this being the site of the former well

LIVING IN HOUSES

gravity wherever possible, and so, considering the size and height of the Priestpopple building/s and its centrally located trapdoor, the layout of the house could easily have accommodated such a brewing process as described here. Bennison explains that the cellar of this 'small' brewery was 2,376 square feet in size (this is where the casks were filled), which is only fractionally larger than the combined footprint of the Priestpopple buildings as shown on the 1863–5 map. Incidentally, Bennison also mentions that this brewery had a 23-foot well. One final piece of evidence is the ramp (the secret passage between our daughter's room and ours): could this have been used for rolling barrels or hauling sacks down?

However, the evidence *against* it being a brewery is also compelling. In Andrew Biggs Wright's 'An Essay Towards a History of Hexham', written in 1823, there is a mention of a brewery in Priestpopple – 'One very considerable Brewery, the property of Mr. Armstrong, is situated in Priestpopple' – but this *does not* refer to this site, but rather one on the opposite side of Priestpopple[10] which was far larger in size. Furthermore, none of the various trade directories between 1822 and 1855 mention any brewer located on Priestpopple, other than Armstrong[11] (and later John Pearson, who took over Armstrong's brewery, the Northumberland Brewery).

At best, then, if this was originally a brewery, it was most likely not a brewery for wholesale distribution, but more likely a small-scale brewery providing beer only for the Coach and Horses Inn next door. As Bennison mentions, 'As the nineteenth century began, the output of beer was not concentrated in the hands of the wholesaling "common brewers" but was also shared amongst beer-retailers, publicans and private home-brewers.' Supporting the theory that the Priestpopple house was, indeed, the brewery of the Coach and Horses Inn, is the fact that in the south-east corner of the building, there is a structure in the wall that suggests that there might have been a doorway connecting it to the Coach and Horses Inn. I think evidence points to it having been a small brewery, probably brewing only once or twice a week,[12] supplying the Coach and Horses with beer until the late 1800s. Hence, the building was feasibly also occupied by the publican James Turnbull.[13]

In its time, the house at Priestpopple has been many things to many people, and what I find most interesting about its history is the fact that at every stage in its history its use seems to exemplify and reflect

PRIESTPOPPLE (c.1700)

the life and times of the market town surrounding it. The workshop at the back was consistently used for more agricultural/craft purposes. It appears to have been used as storage for Fell's Nursery in the 1940s and 1950s, and later it became a joiner's workshop. The combined east and west buildings to the front of the workshop have perhaps had a more interesting history and have supported far more varied uses over time. According to an article in the local newspaper, the *Hexham Courant*, in the 1970s they were the headquarters of the Air Training Corps, Hexham.[14] Later, part of the collection of buildings accommodated a cafe known as The Venice Café.[15]

In the 1980s, some rooms in the building served as the Tynedale Citizens Advice Bureau. According to the Citizens Advice Bureau, there had been a significant rise in enquiries during the 1980s as a result of two recessions and an associated growth in poverty.[16] It is therefore not surprising that this was accompanied by a rise in new bureaux being established, such as the Priestpopple one. Other uses the buildings have had over time include a single room rented out and used for elocution lessons, as well as a carpet warehouse and an antique shop (the building's final incarnation). They have been everything except, of course, a house – that is, until their conversion into a home in 2006; we moved in five years later, in 2011.

2.8 R.A. & J.A. Lowes, carpenters and joiners workshop (at the rear) and The Pine Workshop, antique dealers (at the front)

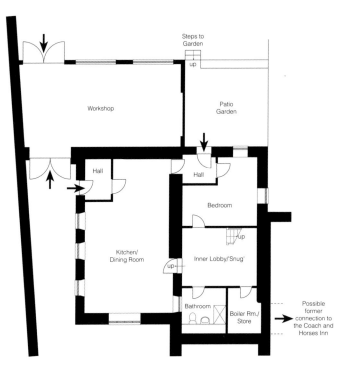

2.9 Priestpopple plans

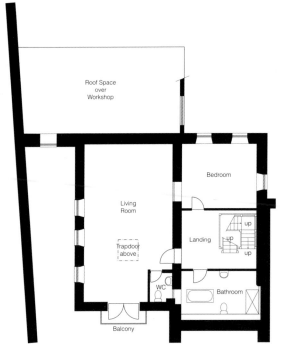
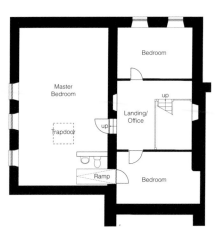

PRIESTPOPPLE (c.1700)

Layout: The House Plan

Since the building went through so many different uses, there is no quintessential, original layout that can be described; rather I will simply describe its arrangement as it was when we lived there.

As mentioned previously, it is accessed through a courtyard and down a cobbled alleyway, at the end of which is the front door. Interestingly, when we first moved in, there was a second entrance which led directly from the courtyard, up a flight of wooden steps and through double-doors directly into the living room on the first floor. We never used these doors, except at the beginning when we moved in our furniture, and since the steps became increasingly rotten (and dangerous to visitors), we removed them and eventually replaced them with a reclaimed, cast-iron balcony.

The cobbled alleyway (which contains the former well) also leads to the workshop – this was a fabulous, self-contained space – nearly 10 metres long with an upper level for storage, a woodburning stove for keeping warm in the winter, and a large sink. We had so many plans for this space, but as it was, like many garages, it became little more than a store and glorified garden shed.

You first entered through a small entrance hall which led to the kitchen – this ran the full length of the house from front to back and was the same size as the living room and master bedroom above. The ground falls gently from front to back with level access achieved at the north, which means that part of the kitchen is below ground and could almost be considered a semi-basement.[17] The kitchen led through one door to the back garden, and through another to an internal lobby and the staircase: a new addition of wood, with open-tread steps, which wound its way round and upwards, connecting all three storeys.[18] The interior hall/lobby, at the base of the staircase, was sufficiently large that we ended up using it as a sort of 'snug', which meant the children could watch TV or play computer games and still be visible from the kitchen. A ground-floor bedroom, a shower room and the boiler/storage room also led off this ground-floor lobby. On the second floor was the large living room, located directly over the kitchen, as well as another bedroom and the main bathroom. This is the floor that contained the 18th-century shuttered windows that visually connected various rooms in surprising ways. The stair continued upwards until the top floor where it emerged onto a surprisingly generous upper

PRIESTPOPPLE (c.1700)

landing, which for us doubled as a home office/homework area for the kids. The final three bedrooms led off this space, the master bedroom being slightly higher than the other two and accessed via three steps. The rear bedroom had two fabulous window seats with views over the garden, whereas the other upper bedroom had only a roof light.

Materials

As mentioned previously, the Priestpopple house is a bit of a hodgepodge of materials, with the oldest part, the east side, being constructed entirely of stone, and the western, slightly newer side, made of a combination of brick and stone; but despite this, I would say that for me the defining material of the Priestpopple house is undoubtedly its stone. One of its internal walls is an extraordinary 30 inches (or more than 75 cm), thick where it connects the newer and older parts of the building. The outer walls of the newer side, although less impressively deep, are still approximately 18 inches (or 45 cm) thick. The external walls consist of a double skin of sandstone masonry with a rubble core. This is not the finely worked ashlar of its close neighbour, Orchard Place (see Chapter 4); rather it is constructed of mostly squared, uncoursed stones. The north-east corner of the older side of the house has large, dressed quoins and elsewhere, including the window surrounds facing the cobbled alley, there are freestone quoins (still identifiably quoins but more roughly cut and irregular in shape). The colour of the stone is mostly a buff or honey-coloured sandstone,[19] but many of the stones contain some ironstone – which gives them more of a ginger tone – so overall the effect is one of a rich tapestry of sandstone colours and textures in the walls.

(left)

2.10 The open staircase running the full height of three storeys. See also the detail of the limewashed interior wall

Another reason that the presence of stone is so forcefully evident *inside the building* is that when the previous owner undertook the conversion, he took the decision not to conceal the interior stonework behind studwork and plasterboard, but wherever possible to leave it fully exposed or paint it with a limewash[20] finish, which served to accentuate the stone's natural, irregular surface. The decision not to hide the interior stonework, but to make a feature of it, undoubtedly helped to retain the vernacular and industrial character of the building, which might have otherwise been lost.

LIVING IN HOUSES

Obviously, with such huge, thick, stone walls, the house was pleasantly cool during the summer months and – especially with the addition of underfloor heating – warm in the winter. However, when inside the building, another effect of the huge mass of stone surrounding you was that it was extraordinarily quiet. It often felt as if the house was located in the middle of the countryside without a single neighbour for miles around, rather than being right in the middle of a bustling market town. This acoustic isolation was one of the more startling effects of its stone walls. Indeed, when the wooden gates in the archway at the front were shut, it felt as if the rest of the world had disappeared, not just visually but acoustically as well.

The Influence and Inspiration of the Creative Reuse of Vernacular, Non-domestic Buildings

What is significant about the Priestpopple house is the fact that I consider it an exemplar of how to convert an historic, vernacular, non-domestic building into a house. This is because the newer parts of the conversion work in harmony with the existing building, emphasising its unique qualities and highlighting its quirkiness. It is hard to state precisely when conversions that radically change the use of historical buildings became popular, but it was undoubtedly influenced, to some degree, by the trend of converting former warehouses into apartments, which originated in New York (and, specifically SoHo) in the 1960s (see Chapter 5 on London Wharf for a longer discussion of the loft-living phenomenon). In the UK, converting and reusing historic buildings is clearly also connected with the establishment of the first conservation areas in 1967 (as part of the Civic Amenities Act of the same year) which are now a mainstay of British planning policies. Historic England estimates that there are now approximately 10,000 conservation areas,[21] which are safeguarded by strict controls over proposed development and demolition.

Furthermore, Derek Latham, in his book on reusing historic buildings, credits the 1975 European Architectural Heritage Year (EAHY) as being particularly impactful, the aim of which was to 'make the public more aware of the irreplaceable cultural, social and economic values represented by historic monuments, groups of old buildings and interesting sites in both town and country'.[22] At the time, the UK government published a book to accompany the European Architectural Heritage Year with the title, *What Is Our Heritage?* It contained photographs of restorations and improvements made between 1972 and 1975, and was intended to both educate and inspire the general public. Peter Burman and Denis Rodwell, in their paper on the UK's response to the European Architectural Heritage Year, suggest that this publication was especially notable for 'the example set by architects in the conversion of disused or derelict buildings as homes and offices for their own use, thereby showcasing what could be achieved'.[23] Burman and Rodwell also concluded that one lasting impact of the European Architectural Heritage Year was 'the realisation that there was limitless scope for imaginative conversion of unused or underused historic buildings'.[24] For my generation of architects, this was simply part of the milieu, the background context against which we were educated – although I do not recall ever being specifically assigned a reuse project at university.

Things are different now. The current buzzwords are 'creative reuse', or even 'creative adaptive reuse', which is essentially the act of breathing new life into formerly disused buildings, while still retaining some of their historic character. Most students of architecture will now undertake at least one creative reuse project at some stage in their education. Furthermore, the Royal Institute of British Architects has recently introduced a new mandatory competence for all architects, Climate Literacy, which includes knowledge of 'retrofit, adaptation, and reuse' as a way of designing buildings that deliver sustainable outcomes and meet the RIBA 2030 Climate Challenge.[25]

According to the architect Derek Latham, creative reuse 'is more than just the conversion or rehabilitation of a property for a new, or continued use. It is a process that harnesses the energy and quality of the original building, whether of special architectural or historic interest or simply a work-a-day redundant building, and combines this with the new energy and activity that the new use brings.'[26] There are some great examples of vernacular, industrial buildings being converted into houses – for example, water towers, carriage/coach houses and stables/mews, mills, railway stations, warehouses and factories, and, of course, barns and other agricultural buildings, to name just a few.

LIVING IN HOUSES

While the television programme *Grand Designs* – which regularly features this type of project – has clearly been influential in encouraging the general public to imagine how such buildings might be transformed into houses, I think that there has been another particularly persuasive project, although this one has probably exerted a more powerful influence on the architectural profession than on non-architects. The Stirling Prize is the most prestigious architectural award that can be given to a building. It is awarded annually, and in 2013 it was awarded for the first time to a creative reuse project. The effect of this should not be underestimated: it is the pinnacle of any architect's career to win the Stirling Prize, and the fact that this could be awarded for a creative reuse project was undeniably momentous.

The project in question was the conversion of a ruined fortified manor, known as Astley Castle, into a holiday home for the Landmark Trust. The building was Grade II* listed but, following a fire in 1978, was in a very poor condition. What was interesting was the approach: rather than rebuild or restore the building, its ruined character was retained, with newly built sections appearing to be almost slotted in behind the jagged facade of the old, making it abundantly clear where old and new met (further emphasised by the changes in materials, the old being stone, the new 'inserts' being brick, glass and wood). The RIBA commented that 'Astley Castle demonstrates that working within sensitive historic contexts requires far more than the specialist skills of the conservation architect.'[27] The architects, Witherford Watson Mann, achieved this through imagination, creativity and meticulous attention to detail.

Personal Lessons Learnt for Architectural Practice

There is one clear lesson that I learnt living in the Priestpopple house and that was the importance of letting traditionally built stone houses breathe. When we were negotiating the sale of the Priestpopple house, we were required, for mortgage purposes, to have a survey conducted. This revealed worrying levels of moisture in the ground-floor walls: 'a level of atmospheric moisture is likely to be high which could be injurious to your health'. The surveyor's clear advice was that if we did not treat it, we would never be able to resell the property as such moisture levels would be clearly off-putting to any future buyers. Their solution was to fully 'tank' the basement – tanking being the process of creating a continuous, fully sealed and impermeable barrier between the dry, inside spaces and the damp, outside world.

As an architect, my experience at the time had mostly been of designing new buildings, so my knowledge of working with stone amounted to little more than knowing that traditional lime mortar is preferable to concrete mortar, as it is less brittle and will move and flex with the stone- or brickwork. I had not, then, learnt about the necessity for stone to breathe and in the face of the Priestpopple house's doom-laden survey, I needed to rapidly educate myself on the topic. Essentially, all air is moist and all stone and brick are slightly porous, meaning that moist air can naturally pass through them (which is a good thing). This process is known as natural vapour transmission. Good interior ventilation will ensure that any moisture passing through the walls is continuously removed through the process of evaporation. However, if anything prevents the movement of air through the stone, the moisture becomes trapped and the water vapour will condense to produce liquid water – and as a result, the stone will become damp. Therefore, the last thing that anyone should do is to tank an old, stone building (this is equally true of chemically injected damp-proof courses), as this will prevent the natural vapour transmission. The dampness that our surveyor had discovered was actually the result of the kitchen area having previously been tanked, causing water to be trapped in the stone.

We chose to ignore the survey report and did nothing. As part of my reading at the time, I read somewhere (and sadly can no longer find the reference) that formerly damp walls, given a chance to breathe, will gradually dry out at a rate of 1 cm per month. Over the six years we lived in the house, I periodically borrowed a damp meter from work to measure the levels of damp in the walls and, sure enough, the so-called 'problematic' walls became gradually drier and drier over time. A little faith in traditional building methods and patience was all that was needed. I am convinced that the previous owner's approach – to repoint the walls with a lime mortar and use breathable, limewash finishes throughout – was the correct one. This was, undoubtedly, a valuable education for me as an architect, and a reminder that we are all constantly learning, regardless of what stage in our careers we are at.

3

Gower Street (1789)

The Story of the Growth of Georgian London

3.1　Sketch drawing of the Gower Street houses

GOWER STREET (1789)

Introduction: My Lived Experience of this Home

The first house that I lived in after leaving Yearnor Cottage was 93 Gower Street, in the middle of Bloomsbury. I was about to take my first tentative steps towards becoming an architect and had secured a place at the Bartlett School of Architecture, University College London (UCL). Like most first-year students, I applied for university accommodation and was duly given a shared room on Gower Street.

I was given a lift to London by my step-father who parked outside the set of three, connected Georgian houses that collectively formed UCL's student accommodation known, then, as 93–97 Gower Street.[1] He helped me with my one bag and, with little ceremony, perfunctorily departed, leaving me to start my new life in London. My room, number 9323, was in house number 93 – or the far left one if looking at the set of three houses – on the second floor (2) and the third of three rooms on that floor (3).

The room, a shared bedroom, would have been quite generous for one person but did not feel particularly large for two people: it was about 5 by 4 metres and contained a couple of single beds, a shared double wardrobe and our own basin. The room did have relatively high ceilings, about 3 metres high, but not so tall as those in the rooms on the ground and first floors. I also do not recall there being much in the way of original mouldings and internal decorative features left, although there was a fireplace, left as a remnant of its former past (Fig.3.2). The room was located at the back of the house, looking towards the back of Chenies Mews (the former stables/coach accommodation), and so was quieter than the rooms facing Gower Street.

The three houses had a very unusual spatial organisation. They were connected via the basements, which was also where the kitchens were situated. Each house had its own kitchen (in probably the exact same location as where the kitchen would have been when they were originally built as family homes). They were also connected, rather strangely, at the third-floor level as well (but not linked via any other floors). This meant that if you wanted a shower, a row of which were located in the basement of number 97, you either had to go down to the basement of number 93 and literally walk through all of the other three kitchens in your dressing gown, towel and soap in hand, or conversely

(left)

3.2   Photograph of me, reading a newspaper, in my Gower Street room; the original fireplace is visible behind me, with dentil moulding beneath the mantel. It was far less grand than the fireplaces on the lower floors

3.3   The entrance to 93 Gower Street, with details such as soot-blackened London stock bricks, external ironwork, including railings and boot scraper, and a semi-circular fan light beneath a brick arch

(right)

3.4   93–97 Gower Street, street elevations

3.5   93–97 Gower Street, rear elevations

LIVING IN HOUSES

go up to the third floor and enter house number 97 that way, and then descend four storeys until you reached the basement.

Of the three, 93 Gower Street was the house that was a bit different; whereas numbers 95 and 97 had their ground floors rendered in stucco to resemble stonework,[2] number 93 was more austere, with its soot-blackened brick entrance, and I recall that I rather grew to appreciate its sombre severity, compared to its flashier neighbours. Of course, I did not truly appreciate, at the time, the fact that I was living in a piece of architectural history. In one of my first lectures at the university, one of our tutors spoke passionately about the beauty of repetitive elements in architecture, citing Georgian terraces as an example, and I do recall returning home and pausing to study the row of Georgian houses on Gower Street, trying to understand what he had meant by this.

History of Georgian London

The story of the building of Georgian London is the story of the first mass construction of housing in England. By extension, this also means that it was the first occasion of a number of other related activities: developer-led housing speculation; the use of standardised building components; catalogues of components, or 'pattern books', especially of decorative features; the organisation of builders into general contractors and subcontractors; the process of writing building specifications (explicit descriptions of what, and how, building products should be used); and, not least of all, the profession of architecture as we would recognise it today. But how and why did Georgian London come about? Just as Yearnor Cottage can be seen as being the product of one building boom (the Great Rebuilding), so the houses of Gower Street can be seen as being integral to the country's next significant building boom – one which, according to John Summerson, author of the classic book on Georgian London,[3] began with the Treaty of Utrecht (1715) and ended with Waterloo (1815); in other words, it coincided with a period of relative peace in Europe.[4] Also, like the Great Rebuilding, this second wave of rebuilding was fuelled primarily by the twin drivers of increased household prosperity coupled with rapid population growth.[5]

GOWER STREET (1789)

The Georgian era refers to a period of time of just over 100 years' duration, encompassing the reign of King George I (crowned in 1714) through to the death of King George IV (1830). Sometimes the Georgian period is also considered to include the reign of George IV's son, William IV,[6] in which case the period is stretched until William's death in 1837 (at which point the Victorian era unequivocally began). The term is often used interchangeably with the Regency period which, strictly speaking, only referred to the nine years when George IV acted as Prince Regent in place of his father, who was deemed incapacitated for reasons of illness, namely 1811–20. The Georgian era was characterised by great social change, as well as by substantial shifts in politics, the arts, literature and, most of all, its distinctive architectural style. Indeed, in a recent survey by a British home improvements firm,[7] it was determined that Georgian architecture was the nation's most recognisable house style (followed by Tudor and Victorian architecture).

If the building boom of this period can be attributed to population growth and wealth, Summerson also suggests that one of its distinguishing characteristics was the importance of taste. Taste can be a nebulous thing at the best of times, but taste in Georgian life unquestionably had its origins in the tradition of the Grand Tour, this being a trip taken by young, upper-class men around Europe and lasting anywhere between a few months and several years. One primary reason for the Grand Tour was its educational purpose, and hence the trip typically included visits to sites of architectural renown, particularly in Italy, and sites of antiquity in Rome. Young men were encouraged to observe, study, sketch and paint these buildings or ruins, and being knowledgeable about classical architecture was an expected component of any gentleman's education. It is interesting to note that the golden age of the Grand Tour happens to coincide precisely with the building of 93–97 Gower Street in Bloomsbury, and it is no coincidence that many features of Georgian architecture are reinterpretations of the classical architecture that had been so admired on the Grand Tour. It could therefore be argued that the upper classes had received an architectural education (or at the very least, an education in architectural taste), unlike that of any previous generation; all that was needed was an outlet for it, a means by

63

LIVING IN HOUSES

which such knowledge could be applied to the real world – and that opportunity was poised to present itself during the building boom that was Georgian London.

Let us now turn our attention to Bloomsbury, the area of London in which Gower Street is located. Bloomsbury is one of the best examples of Georgian London, with many well-preserved terraces of Georgian townhouses. This part of Bloomsbury was developed by generations of the Dukes of Bedford, or the Russell family,[8] and so the story of this family and their development of Bloomsbury is effectively the story of Georgian London's building boom in microcosm. So why did the Dukes of Bedford suddenly decide to engage in the speculative development of housing, aside from obvious financial gain? There are three key players in the development of the Duke of Bedford's Bloomsbury land: the 4th Duke, John Russell (1710–71), his wife Gertrude Leveson-Gower,[9] and their grandson, the 5th Duke, Francis Russell (1765–1802). It was Francis Russell who, in collaboration with his grandmother, effectively built Gower Street, naming it after Gertrude's family, the Earls of Gower. It could be argued that the development of Bloomsbury arose because of a unique and fortuitous constellation of circumstances. First, the northerly extent of London in the latter half of the 18th century more or less followed the line of Great Russell Street[10] (now best known as being the location of the British Museum); a small section of the Bedford Estate lay to the south of Great Russell Street, but the vast majority of it, as undeveloped farmland, lay to the north. In other words, the only way in which London could be developed beyond its then northern boundary, in this part of London, was on land belonging to the Russell family. Second, there were already some compelling examples of experiments in speculative building in the Russell family: John Russell's great-great-grandfather was the 4th Earl of Bedford who had been responsible for developing Covent Garden in 1630, while another of John Russell's ancestors, his great-grandfather, Thomas Wriothesley, 4th Earl of Southampton, was also a pioneer speculative builder, building Bloomsbury Square in 1665. Therefore, John had precedents of speculative development through both his paternal and maternal grandparents' families. Third, the Russell family had the financial capital to underpin the new development. The influence

GOWER STREET (1789)

of the construction of Bloomsbury Square, built by John Russell's great-grandfather in 1665, is particularly germane to this story since Summerson suggests it firmly established the three core principles of London's future Georgian developments: an aristocratic lead; mixed development (squares, streets, houses, markets, churches); with a speculative builder as middle-man. Summerson concludes: 'Here we have the beginning of that system of speculation by hereditary landlords which brought half [of] London into being.'[11]

Although it was John Russell who began the development of Bloomsbury, it was his grandson, the 5th Duke, Francis Russell, who finished it. Francis had lost both his parents by the age of three and inherited his grandfather's title in 1771, at the age of six. He was, presumably, raised by his grandmother, the Duchess, and it was his grandmother's determination to carry on her late husband's work that led the two of them, in collaboration, to finish the development. Francis spent 1784–6 on the Grand Tour,[12] returning when he was 21, and less than three years later began the development of Gower Street, starting with, among others, numbers 93–97 – and so the house that I lived in was one of the very first to have been built.

Essentially there were two types of speculative builders in Georgian London: those who developed both the land and the houses (the Dukes of Bedford fell into this category), and those who developed the houses only (these were often developed by builders and craftsmen, frequently formed into small collectives). The way in which Bloomsbury would have been developed is that the plots of land would have been laid out in such a way as to maximise frontage (in other words, profit), leading inevitably to an unusually narrow house width, often 24 feet wide (7.3 metres) or less; then the plot was leased to a separate, speculative builder to develop. The *Survey of London*, originally published by the London County Council in 1949, describes the development of the Gower Street houses: 'The first six houses on each side, Nos. 87–97 (west), and Nos. 88–98 (east), are on the site of Cantlowes Close and building leases were granted for their erection by Francis, Duke of Bedford, in 1789.'[13] It is not known who was the architect or builder[14] for 93–97 Gower Street, but they most likely consisted of a main contractor (or 'master builder') using a group of trusted carpenters, bricklayers, tilers, plasterers, plumbers and

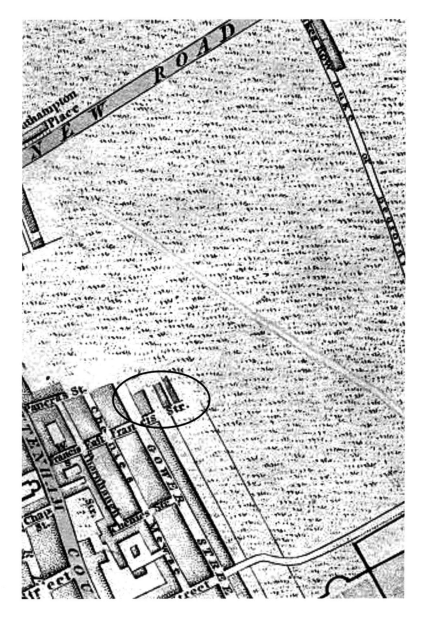

3.6 Excerpt from *Cary's New And Accurate Plan Of London And Westminster, 1795,* showing the extent of Gower Street's development. 93–97 Gower Street (circled) is one of the last houses on the west side of the street

decorators, this essentially being the beginning of the modern system of general contractors and subcontractors. As Summerson observed: 'Sub-contracting was an essential and striking feature of the Georgian building industry. A very large part of the ordinary tradesman's work was done for his fellow tradesmen.'[15]

On *Cary's New And Accurate Plan Of London And Westminster, 1795,* drawn less than six years after 93 Gower Street was built, you can easily see that the 93–97 Gower Street houses are situated on the very edge of the development, in the block bounded by Gower Street to the east, Francis Street (Torrington Place today) to the south and Chenies Mews to the west. It is striking that there is nothing but fields between this block of houses and the New Road (now Euston Road). Indeed, Gower Street simply peters out. By the time, however, that *Cruchley's New Plan Of London Improved To 1827* was published, this entire area of Bloomsbury had taken the form that we would recognise today.

Finally, it is just worth noting that, unlike many of the other houses in this book, the former occupants of 93–97 Gower Street have been well documented via a number of different sources.[16] Bloomsbury was a solidly professional, middle-class neighbourhood, and for the most part, numbers 93 and 95 appear to have originally been the homes of doctors and surgeons. This fits with a description of Gower Street from UCL's Bloomsbury Project[17] that suggests that 'medical men were the main residents of the street at this time'.[18] Only number 97 had a different early occupant, namely the Reverend Thomas Rackett[19] (1757–1841), who lived there for nearly 20 years and, as well as being a clergyman, was also a writer and scholar, expert in many fields, and member of multiple learned societies. After his departure in 1842, number 97[20] also became occupied by a surgeon.

Layout: The House Plan

I have already described at the beginning of this chapter how the 93–97 Gower Street houses had been converted into student accommodation by connecting them through their basement and attic floors. It is far more interesting to try to understand how the houses might have been laid out when they were first built as family homes. An article for the Temple Bar magazine, written in 1893, describes the overall situation of these houses: 'The houses in Gower Street are solid and substantial without, comfortable and roomy within. They all have long gardens, in some of which are venerable trees . . .' and goes on to describe how one of the occupants 'used to say that the house was the pleasantest he ever occupied. He could look over the fields as far as Hampstead, Highgate, and Islington.'

LIVING IN HOUSES

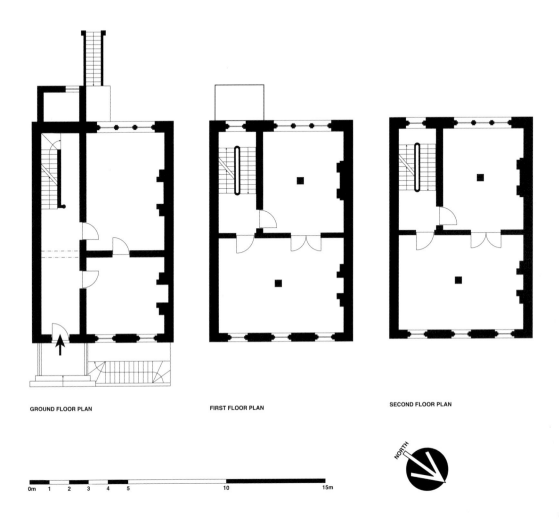

3.7 Original layout of a Gower Street house

The layout of Georgian townhouses was remarkably consistent and there were good reasons for this: if the frontage were to be kept as narrow as possible, for purposes of maximising profit, then it prohibited houses being more than a single room wide. A typical facade was just 24 feet wide,[21] and stairs were required for accessing upper floors, so one room wide was as much as could be squeezed in. Equally, because of the necessity for light, there could only be a single room at the front and a second at the back, so the houses

68

GOWER STREET (1789)

were essentially extended upwards, with pairs of rooms stacked on top of each other. This resulted in the distinctive tall, thin, Georgian townhouse proportions. Each storey became successively shorter, which also induces a slight optical illusion of making the building seem taller than it actually is.[22] Each floor had different functions which varied only slightly from house to house: the ground floor was for dining (to minimise the distance from kitchen to table since nobody wants cold food) plus a library/study; formal entertaining therefore necessitated shifting the reception rooms to the first-floor level as a sort of *piano nobile* after the fashion of Italian palazzos; the subsequent floors accommodated family bedrooms; and finally

3.8   Here you can see the extent of the 'area' or 'airy' surrounded by railings and the steps descending down into the kitchen/service basement level

LIVING IN HOUSES

the attic (beneath an uninsulated roof and hence cold) was always reserved for the servants' bedrooms.

Another feature of these houses was their semi-basement, produced through the process of road building. The original ground level of 93–97 Gower Street is evident only at the back, where it is level with the garden and Chenies Mews; in contrast, the level of Gower Street at the front has been partially built up. The basement level was excavated by approximately a third of a storey, and the soil used to build up the road level by the same amount. Additionally, steps leading from street level to the ground floor complete the final third of the basement's height, as well as creating a more imposing entrance. This meant that activities such as cooking could be visually (and potentially olfactorily) hidden from any arriving visitor. Most London Georgian houses with such a sub-basement also had a small courtyard/lightwell 'area' at the front known colloquially as an 'airy'. Part of the genius of this arrangement was that coal cellars could be located beneath the pavement, facilitating quick and easy coal deliveries via a covered coal-chute in the pavement. Stairs leading from the pavement to the 'area' facilitated easy deliveries to the kitchen which, along with the scullery, pantry and any ancillary service rooms, was located in the basement. As mentioned briefly, the stables and/or coach house were usually located behind the house in a *mews*; in the case of Gower Street this was Chenies Mews. The beauty of this layout was that it was surprisingly flexible and egalitarian: it could be used as the basis for upper-class houses as well as those of the middle and lower classes, with only minor variations (that is, varying the numbers of storeys, the width of the frontage and the inclusion/exclusion of mews).

Materials

It is interesting how three of the characteristic features of Georgian architecture can be attributed to regulations that arose in the aftermath of the Great Fire of London (1666) and were all intended as measures for reducing fire-spread: recessed windows, parapet roofs and cornices. All of these building features were intended to ensure that there was no exposed timber on the facade of the building: the wooden eaves

GOWER STREET (1789)

are hidden behind the parapet and cornice, and the wooden window frames, while unable to be hidden entirely, are at least recessed as far back as possible, rather than being in line with the facade. The recessing of the windows in this way had an additional, unforeseen effect of making the building appear more solid and substantial, with the windows as holes seemingly punched through the solidity of the brick or stone wall.

Georgian window-openings cannot be mentioned without a consideration of the sash window. Essentially windows fall into three broad types: fixed glazing (which do not open: Georgian fanlights above doors are a type of fixed glazing), casement windows (a hinged window opening like a door), and a sash window (where one part of the frame slides past the another to open it). Sash windows, per se, were not a new invention: Yearnor Cottage, in Chapter 1, had sash windows, but they were *horizontal* sash windows. Obviously, if window panes slide horizontally, they are relatively easy to construct since all a carpenter needs to do is to make grooves for the frames to slide along. However, the problem with horizontal sash windows is that they lend themselves, naturally, to being wider than they are tall, namely more horizontal. The tall, thin proportions of a Georgian terrace house require, from an aesthetic point of view, tall, thin windows; compositionally, the facade would simply not look 'right' if it contained low, wide windows.

However, there is a problem with vertical sash windows: on pushing/sliding up a window, how do you keep it in place, since gravity will want to make it slide back down again? The answer is, and was, to use counterweights, perfectly balancing the weight of the moveable window frame, such that the window appears to magically stay in whatever position it has been placed. In fact, you need not just weights, but an entire counterbalancing system including cords and pulleys, and this is a massively complex construction problem, especially if you then wish to conceal the ingenious mechanism. The ultimate solution is that the counterbalancing system is housed in a 'box' hiding the weights and pulleys from view, with only the sash cords visible, and this is why sash windows of this kind are sometimes referred to as box sash windows.

According to two experts on the history of the sash window, Hentie Louw and Robert Crayford, it emerged about 1670[23] in London. However, they stress that it took decades of experimentation by

LIVING IN HOUSES

craftsmen to attain the form that became commonplace in Georgian London; indeed, they suggest that it was only by 1720 that the technical development of the sash window had been finished, with all teething troubles resolved. In other words, the maturity of the box sash window occurred exactly in time for the beginning of the Georgian building boom.

The Influence and Inspiration of the Georgian Terraced House

It cannot be underestimated how influential the Georgian townhouse has been. 'Mock Georgian', 'Neo-Georgian' or even 'Pseudo Georgian' is a style that is built in its thousands today,[24] but interestingly enough, rarely for terraced townhouses such as the long stretches of terraces in Gower Street. Rather, such Neo-Georgian houses are more likely to be found as a style for detached or semi-detached, new-build homes. What makes these houses Neo-Georgian? Typically, such a style is denoted by a few token features: the odd keystone lintel above a window, a vague suggestion of pilasters or columns flanking the front door, with an obligatory fan light beneath a miniature pediment or even an attempt at an entablature. In other words, a collection of architectural elements intended merely to suggest period style. However, the fundamental aspect of Georgian interiors – the proportions and height of rooms and the subtleties of its planning and layout – are entirely omitted. Once through the door, any pretence of being inside a period property disappears – these mock Georgian properties are frequently 'window dressing' in every sense of the word.

Perhaps the true influence of Georgian London is not to be found in these mock period developer-built estates, but rather in the essence of the terrace itself. It would be untrue to say that the terrace house had not existed prior to the Duke of Bedford's experimental development, but what was truly influential about the Georgian London terrace was the sheer scale of it – the array of identical, or near identical, houses stacked in a relentless ordering of sameness. The definition of the terrace, therefore, is where a house shares party walls[25] on both sides with different houses, but at least all three (the smallest possible number for any terrace) houses sharing similar proportions, massing, materials and architectural features – in other words, style. According to John Summerson: 'The Great Queen Street houses [built around 1637][26] were reputed, in the eighteenth century, to constitute "the first regular street in London".' He goes on to say: 'They laid down the canon of street design which put an end to gabled individualism, and provided a discipline for London's streets which was accepted for more than two hundred years.'[27] The Georgian terrace can therefore be considered one of the great contributions, not only to domestic architecture, but to urban design.

It would not be an underestimation to say that architects are currently in the process of rediscovering the terrace house in new and exciting ways. Although during the 20th century there were some notable examples of architects dabbling with the terrace house as a form, they are not particularly plentiful. Rare examples include the short terrace of four houses on Genesta Road in Plumstead, built in 1935 by Berthold Lubetkin and A.V. Pilichowski, as well as Ernő Goldfinger's Willow Road terrace (consisting of merely three houses), built in 1939, which, together, are probably the only two modernist terraces in the UK.

As we move through the 20th century, there are some important examples of terraces from the 1950s and 1960s. For example, many of the houses designed by Geoffrey Townsend and Eric Lyons (through their company, Span Developments Limited) were two-storey terraced houses, of which there are numerous excellent examples in Blackheath,[28] as well as those found in the village of New Ash Green in Kent. Moving forward again through time, to the 1980s, we arrive at the high-tech style (think curvy and metallic) terraces known as 1–12 Grand Union Walk, by Nicholas Grimshaw & Partners, which are now Grade II-listed and located just down the road from where I eventually came to live for many years in Camden (also see Chapter 9 for a discussion of another Georgian-inspired terraced house in Elm Village, Camden).

But it is at the start of the 21st century that the terrace house really seems to be coming into its own again. Three examples come to mind as being particularly influential, the first being the sustainable housing development in Sutton, south London, known as BedZED (Beddington Zero Energy Development), completed in 2002 and designed by BedZED in partnership with Bill Dunster Architects. It is a mixed-development scheme, but the houses – instantly recognisable because of their fully glazed facades (to maximise heat gain from the sun), gently curved roofs and colourful chimneys – are arranged in long, parallel, south-facing terraces.

The second prominent example is Urban Splash's Chimney Pot Park scheme in Salford – not a new build but a regeneration – built in 2007 after eight pairs of unwanted terraces (consisting of 349 homes in total) were entirely remodelled and modernised by the architects ShedKM, demonstrating how transformative regeneration can be. And it is not too much of an exaggeration to draw a line connecting Chimney Pot Park to my third example, Goldsmith Street terraces, the 2019 Stirling Prize-winning design of social housing designed by Mikhail Riches with Cathy Hawley, which were also certified Passivhaus and, like the BedZED development, have terraces running east to west, permitting south-facing facades.

Why are terraces becoming popular again? I think it is a combination of the need for low-rise yet high-density developments, a recognition that terrace houses can be some of the most sustainable forms of housing (as per the BedZED development) due to their inherent reduction in external walls (hence minimising heat loss), and finally, perhaps, also due to a new-found respect for community, coupled with a sense that as a society we have, potentially, now passed 'peak individualism'.[29] I look forward to the terrace's next stage of architectural evolution.

Personal Lessons Learnt for Architectural Practice

While I did not pay too much attention to my tutor[30] all those years ago, talking about the beauty and elegance of repetition, the comment has obviously stayed with me over the years. But I think that if there was anything that I learnt from living and studying in Bloomsbury, it was an appreciation of brick. Having grown up in Leicestershire, with frequent visits to Leicester, which is essentially a red-brick city (so much so that there are now numerous bricks available which are variations of 'Leicester' red), I just do not think that I ever really looked – properly

GOWER STREET (1789)

looked – at bricks until I came to live in London. Red bricks had been so much of a backdrop to my childhood, including the lovely handmade bricks of Yearnor Cottage, that I never gave them a second thought. I suspect, though, had I been asked in my childhood, I would have said that I did not really like red-brick houses. Later, I certainly recall having conversations with my fellow architecture students about the merits of yellow London stock bricks, compared to red stock bricks, and whether blackened bricks should be cleaned to reveal their true colour (no real consensus on this one) or, even worse, painted black. In short, at a time when bricks were deeply unfashionable in schools of architecture, being immersed in Georgian Bloomsbury made us look at them again and reconsider their values.

4

Orchard Place (1824)

The Story of a Regency Villa Fallen on Hard Times

4.1   Sketch drawing of Orchard Place

ORCHARD PLACE (1824)

Introduction: My Lived Experience of this Home

My mother had decided to move to Hexham to be closer to our family. We had probably looked at about 10 houses (both flats and larger houses with separate annexes), and nothing seemed to fulfil her requirements, before she showed me a listing – surprisingly not for a residential property, but for a commercial one – just over 100 metres from our Priestpopple house. I had been aware of this property but had previously dismissed it as an unviable option; however, I readily agreed to accompany her on a viewing, just out of curiosity.

1 Orchard Place was an utter mess – there is no other way of describing it. It was classified as a commercial property, indeed it had not been used as a house for at least 81 years (as I later discovered). The front section was a retail property: it had formerly been used as a shop which had closed five years earlier. The back part was classified as offices which had probably not been used as such since the 1980s. The rear office rooms were full of solidly built fitted cupboards, threadbare commercial carpets and desks huddled in random clusters, as if lost. The needs of the shop at the front had necessitated the removal of many of the original interior walls in order to make a larger, more expansive retail space, and the addition of changing rooms (it had been a dress boutique) as well as a huge, semi-circular reception desk. Once you began to delve into the bowels of the building, it was clear that there was a damp problem, probably woodworm, possibly wet or dry rot, and clear evidence of subsidence. Basically, it was unloved, abandoned and in a terrible state, and anyone with half an ounce of sense would have walked away without a backward glance. And yet . . . there were glimpses of parts of carved fire surrounds peeking out from behind the modern reception desk, exquisite mouldings in the ceilings, well-proportioned rooms (if you could imagine the original walls reinstated) and large sash windows. It wrung my heart to see such a handsome building chopped up, messed around with and then heartlessly abandoned.

When we first visited it, the building had already been vacant for five years and its condition was steadily deteriorating. The reason why it had been left empty for so long was that there was not a high demand for more offices/retail space in our Northumberland market town, it

LIVING IN HOUSES

was too large for a single-family dwelling, but the layout was equally unsuitable for carving up into smaller flats. Apparently, a number of developers had viewed the property with an eye to converting it into multiple flats, but the layout, particularly the location of stairs and services, did not lend itself readily to this sort of sub-division. In fact, as it turned out, one of the few things that it could lend itself to was a large family home with an attached granny annexe. We had it surveyed just two weeks later and subsequently completed the purchase by September 2016. Every step of the way we were advised (by a local authority planner, our solicitor, different builders and even architectural colleagues) not to proceed with our plans of converting it back into a house. But like many things, the aspects we had anticipated would be problematic were not: the roof was sound; there was no dry or wet rot, just typical (and more easily remedied) damp problems; the woodworm was limited and treatable, and the obvious signs of subsidence turned out to have dated from around the 1860s and thankfully nothing had moved, in any significant way, for over 100 years. The unanticipated setbacks were the presence of asbestos (all possible types and in many, many locations[1]), the fact that when we removed one of the marble fire surrounds for restoration, we discovered that it was holding up the gable wall of the house (thank goodness for steel shoring posts) and the 8-foot-tall, stone garden wall that subsequently blew over in a storm. Admittedly, it has been a proverbial money-pit: I discovered that even being an architect does not prevent escalating costs in a project like this, when you never quite know what you will discover when you start 'removing' or 'uncovering' parts of the building fabric.

In essence, we lived continuously on a building site for four years and now count the builders as members of our extended family, but we have been rewarded with a remarkable building about which we are still uncovering the history. So, what is my experience of living in this house? I simply love the tall ceilings – they are literally uplifting. The effect of the large sash windows is light and airy rooms. The master bedroom was an unforeseen surprise since its double-aspect windows ensure we receive both morning and evening sunlight – pure joy! But most of all I think I love the elegant, mahogany, gently curved staircase handrail, and holding it, as I come down stairs, is a genuine tactile pleasure.

ORCHARD PLACE (1824)

History of 1 Orchard Place

The history of 1 Orchard Place dates back to at least 1733, when land of about an acre in size, known as 'The Barn Garth',[2] came into the ownership of a William Head and was to remain in the Head family for 132 years. Upon this land lay three barns (and it is probable that the house's coach house, which appears older than the main house, is either built upon the site or incorporates part of one of these original barns).

In 1824, the estate came into the possession of notable Hexham worthy Charles Head[3] – presumably a descendant of William Head – and included the 'said Dwellinghouse, Garden and premises . . . together with all and singular Outhouses, Edifices, Buildings . . .'[4] and the house, now known as 1 Orchard Place, was built. Charles Head was born in Chollerton, Northumberland, in around 1794 and is described variously as a gentleman, a farmer with 21 acres, a banker[5] and a solicitor, with his practice located at 1 Meal Market in Hexham for what appears to be most of his professional life.

Orchard Place first appears on Wood's 1826 *Plan of Hexham*, and at this stage it consisted only of the front part of the present house (plus the coach house and its stone archway entrance, now a scheduled ancient monument) and was located at the then very edge of Hexham, looking outwards in a south-easterly direction towards Dipton Wood. In a book on the gentleman's house by Robert Kerr, in 1865,[6] he describes the prospect of a house being 'the view from its windows; this being considered with relation, first, to the landscape, and secondly, to the light in which that is to be seen'.[7] There is no doubt that, when first built, 1 Orchard Place's prospect must have been exceedingly fine[8] and it must have felt distinctly rural, despite enabling a mere five-minute walk for Charles to go to work.

The house, as originally built by Charles, was two storeys high with a basement; however, the land slopes from front to back, so the basement level at the front becomes ground level at the back. This difference in height was further exaggerated by building up the ground level at the front to form a plinth in front of the house, which also serves to make the house appear a little grander, and a little more detached from the street, than it might otherwise have been. In many respects this is reminiscent of how 93 Gower Street, built only 35 years earlier, was similarly raised up

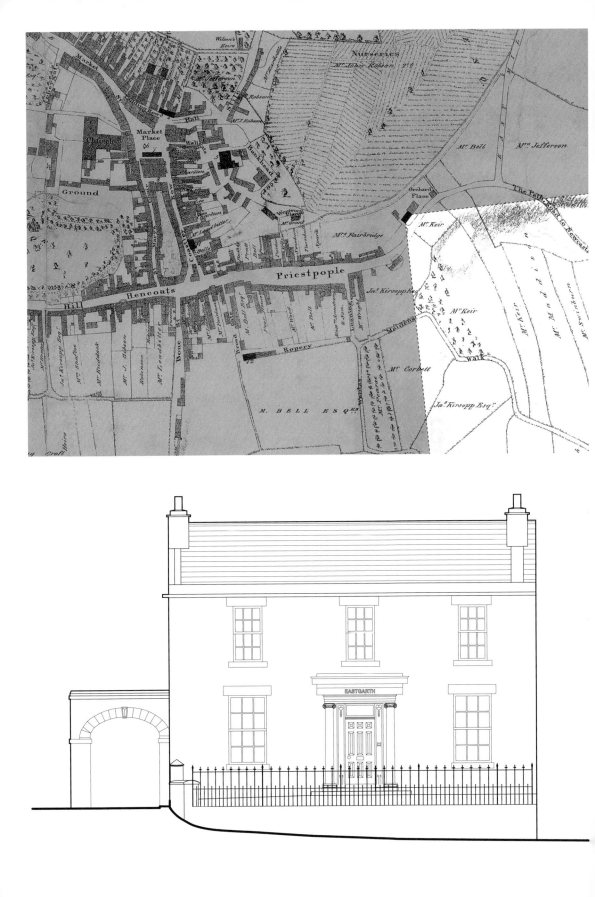

(left)

4.2 The rural prospect of (or view from) 1 Orchard Place superimposed on Wood's 1826 *Plan of Hexham*

4.3 Front elevation of Orchard Place

(right)

4.4 The entrance to Orchard Place showing the entablature and former Eastgarth name carved into the frieze

at the street level. The house is built of local sandstone, with the front elevation constructed of ashlar (finely dressed stone cut into regular sizes) and the remaining external walls made from random coursed sandstone with ashlar quoins and dressings. The entrance has a central Ionic portico with detached columns and side niches.

When first built in 1824 it was a detached house, but very rapidly it was joined by first two, and then a third, additional houses to the east, the first two being built the following year, immediately turning it from a detached villa into a terrace. It is unclear whether it was originally intended to be part of a terrace – as its design certainly resembles that

4.5 Orchard Place carved above the terrace

of a detached villa – or whether this was an afterthought. However, a document,[9] dated 1824, describes Charles' ownership of the house as excluding 'the East Gable of the said Dwellinghouse which is agreed shall be a party Gable between the said Charles Head and the owner of the adjoining Dwellinghouse where erected . . .' Since the other three houses are built on land owned by the Head family, perhaps Charles was simply unable to resist a little small-scale, speculative house building of his own.[10] Whatever the reason, the house now forms the end of a terrace of four houses which, together, have acquired a collective and enduring identity as Orchard Place, which is proudly proclaimed on a carved parapet above Nos 2 and 3.

The house remained in the ownership of Charles Head until 1845 when he and his wife Betsy moved to Hackwood House, a Tudor gothic villa built for them by the renowned architect John Dobson[11] of Newcastle.

By the time the next map of Hexham – the first Ordnance Survey map of 1863 – had been published, a rear extension to the house had been added, but not in the position of the current extension, which is first shown on the 1897 Ordnance Survey map. The current extension, therefore, must have been added between 1863 and 1897, making the rear part of the house mid-Victorian. Since the next owner, leather and wool merchant Henry Bell, died in 1875 and he was most likely responsible for building the extension,[12] this part was probably built in the 12 years between 1863 and 1875. The house remained in the Bell family for nearly 60 years, until 1919, making them the house's longest inhabitants.

After the Bell family's departure, the house endured a rapid succession of owners and tenants, until 1936 when it was sold to Hannah Mark – previously the landlady of The Tanners Arms public house in Gilesgate, Hexham – for £600. She purchased the house to turn it into a drinking establishment, calling it the Eastgarth Club,[13] and it remained a drinking and social club for 18 years, until 1957 when

ORCHARD PLACE (1824)

she leased it to the National Farmers Union as their Hexham office. At this stage, an inventory was made of the Eastgarth Club's fixtures and fittings, including a bar area 'in the front room', covered with linoleum, and 40 feet of upholstered benching in 4 × 10-foot sections. It remained the NFU's office until Hannah's death in 1967 when it was sold or leased to a veterinarian, John Pickering, to use as a practice.

In the 1980s, the house served as offices for a firm of accountants, and finally, in 2008, it was sold to be turned into a short-lived dress boutique which closed in 2011. The property then remained empty until we bought it with the intention of restoring it back into a family home, the first time it had been used as a house for at least 81 years.

Layout: The House Plan (and the Typical Regency Villa Plans)

Plans of similar houses from the time are invaluable for working out what the original layout of 1 Orchard Place might have been, and the closest I have found was published in Richards' book on the history of the English house.[14] This illustration (Fig.4.7) shows a Regency villa dated 1823, just two years before the front portion of 1 Orchard Place was constructed. This plan shows a highly symmetrical layout, with a centrally placed hall leading to a rear, curved staircase. The rooms are divided symmetrically either side.

If we overlay Richards' plan of the typical Regency villa form onto the plan of 1 Orchard Place we draw the following conclusions: the room in 1 Orchard Place to the right of the hall upon entering the house was most likely the parlour. This is the only room that occupies the full depth of the house, with windows overlooking both the front and back. This is also the room that contains the grandest marble fireplace and has the most ornate cornice of any room (consisting of a pattern of oak leaves and acorns) which supports the premise that it was the parlour, the room for receiving guests. To the left of the hall, at the front, was a smaller room, most likely the dining room; and finally, the smallest room on the ground floor, immediately behind the dining room, was probably Charles Head's library/study.

We can be sure that the kitchen was originally in the basement (opening onto the rear garden, before the rear part was built) since in

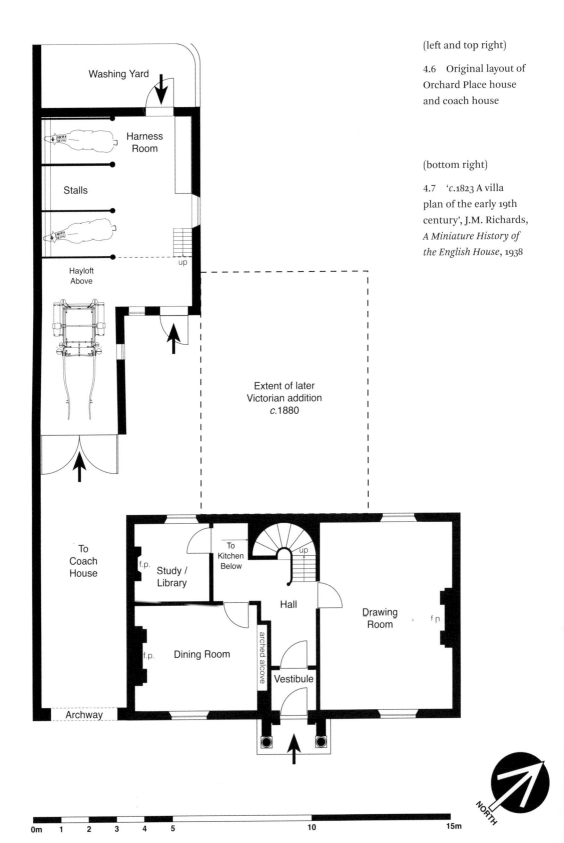

(left and top right)

4.6 Original layout of Orchard Place house and coach house

(bottom right)

4.7 'c.1823 A villa plan of the early 19th century', J.M. Richards, *A Miniature History of the English House*, 1938

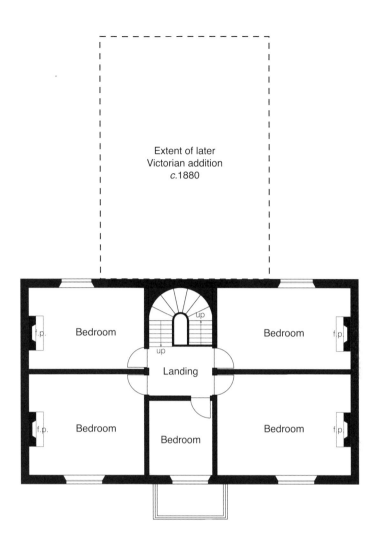
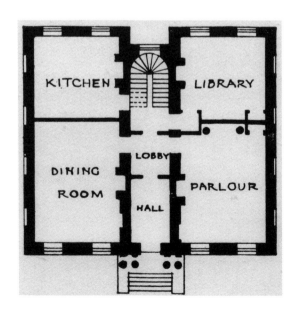

4.8 A reconstruction of the layout of the coach house at Orchard Place

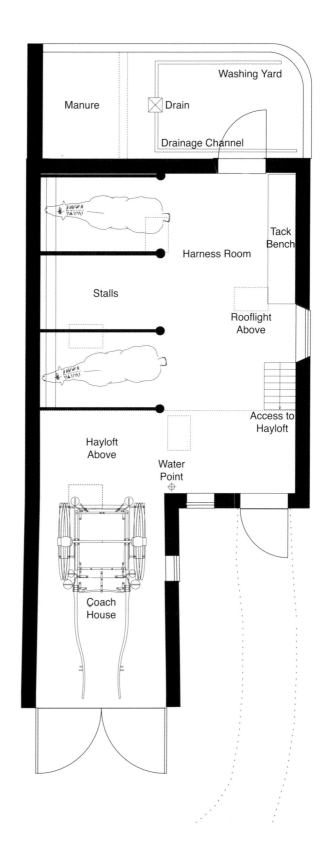

ORCHARD PLACE (1824)

the inventory of 1957, when the building was leased to the NFU, it states that the basement still contained a black metal range/stove of a 'plain' type. The kitchen was quite large, occupying half of the basement, and so probably doubled as the Servants' Hall. Of the other basement rooms, one was clearly the coal cellar (its blocked-up coal hole is still visible), one the wine cellar (still containing the square, stone alcoves), another the larder (having hooks in the ceiling, presumably for hanging meat) and another the store room. Upon moving in, we found two boards containing rows of servant bells, and some of the bell-wires still run down into the basement. The first extension to the rear of the house was just one storey high and was probably built to house a new scullery and possibly additional servant rooms. Upstairs originally consisted of five family rooms, with no provision for live-in servants and no separate bathroom. When Henry Bell built the second extension, this would have provided him with much needed additional bedrooms on the top floor, an additional drawing room on the ground floor, and extensive additional servant rooms at the basement level (allowing, probably for the first time, live-in servants).

We have also spent some time trying to work out what would have been the original layout of the house's coach house. Some clues were left behind: although part of the hayloft still existed, empty joist 'holes' in the stone walls gave an indication of the full extent of the original hayloft,[15] and when we removed the modern concrete floor, we discovered the original grooved floor contained extensive drainage channels, suggesting that horses had been stabled in the double-height space. The 'courtyard' space outside also had good drainage and drainage channels, which suggests that this might have been the stable's washing yard. We have also looked at plans of other coach houses and stables from the Regency period for guidance. John Stewart's 19th-century book on horse management, states that smaller stalls were more typical than larger loose boxes and that stall sizes were between 5½ to 6 feet wide by, at most, 9 feet. The 'coach' for a local solicitor of 1824 was most likely a modest phaeton, curricle or chaise drawn by one or two horses. Possibly a horse was kept for riding, and a spare stall may have been available to accommodate a visitor's horse,[16] and that is probably all the horses that were stabled in our coach house. Our best 'guess' plan of the original layout of the coach house is shown in the illustration.

LIVING IN HOUSES

Materials

One of the most noticeable features of 1 Orchard Place is its entrance with stone columns. I mentioned earlier that they are of the Ionic order. Even a couple of generations ago, an architect was expected to be fully conversant with the classical orders, and I was probably the first generation for whom it did not really matter but it might still be useful. As a rule of thumb there are three column types: the Doric, or the plain one, the Ionic, with spiral scrolls (or volutes), and the Corinthian, the one with leaves. When we moved into 1 Orchard Place, one of the Ionic column capitals was severely decayed and we took the difficult decision to have it replaced. A replacement capital was carved by a firm of stonemasons from Darlington and is a perfect match for its twin. The process of installing it was quite fascinating. How do you slide a column capital into place, without disassembling the entire portico? The answer is that the base of the capital has holes in it, into which fit pegs.[17] These holes line up with corresponding holes at the top of the column shaft, and when the capital slides into place, the pegs drop down into the holes in the shaft connecting the two, ensuring that there can be no lateral movement – how ingenious.

Another interesting material aspect of the house is its lath and plaster interior walls. If you recall, in Yearnor Cottage, some of the original walls were still made of wattle and daub, and lath and plaster is very much the descendant of this earlier material. Instead of the twigs used previously, laths are pliable strips of wood, often of oak or hazel, laid horizontally with small gaps between them and held in place by vertical timber studs. The plaster was made of lime and mixed with horse hair to give it a little reinforcement (rather like the glass fibres in fibreglass plastic). The plaster was pressed into the laths, forcing its way between the horizontal gaps between adjacent laths. This is an important part of the process because, as the plaster oozes out of the other side of the laths, it slumps slightly, forming a 'key' which, when dry, holds the plaster in place. In one area of the house, where the plasterwork was in a particularly poor condition, we had to remove it, exposing the original laths which, when 'naked', I found strangely beautiful (Fig.4.10). Fortunately, we were able to retain all the laths, and the process provided a fleeting glimpse into past building crafts that have long been lost.

(right)

4.9   The replacement Ionic column capital ready to be installed

(below)

4.10   Exposed laths during the restoration work

LIVING IN HOUSES

Incidentally, I have one final thought about lath and plaster walls to share. For the first time, I truly understand why the Georgians had picture hanging rails in their houses. Trying to hammer a hook into a lath and plaster wall is, literally, a bit 'hit and miss': it is really not the best surface to hang *anything* from. Far better to install a long wooden strip, which can be both glued (and has a large surface area for gluing) as well as nailed periodically into the vertical studs. This then provides a very stable way of hanging pictures without damaging the plaster every time you try to hang a painting.

The Influence and Inspiration of the Regency Villa

What do we mean by 'villa' and why have I been referring to 1 Orchard Place as a Regency villa, not merely a townhouse, which arguably it could also be described as? The word 'villa' clearly sounds Italian, and, indeed, it is the Italian word for a country house or farm, but architecturally, it is a word that has a very specific set of meanings and connotations: Dana Arnold suggests that 'The villa remains one of the most potent architectural forms in western culture.'[18]

From an architectural perspective, villas can be held to have had four waves of popularity, with each subsequent generation rediscovering and being influenced by the previous one. The first wave of villas were the villas of antiquity, the original villas – these were Roman country houses, on the edge of the city, to which wealthy, upper-class, Roman citizens would flee to escape the heat of the city during the summer months. Very little was written about these, and their inspiration was found mainly in their ruins. These in turn influenced Renaissance architects who attempted to recreate them, one of the most important being Andrea Palladio who was renowned for them. Palladio's villas are recognisable for their strong symmetry and geometric plans, their proportions, often with a temple front, and their use of the classical orders. Renaissance villas then influenced the third wave of villa architects in the 18th and 19th centuries. As mentioned in the previous chapter, this was the era of the Grand Tour, when any young gentleman, or indeed aspiring architect such as Inigo Jones, toured Europe and, principally, spent time in Italy where they would have visited numerous

ORCHARD PLACE (1824)

Renaissance villas. And so the Georgian or Regency villa became the third incarnation of this building type. The final wave, which I will discuss soon, came in the 20th century, and arguably, we are still riding this one.

But before I move onto the current influence of villas, I need to say a little about what they are and what sets them apart from ordinary houses. What is interesting about the first, second and the early part of the third wave of villas is that they were designed for the aristocracy or upper classes as what we might now term 'bolt holes', located somewhere outside, but close to, the city. Ackerman suggests that 'The villa cannot be understood apart from the city; it exists not to fulfil autonomous functions but as the antithesis to urban values . . . its economic situation is that of a satellite.'[19] Mostly, the owners were people who already possessed townhouses and large country estates, and it is important to note that villas were not grand country houses, but were distinctly inferior and secondary to them. They were designed primarily for pleasure and were not necessarily large; in Charles Middleton's book on the villa, he states that 'elegance, compactness and convenience are the characteristics of such buildings'.[20] They were designed to be *looked at* (and can be considered a little 'showy') as well as to delight in their rural setting, or to be *looked from* (also known as their 'prospect').

But between the Georgian villas of the early 18th century and the Regency villas of the early 19th century, a transformation took place. Instead of villas being a second or third house for only the wealthiest of society, they began to be built as the primary home of the upper middle classes. In Lawrence and Chris's book on the period house, they discuss how a scheme of villas built in the 1820s in St John's Wood in London created the first villa suburb or 'gracious, detached houses standing in their own grounds on the outskirts of town'.[21] They go on to describe how this became the prototype for similar developments on the edge of other towns. In Loudon's book on the principles of designing villas, written in 1833, he says how 'every man who has been successful in his pursuits, and has, by them, obtained pecuniary independence, may possess a villa'. He continues: 'it is not necessary that the dwelling of the villa should be large, or the land surrounding it extensive; the only essential requisites are, that the possessor should be

LIVING IN HOUSES

a man of some wealth, and either possess taste himself, or have sense enough to call to his assistance the taste and judgement of others, who profess to practice this branch of design'.[22] Charles Head, and the house he built at 1 Orchard Place, can very much be seen as an epitome of this, built for an upper-middle-class professional, on the edge of town, and intended for use as the primary, family home.

In the 20th century, the idea of the 'villa suburb' and the suburb became practically synonymous, and the large suburban detached, or semi-detached, house can easily be held to be the direct, yet democratised,[23] descendant of the villas of the past. Indeed, John Summerson, writing in 1959, says, rather disparagingly, 'In the last three decades of the century "villa" became a very common word indeed, probably for the snobbish reason that it seemed to give an air of distinction to a house that was not quite big enough to earn distinction by its dimensions.'[24] If we return to the idea that location, a pastoral setting and its outward appearance are all critical to the design of the villa, is it any surprise that 20th-century architects fell in love with the idea of the villa? And, considering Loudon's observations, for those able to afford it, clients could rely on architects with 'taste and judgement' to build such a villa for them. Hence, some of the most famous 20th-century houses are villas, from Le Corbusier's Villa Savoye[25] to Frank Lloyd Wright's Fallingwater, and a quick trawl through recent winners of the RIBA's House of the Year award reveal many entries that could easily be described as villas: the villa is alive and flourishing.

Personal Lessons Learnt for Architectural Practice

Most of the lessons that I learnt as an architect, through this house, have been lessons on 'how to fix things that have gone wrong'. It is interesting how, once you have experienced something – however difficult or stressful it seems at the time – having got through the other side, it then loses its future power over you. For example, as an architect I thought I knew all about asbestos (theoretically at least); and frankly, I always hoped that it was something I would never have to encounter. My record of zero asbestos experiences came abruptly to an end with this job. The sheer volume of asbestos in 1 Orchard Place was surprising

ORCHARD PLACE (1824)

(for what should have been a domestic property). It was found in 10 separate locations, including in vinyl floor tiles, in the adhesive sticking the vinyl floor tiles to the floor, in a high-level toilet cistern, beneath the office carpets, as insulating board fixed to some of the doors, on the corrugated roof over the yard behind the coach house, on almost every fire surround (as an insulating backing board to the 'modern' electric bar heaters), and even in the soffit that had been added to the underside of the portico. In other words, this house was the epitome of an architectural, asbestos nightmare. In the end, however, it was not such a disaster: the professionals came in, donned their protective suits and simply did the job of removing it. It took about a day and added a little to our unforeseen costs. I can truly say that the fear of discovering asbestos on a job has now lost its hold over me, and should I encounter it again, it will be with far greater pragmatism than before.

On a more delightful note, through living in this house I have finally learnt something about marble. When we moved in, I was obviously aware that we *had* fireplaces, that some were more ornate than others, and that at least one was clearly made of marble. One fireplace, however, had been painted over with thick, beige paint, and it was not until we removed it for restoration that we had any idea what lay beneath. I cannot honestly say that I had been a big fan of marble, and so it was without any particular anticipation that I awaited the results of the restoration. However, what lay beneath the layers of paint proved to be a great surprise. The fireplace in the (probable) former dining room was made of a type of marble called *bleu fleuri*, an astonishingly rare marble from the quarries of Seravezza in Tuscany. The colour is a sort of greyish, powder blue with a contrasting indigo veining, a combination that is particularly attractive, even to a marble philistine such as me.

Another fireplace, which was located in the Victorian extension, appeared to be made of marble (and is even called Frosterly Marble), but is not marble at all, but rather made of limestone. Frosterly Marble, as the name suggests, is from Frosterly in County Durham. When polished, it is mostly black, but contains the white fossilised remains of former sea creatures such as crinoids, as well as coral, pieces of shell and even leaf fragments. The 'marble' dates from the Carboniferous period, 325 million years ago, and I find it remarkable that I can sit in my own home, gazing upon such an ancient slice of geological history.

5

Wharf Place (*c*.1902)

The Story of Warehouse Loft-living and Yuppies

Introduction: My Lived Experience of this Home

I found the flat in London Wharf when I was living in the Haberdasher Street flat (see Chapter 7) and which I had been poised to buy. Before doing so, as a first-time house buyer, I decided to check out the prices of similar properties. Unsurprisingly, I stumbled upon another flat, for the same price, but approximately one mile further east, on the border between the London boroughs of Hackney and Bethnal Green. This other flat was about twice the size of my small Haberdasher Street flat (two bedrooms instead of one, two bathrooms instead of one, and practically double the useable floor area). This flat was in London Wharf.

London Wharf was then a newly converted, loft-style, four-storey factory/warehouse on the Regent's Canal (Venice-style, the warehouse walls plunged straight down into the water, forming part of the edge of the canal).

It was the early winter of 1991 when I serendipitously found the flat, and I soon discovered that the developers were unusually desperate to sell, and to sell quickly. It transpired that flat number A1 was the last-remaining of the 36 newly converted flats to be sold, and house prices, especially in London, had been steadily plummeting since the house price crash of early 1989. Furthermore, the year 1991 also holds the dubious fame of being the year of peak house repossessions in the UK: 75,000 homes were repossessed that year.[1] Looking back now at graphs of house price trends, I see that when I bought London Wharf it had already been three years since the crash, and those were three years of unrelentingly falling houses prices; they continued to fall for another five quarters after I moved in, not bottoming out until the second

(left)

5.1 Sketch drawing of Wharf Place

95

LIVING IN HOUSES

quarter of 1993. It is easy, therefore, to see why the developers were so keen to be rid of their last flat.

There were many aspects of the flat that appealed to me, but the three main ones were its industrial aesthetic, its exceptionally tall, floor-to-ceiling height and its proximity to the water. I will quickly describe each of these, and what was their appeal, in turn. First, considering its industrial aesthetic, it had previously been a factory and warehouse, and its utilitarian brick walls and large windows represented a trend of living in former industrial buildings that very much epitomised the zeitgeist of the time (more on this in the next section). But like many others, I was seduced by the former industrial, slightly edgy and unconventional style of it. I very much liked the idea of living somewhere with a bit more history and character, and frankly, just a little less 'ordinary'.

Second, its floor-to-ceiling height was almost 4 metres (3.9 metres or 13 feet), and I have already described in the previous chapter (Chapter 4 on Orchard Place, a house with similarly high ceilings) how uplifting I find high ceilings to be. But another interesting fact about London Wharf was that, proportionally, its living room was as tall as it was wide; furthermore, the length of the room was more or less double its width. This meant that the dimensions of the room were approximately a 'double-cube' proportion (simply imagine two dice placed side by side on a table). A small note on room proportions here: I was taught, as an architecture student, that the double-cube was one of the ideal, classical proportions for a room. In 1622, Inigo Jones designed the hall of the Banqueting House for King James I and used double-cube proportions (although admittedly his 55 × 55 × 110 feet were rather grander a scale than London Wharf's humbler 13 × 13 × 26 feet). Inigo Jones' influence was such that the trend had been set. Many other architects followed his lead and numerous Georgian/Regency home owners aspired to have their own double-cube room. I was immediately aware of London Wharf's living room's unusual proportions and it certainly contributed to the flat's allure.

Third, one feature that I absolutely loved about this flat was its proximity to the canal. The living room had full height, floor-to-ceiling, French windows leading to a small Juliet balcony that overhung the waters below. On sunny days it was possible to fully open these doors and sit looking out over the canal. Canal boats would frequently pass by and people would wave and say hello as they slowly chugged past the

5.2 Photograph of me in the living room of 1A Wharf Place, showing the tall floor-to-ceiling heights

window. Finally, another effect of the water – which I had never thought about before living in London Wharf – was the way that, on sunny days, the sunlight reflected off the water and formed little animated ripple patterns on the white walls. It was the first time that I realised how sunlight and water can transform architecture. In summary, the combination of the flat's industrial aesthetic, its rooms' proportions and its relationship to the canal were more than enough to convince me to buy it.

5.3 A view of the London Wharf building from the canal, showing how the walls go straight down into the water, forming the edge of the canal. The bridge in the distance is known as the Cat and Mutton bridge

LIVING IN HOUSES

History of London Wharf

The street on which the London Wharf warehouse is situated, Wharf Place (or Wharf Road as it was originally called), owes its existence solely to the Regent's Canal, an 8.6-mile-long canal linking Paddington to Limehouse. The canal was begun in 1812, completed in 1820 and subsequently named in honour of the Prince Regent. In 1817, a map of London indicating the intended route of the canal was produced by the publisher, William Darton.[2,3] This route shows the proposed canal crossing Pritchard's Road (at that time called Ann's Place and Trafalgar Place) and Sheep Lane (which now only exists to the north of the canal, the southern part having disappeared after the canal was built). Wharf Road was built around 1852, joining Pritchard's Road to the east and then turning to follow the edge of the Regent's Canal, heading south-east until coming to a halt at the boundary of the Imperial Gasworks, built around 1860/61.[4] Wharf Road was clearly laid out with the purpose of serving the canal-side wharves, hence its name.[5]

Fascinatingly, there is a first-hand account of what Wharf Road was like in 1898 (before London Wharf was built) written in a notebook belonging to George H. Duckworth. Duckworth was one of the assistants working on Charles Booth's survey, *The Life and Labour of the People in London*, undertaken between 1886 and 1903.

In Duckworth's notebook entry of 1 April 1898, he describes his route and his impressions of the area as he walked around:

> North up Pritchard's Road to Ada Place. Windows broken and patched, children and women dirty and ragged, 'like Gales Gardens'. Db. [dark blue] as map. 2 storey houses. East to Wharf Road. 2½ stories, rough, bread and mess in the street . . . db [dark blue]. Wood wharves at the South and North ends backing on the canal. South down Pritchard's Row – a mixed road, at the north end shops, at the south 2 storied houses like the Old Bethnal Green Road in character. It looks pink as far south as Caroline Place, then there are broken windows and it is no better than purple.[6]

Duckworth's reference to colours may sound confusing but he is referring to Booth's classification for streets in which he methodically

100

WHARF PLACE (c.1902)

5.4 A sketch map of George Duckworth's walk around the district on 1 April 1898

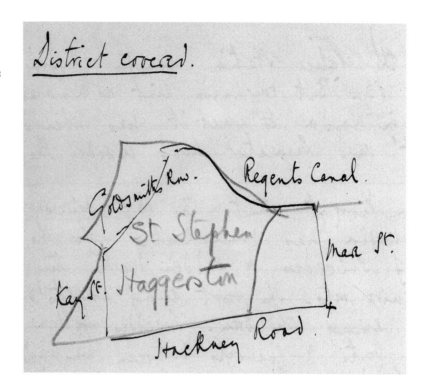

coded every street in London with a colour indicating its level of poverty. 'Dark Blue', which Duckworth judged London Wharf to be, was classified as being 'Very poor, casual. Chronic want'. In contrast, Duckworth judged Pritchard's Row to be pink, that is, 'Fairly comfortable. Good ordinary earnings', but turning into purple, 'Mixed. Some comfortable others poor'.[7]

At the time that Duckworth was walking around, keenly seeking out signs of poverty, the site of the present-day London Wharf warehouse conversion consisted of a row of modestly sized terrace houses. When first built, these houses had gardens backing onto the canal; later a coal wharf was established at one end and a wood wharf at the other end, effectively sandwiching the houses between them. By the 1890s the wood wharf had turned into a saw mill, the coal wharf had been renamed 'London Wharf' (Fig.5.5) and the entire row of terraced houses had collectively lost their gardens when they had been transformed into an industrial 'yard' serving the wharves. It was

5.5 Pritchard's Road, by the Cat and Mutton Bridge, 1903

in this rather reduced and beleaguered state that Duckworth found the terrace, while walking down Wharf Road.

In the 1901 census, there is a handwritten note on the census form observing that houses 3 to 17 were not in occupation, namely the terrace houses on the canal side. I presume that these had been deliberately vacated prior to demolition, since by the time of the 1911 census the odd-numbered houses had disappeared entirely and been replaced by a single, monolithic, brick warehouse building, known then as Red Star Wharf (but later renamed London Wharf). The earliest official document on which Red Star Wharf is named is an electoral roll from 1905; therefore the factory/warehouse which, decades later, housed my flat was most likely to have been constructed between 1902 and 1904 and was originally called Red Star Wharf. But if this is when it was built, for what purpose was it built?

One clue to the factory or warehouse's original function can be found in the census records. In the 1911 census (the first census after

WHARF PLACE (c.1902)

the building's construction), a certain Lewis William Blight is recorded as living in Red Star Wharf, and is described as being the 'Manager [of the] Wharfingers and Stationers'. I believe that from the moment it was built, the building was both a factory and warehouse for the manufacture and storage of paper products. Paper-making was a very common industry in Bethnal Green, and so this was typical of the borough and its location.[8] This also corresponds with later records, when Red Star Wharf is given as the address for a factory belonging to a firm of stationers known as J.S. Darwen & Company. In a paper trade directory of 1923,[9] the entry for Darwen (J.S.) & Co., Ltd. shows them producing the following paper goods:

Strawboards, Wood Pulp Boards, Leather Boards, Ticket Boards, Mounting Boards, Pasteboards, Cardboards, 'Hempite' Fibre Boards, Folding Box Boards, Billiard Shade Boards, Corrugated Boards, and Papers; all kinds of Papers – Printings, Tissues, Browns, Manillas; all kinds of Fancy Papers – Coloured Flint, Enamel and Surface Papers, Embossed Papers, Gold and Silver Papers, Imitation Cloth and Leather Papers, Marble and Calico Papers, etc.; Glue, Box Calico, Tapes, Wadding.

Wharf Road was eventually renamed Wharf Place on 21 February 1938, taking effect from 1 July 1938. In 1937, London County Council proposed that it should be renamed as an extension to Ada Place (an existing road linking Wharf Place to Pritchard's Road), but this never happened as Messrs Darwen & Sons, the sole objector, pointed out that his wharf was the only premises in the street.[10] In a nice touch, however, when new houses were built recently on an extension to Wharf Place, adjacent to the former Red Star Wharf (or London Wharf) warehouse, this section of new road was named 'Darwen Place' after Darwen's paper factory.

City Directories dating from 1940 and 1941[11] show that the building continued to be used as Darwen's paper factory, which must certainly have been its function when it suffered bomb damage during the London Blitz. The Architects' Department of the London County Council (LCC) produced extensive 'Bomb Damage Maps'[12] that used colour codes to indicate the location, extent and type of bomb

103

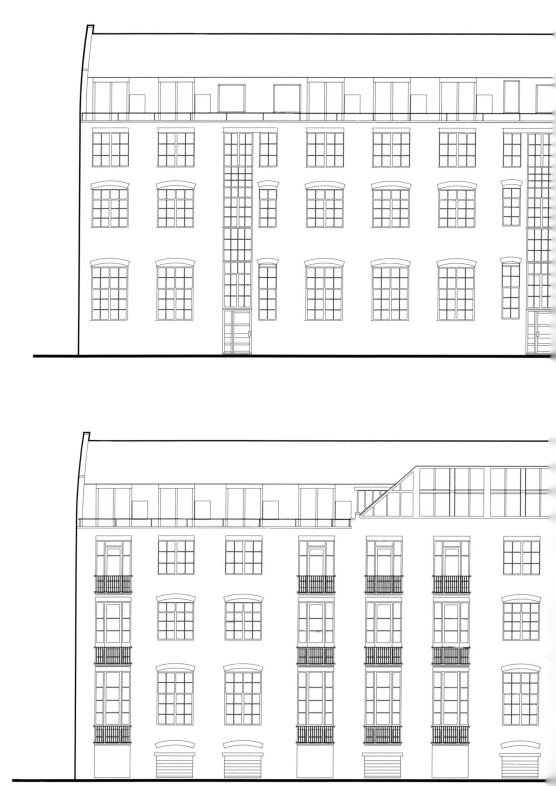

5.6 Street elevation (top) and canal elevation (bottom) of Wharf Place

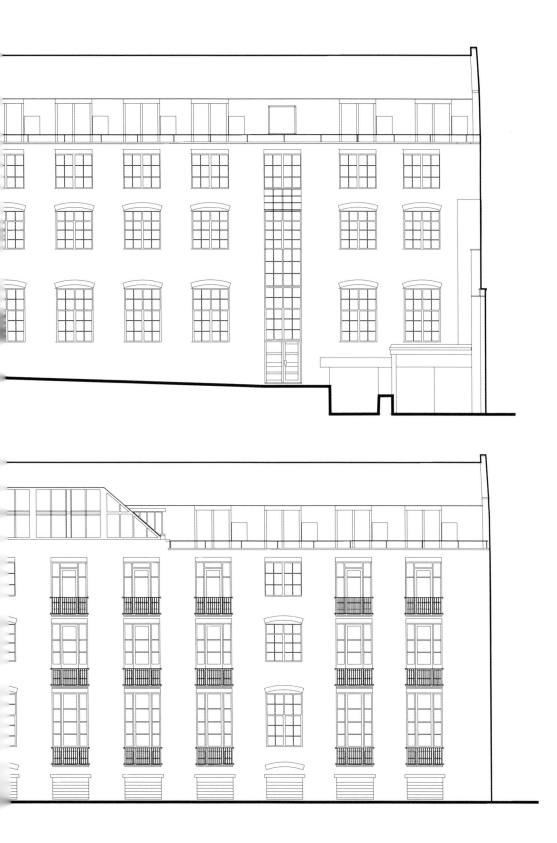

LIVING IN HOUSES

damage to London's buildings. The whole of the Red Star Wharf building is shown as having suffered from minor blast damage, but the central third was more severely affected than its two ends. What is strange is that all the surrounding buildings are intact, showing no bomb damage, so the bomb must have fallen close to, but not on, the warehouse, and without damaging any other buildings in the vicinity (could the bomb possibly have fallen into the Regent's Canal?).

The next notable event in the history of the building was a dramatic fire that took place in the 1980s. An article in the local *Hackney Gazette*, 16 November 1982, describes how the police were on the verge of evacuating hundreds of sleeping families from their homes, in the vicinity of London Wharf, amidst fears that the fire in the warehouse might spread to the adjacent gasometers, which were, at the time, still in use and, hence, full of highly combustible fuel. The newspaper article goes on to describe how 'more than sixty firemen battled for four hours to stop flames reaching the gas storage tanks behind the blazing building'.[13] This dramatic moment was captured by a local freelance photographer, Harry Austin, 'who chased fire engines back in the day'.[14] The accompanying black and white photograph in the *Hackney Gazette* is far less dramatic than Harry Austin's 'blazing inferno' photograph (Fig.5.7); instead it depicts the final stages of the fire when it was little more than damp, smouldering embers. In this photograph the interior of the warehouse is clearly visible and it is evident that what is left of the building is little more than an empty shell. The article concludes with a description of the owner of a toy firm – who was then renting the warehouse (and which was full of toys and games in preparation for Christmas) – as being too shocked to speak to reporters. Therefore, after being a paper factory, perhaps the warehouse's very last industrial use was as a warehouse for toys.

It appears that this was, in fact, a second fire as an earlier fire was recorded as having occurred in June 1980.[15] I therefore suspect that it was after this second fire that the warehouse was sold to developers for conversion into flats. If we remember the house price crash from early 1989, I would suggest that it is highly unlikely that anyone would have started a residential conversion at such a financially precarious time and that the plans to convert it must have pre-dated 1989. Since the second fire took place on 15 November 1982, and the damage

5.7 Factory fire, Wharf Place

Table 5.1 Timeline of events in the warehouse's history

DATE	EVENT
1902–4	Construction of warehouse known as Red Star Wharf
1904–1970s	Stationers, paper factory and warehouse (J.S. Darwen & Company)
1940s	Bomb blast damage
1964–72	Winding-up and closure of J.S. Darwen & Company
1970s–1980s	Toy warehouse (Orwell Supplies Ltd)
1980 and 1982	First and second fire
1983–8	Conversion into flats and renamed London Wharf
1989	Property price crash
1992	Last flat sold (to me)

LIVING IN HOUSES

was extensive (judging from the photographs), it is unlikely that the building's fire-damage was repaired and it returned, temporarily, to its former function as a warehouse before being sold for change of use into flats. It is more likely that it remained empty, post-fire, until its potential for residential use was spotted and exploited.

History of Loft-Living

According to Sharon Zukin, who wrote the definitive book on the history of loft-living, this phenomenon can be traced back to the beginning of the 1970s. Interestingly, unlike many other writers, she does not attribute this solely to the United States; indeed, she writes: 'This new housing style emerged along the canals of Amsterdam, near the London docks, and in the old sweatshop districts of New York.'[16]

Zukin argues that the growth of the loft market was the result of a combination of a number of different factors. First, there was a decline in manufacturing in city centres, leading to an excessive supply of empty lofts (although Zukin cautions that the reasons for the decline are complex and there is an argument that, for New York at least, part of the decline of manufacturing was the result of politics and a deliberate policy to drive working-class people from urban centres). If there was an increase in the supply of vacant, former industrial buildings, there was, fortunately, also a commensurate increase in demand. This demand began in New York when artists, who had been living and working illegally in lofts, gained the legal right, in 1964, to continue to do so. But why did people, and not just artists, in the early 1970s suddenly decide that they wanted to live in lofts? Zukin suggests that this was also part of the zeitgeist: old factories had become symbolic of post-industrial society just at the same time that people began to develop an increased sense of history and of the heritage of buildings (see Chapter 2 on the former brewery at Priestpopple). Eventually, one consequence of this was a potential new financial market for real estate agents and developers, which they were quick to exploit. Indeed, by the end of Zukin's book there is a sense that loft-living was an unintended consequence of numerous trends, policies

WHARF PLACE (c.1902)

and market forces. In an article on the style of the 1980s by Josh Sims, for the *Financial Times*, he suggests that by the start of the 1980s, open-plan loft-living had become a cliché primarily associated with yuppies (an acronym for 'young urban professionals') since such spaces were 'perfect for a flashy decade'.[17]

Layout: Typical House Plans

The London Wharf warehouse building is deceptively massive. Originally it was three storeys high, with a semi-basement area (which became a residents' parking garage after its conversion). During the conversion a mansard roof was added, providing an additional fourth storey – now known as an 'upward extension' – meaning that today there are four storeys of flats in total. The original building tapers slightly, with the northern end being a little over 12 metres deep (front to back), but the southern end, where my flat was situated, being nearly 16 metres deep. The building is over 50 metres long and was divided into three blocks during the conversion: A (the southern block, nearest the gasometers); B (the middle block); and C (the northern block, nearest the Cat and Mutton[18] Bridge). Each block is organised around a central staircase, with three flats per floor, so one staircase serves 12 flats in total (twice as many as the Haberdasher Street, purpose-built flats, see Chapter 7). Two out of every set of three flats are roughly L-shaped and span the full depth of the building, making them dual aspect. (Given the building plan tapers, the flats at one end are more 'skewed' L-shapes than at the other end.) For the L-shaped flats, it is typically the living room that looks out over the canal. In contrast, the middle flat of the three faces in one direction only, towards the canal, and therefore both bedrooms and the living room/kitchen are oriented in that direction.

My flat was one of the L-shaped ones, and being situated at the larger end of the building, was fairly orthogonal. It was also on the ground floor and therefore had the tallest floor-to-ceiling heights compared to the flats on subsequent floors. The entrance to my flat was immediately to the left of the communal stairwell and led, in turn, to a large central 'hallway' area which was nearly 6 metres long

109

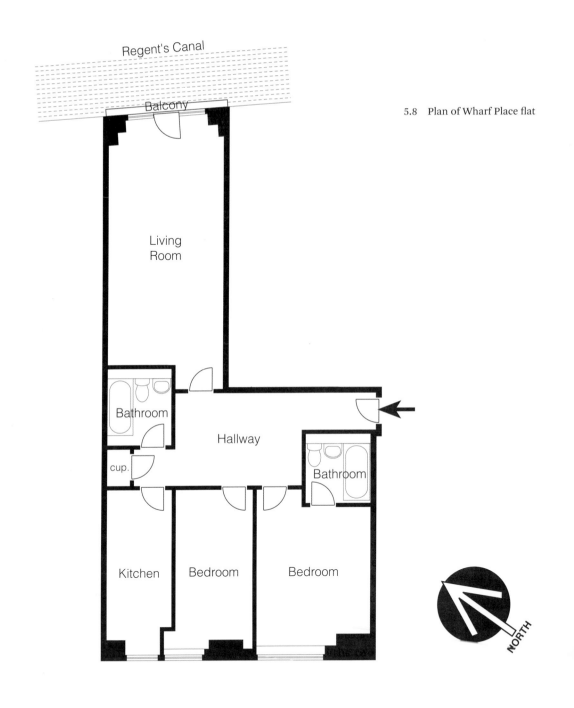

5.8 Plan of Wharf Place flat

WHARF PLACE (*c.*1902)

and over 2 metres wide. This was a very strange space: far too large to be a conventional entrance hall, but with all the doorways to the other rooms leading off it, it was not really possible to do much with it. I do recall visiting neighbours who had turned this space into a (slightly awkward) dining area, but I simply kept my bicycle in it and a comfortable chair to sit in when talking on the land-line telephone (at a time when you still had to be in a fixed location to talk on the phone). On the street side of the hallway there were two bedrooms, with the master bedroom having its own en suite bathroom.

The second bedroom and the kitchen effectively shared a single window, which meant that from the inside each had a half-window that was uncomfortably and inelegantly wedged against the wall. The kitchen itself was long and thin – very much a 'galley' kitchen – but was a good enough size for the flat. Indeed, the flat was very generously sized and spacious. Both of the small bathrooms had false, lowered ceilings (otherwise their proportions would have felt very strange, being taller than their width), which meant that each had a sort of 'loft' storage space above it, accessed via a hatch, which was extremely useful. The *pièce de resistance* of the flat was undoubtedly its large living room, with a balcony overlooking the canal. It was light and spacious, and the views of the canal were superb.

Materials

The London Wharf building is essentially a steel frame building with a London stock brick exterior. The use of iron or steel as the primary structure of a building is a relatively new innovation in the long history of architecture. In Britain, it was the Georgians who first started using cast-iron components in their buildings. After all, the famous Iron Bridge in Coalbrookdale, Shropshire – the first iron bridge in the world – was constructed as early as 1779, and it is natural that this engineering knowledge would have eventually found its way into the design of buildings as well as bridges. Certainly, the Georgians were prolific users of metalwork in their houses, but this tended to be the use of cast and wrought iron for decorative details, railings, gates and balconies, rather than for structural purposes. The architect John Nash,

5.9 Street elevation of London Wharf; the two windows at the bottom right were my bedroom/kitchen windows

LIVING IN HOUSES

who designed the Royal Pavilion in Brighton, Sussex as a residence for the Prince Regent, was the first to use cast iron structurally using cast-iron trusses, arched ribs and cast-iron columns, mostly hidden from view within its walls. The Brighton Pavilion was completed in 1822, and according to the Georgian Group, at the time Nash claimed to be 'the principal user, and perhaps I may add the introducer of cast-iron in the construction of floors of buildings'.[19] By the end of the Regency era, cast-iron beams and columns were starting to be used in all kinds of buildings, including houses.

However, it was really the Victorians who embraced the use of metal-framed buildings, particularly for industrial buildings such as warehouses, mills and factories. Initially, like the Georgians, they used cast iron, but later they replaced iron with steel. Once the switch from cast iron to the much stronger steel had been made, the possibilities became limitless. Steel was introduced around 1885 and had become the dominant structural form of metalwork by 1890. Therefore, when London Wharf – or Red Star Wharf as it was originally called – was built, its use of steel frame construction constituted a relatively new, cutting-edge technology.

What a steel frame building permitted the builders or architects to do was to span far larger distances than would have been possible using load-bearing masonry construction. For a building such as a warehouse or factory, this meant that the spaces inside – often a single, open space punctuated with the occasional cast-iron or steel column – could be used far more efficiently and flexibly. For warehouses, this simply meant more storage, as items could be packed together far more efficiently. If Red Star Wharf had been more factory than warehouse, a long, open space would have been necessary as the paper manufacturing process at that time required a long, unobstructed, continuous run of machinery to allow the passage of paper.

Sadly, the developers responsible for the conversion of the warehouse into flats chose to hide its structure behind plasterboard walls. I suspect that this was done, at the time, for reasons of fire safety and economy. In the UK, building regulations require that in the event of a fire, any structure must be able to retain its structural integrity for a specified duration. This is known as the structure's

WHARF PLACE (c.1902)

fire resistance and it applies equally to both new structures as well as to the refurbishment of historic buildings. There are a number of ways that a steel structure can be protected against fire and the choice typically depends on whether the structure is to remain visible or be hidden. If wanting to build cheaply and quickly (which, most likely, characterised the conversion of London Wharf), then the simplest thing to do would have been to build a 'box' around the beams and columns using fire protective boards, thus concealing them. However, I suspect, that were the building to have been converted now, far more attention would have been made to not only retaining any original warehouse features, but to emphasising them, and therefore an architect today would probably try to expose the steel structure wherever possible.

The Influence and Inspiration of Warehouse Conversions

On the one hand, it would be easy to say that the influence of warehouse conversions and loft-living is far more evident in interior design than architecture. The fact that it is now possible to buy 'brick effect' wallpaper to mimic the bare, exposed brickwork so redolent of many warehouse conversions perfectly encapsulates this statement. However, rather than interior design, I would like to discuss the influence of warehouse conversions on architecture.

The Regent's Canal has been the backdrop – perhaps even the inspiration – for some particularly interesting and innovative buildings over the years, from the elegant, 19th-century, stuccoed villas and Edwardian mansion flats of Little Venice, near Paddington Basin, to Berthold Lubetkin and Tecton Group's Gorilla House and Penguin Pool for London Zoo – through which the canal runs – in addition to the zoo's Snowdon Aviary by Cedric Price and Frank Newby, Terry Farrell's postmodern TV-am building (see Chapter 7 for further discussion of this), and Nicholas Grimshaw's high-tech style terrace of houses – looking as if they have been assembled from aeroplane parts – in the middle of Camden. In fact, the Regent's Canal can be thought of as a necklace, along which a number of beads of architectural 'gems' have been strung. But since the turn of the millennium, most of the new

LIVING IN HOUSES

buildings constructed along the canal have been either housing or mixed-used buildings containing a large proportion of housing.

What is interesting about many of the newly built housing developments along the canal is how much many of them seem to owe their outward form to the former industrial heritage of the canal, often sitting next to converted warehouses, of which London Wharf is a splendid example. Interesting examples include Hawley Wharf, a mixed-tenure scheme by Allford Hall Monaghan Morris completed in 2018 on a triangular site of land between Chalk Farm Road, Hawley Road and the Regent's Canal.[20] The block of housing which faces Hawley Lock, and is directly across the water from Farrell's TV-am building, unquestionably appears warehouse-like, with its strongly expressed brick frame and large windows, which sensitively match the industrial, vernacular character of the canal locks and adjacent brick railway arches.

Another, earlier scheme on the Regent's Canal – also by Allford Hall Monaghan Morris, and adjacent to the Queensbridge Road – is Adelaide Wharf, a mixed-tenure housing scheme completed in 2007 and occupying the site of a former timber wharf. Winning many awards, including *Building Magazine*'s 'Housing Project of the Year', it clearly makes reference to the warehouses that once occupied this area of Hackney. Among its most striking and memorable features are the brightly coloured, protruding balconies which, the architects explain, are intended to be a reference to packing crates.[21] What I find more interesting is the way in which the large balconies are supported by what appears, at first glance, to be crane arms cantilevered over the top of the roof, making them appear less like a stack of packing crates and more like a giant, continuous bucket elevator (or grain leg).

The Wenlock, by Hawkins Brown Architects, completed in 2019, overlooks Wenlock Basin, in the centre of Islington. Its appearance clearly mimics the typical warehouse materials of a brick frame which, in this case, the architects have combined with timber infills and recessed balconies. They confirm that 'The building references the solid warehouse massing of traditional canalside architecture.'[22] And this building is just a few hundred metres across Wenlock Basin from another of their schemes, called The Cube, which shares some of The Wenlock's industrial characteristics – but with more irregular

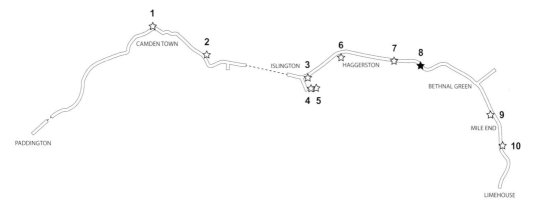

KEY

Recent warehouse-inspired or industrial heritage-inspired housing schemes include:

1. HAWLEY WHARF BY ALLFORD HALL MONAGHAN MORRIS (2018)
2. KING'S CROSS GASHOLDERS BY WILKINSON EYRE ARCHITECTS (2018)
3. THE WENLOCK BY HAWKINS BROWN (2019)
4. WHARF ROAD BY POLLARD THOMAS EDWARDS (2018)
5. THE CUBE/BANYAN WHARF BY HAWKINS BROWN (2015)
6. HACKNEY TOWERS BY DAVID CHIPPERFIELD AND KARAKUSEVIC CARSON (2019)
7. ADELAIDE WHARF HOUSING BY ALLFORD HALL MONAGHAN MORRIS (2007)
8. LONDON WHARF
9. WESTFIELD STUDENT VILLAGE BY FEILDEN CLEGG BRADLEY STUDIOS (2006)
10. CANDY WHARF BY YEATES DESIGN (2007)

5.10 Recent warehouse-inspired or industrial heritage-inspired housing schemes

massing – and consists of a hybrid structure, combining steel with cross-laminated timber, before being clad in timber.

Still in Islington, and very close to these two schemes, is a particularly interesting housing scheme known as Wharf Road, designed by local architects Pollard Thomas Edwards, and built between 2016 and 2018 for Family Mosaic and the Peabody Trust housing association. The industrial, manufactory aesthetic is evident in this project, including the way its layout mimics an arrangement around two 'wharves', or gardens, which, rather than being water inlets, are in fact, in this scheme, 'garden wharves' for its residents. Their saw-tooth roofs are unmistakably reminiscent of factory roofs, and the end of each of the housing blocks – which terminate on the canal – features a protruding black-clad box, slightly overhanging the canal, which is evocative of cantilevered housings for hoist pulleys (known as lucams).

In summary, the canal context has allowed the architects of many of these recent, warehouse-inspired housing schemes to build higher, at a greater density and with features such as larger-than-average windows, than they would otherwise have done if the scheme had been sited elsewhere. It has allowed them to move away from more

WHARF PLACE (c.1902)

(left)

5.11 View from the corner of Broadway Market towards the canal, London Wharf and the gasometers beyond

traditional notions of what a residential scheme 'should' look like, and in doing so have been able to design some truly great, award-winning projects.

Finally, any discussion on industrial, canal-side architecture would not be complete without a brief mention of Wilkinson Eyre and Jonathan Tuckey's design to convert the King's Cross gasholders into apartments. The Grade II-listed, cast-iron gasholders, originally constructed in 1867, have been an integral part of the King's Cross railway land and the Regent's Canal for over a century. Their recent conversion into 145 apartments was completed in 2018 and has ensured that they will remain part of this landscape, with their new function, for the foreseeable future.

Personal Lessons Learnt for Architectural Practice

I was wondering what, if anything, I had really learnt, as an architect, from living in London Wharf, when I came across an old photograph. The photograph captures my father standing on the balcony over the canal with an expression of fierce concentration on his face. His hand is poised, mid-air, caught in the act of throwing a piece of bread: he was feeding the ducks from my living room. It made me think that, as architects, we so often become obsessed by the 'grand gesture' or the 'statement' design move – the one thing that we want to do that will stop everyone in their tracks, cause them to look on in awe, and enable us to be remembered – that we often overlook the little things. By 'little things', I don't mean the architectural details – after all, it was Mies van der Rohe who memorably said 'God is in the details', and these are rarely overlooked by any half-decent, or aspiring to be half-decent, architect. Rather, I mean the small, incidental pleasures of being in a place – the *small gestures* if you like: a cosy reading nook, a framed view from a window, the reflection of water on a plain wall and the simple joy of being able to feed the ducks from your living room. Architecture is unquestionably about design, but first and foremost it is about people and people's lives, and if we can facilitate such small pleasures, such little moments of joy, in people's lives in our buildings, is that not worth all the grand gestures put together?

6

Bradwell Road (1902)

The Story of an Edwardian Semi-detached House Absorbed into a New Town

6.1　Sketch drawing of the Bradwell Road semi-detached houses

BRADWELL ROAD (1902)

Introduction: My Lived Experience of this Home

We moved from Camden (see Chapter 9) to Bradwell Road in Milton Keynes when I was pregnant with my second child. We wanted to be within a short walking distance of the train station and that, essentially, meant the village of Loughton, one of the original villages that had been absorbed by the new town of Milton Keynes. The house was one of only two we looked at: it was the right price and the right size, had a generous, but not too large, garden and the best position in the whole of the village of Loughton (arguably in all of Milton Keynes, in my biased opinion). Apart from its mirror image, house-twin next door (it was an Edwardian semi-detached house) there were few houses in its immediate vicinity. The house looked out across open fields, then occupied, picturesquely, by a pair of horses. The Loughton Brook flowed past just in front of the house (with a little bridge over it for our children to play 'Poohsticks'), and in the far distance the medieval church of All Saints, Loughton, sat on top of a hill. The view from our house gave no indication that we were in the middle of a new town and just ten minutes' walk from its modern, glass and steel train station.

6.2 Aerial photograph of the Bradwell Road house

LIVING IN HOUSES

I instantly fell in love with the house for its prospect (its view from the house), but my decision to buy it was consolidated by the delightful, small details of the house: its porch; its elegant roof ridge finials; its wrought iron, monkeytail window fasteners inspired by Arts and Crafts designs; and its terracotta, decorative string course mouldings. Within months of moving in, my daughter was born, at home, in the living room.

History of Milton Keynes and its Original Villages

The house is situated in Loughton, which is one of the original villages of the new town of Milton Keynes. The new town was not built on a greenfield site, but rather incorporated a number of existing small towns (Stony Stratford, Bletchley, Wolverton and Newport Pagnell) as well as numerous villages and hamlets into its vast, gridded plan. Loughton was one of these villages and was first recorded in the Domesday Survey of 1086. Interestingly, just immediately behind our old house is located the archaeological remains of a medieval, moated site containing fishponds, house platforms (the remains of seven houses) and other earthworks, almost all that remains of the former parish of Little Loughton.[1] These earthworks are now a scheduled ancient monument. It is possible that this fishpond complex was constructed by the Piggott family, who were also known for their rebuilding of Little Loughton manor house; therefore it may be that the land on which our house was eventually built was once owned by the Piggott family.[2]

Bradwell Road runs through the centre of the village, and before Milton Keynes existed it connected the former villages of Shenley Church End and Bradwell, hence its name. The first map of Bradwell Road is from the 1880s[3] and shows hardly any houses located on Bradwell Road between the Loughton Brook and Shenley Church End, and this situation had not changed by the publication of the next map in 1900. This pair of houses, built in 1902, therefore appears to be the first of the 'new' houses to have been built on Bradwell Road. By the 1920s, however, a whole string of houses had followed, effectively lining Bradwell Road with a continuous development, connecting our house, near the centre of Loughton, to the next village, Shenley Church End.

6.3 View of the front of the house demonstrating its quintessentially Edwardian characteristics

Key
1 Ridge tiles and roof finials
2 Plain bargeboards
3 Terracotta plaque
4 Timber-framed patterns
5 Moulding/string course
6 Colour/stained glass
7 Canted bay window
8 Casement windows
9 Terracotta sill bricks

6.4 View along Leys Road, showing the house on the corner, c.1910

Some aspects of the house still owe allegiance to the Victorian era, but its features undoubtedly 'tick all the boxes' for being a quintessentially Edwardian house. Externally, these are: casement windows; stained/coloured glass; a bay window; ridge tiles and finials; a wooden porch; a terracotta plaque; plain bargeboards; a timber-framed pattern in the gable; and an Art Nouveau-inspired letterbox (Fig.6.3). Internally, these features are: wrought-iron window fasteners; a leaded glass transom window; quarry tiles on the floor; tiled fire 'cheeks' (the angled part immediately next to the grate); and a cast-iron fire surround and grate.

It is debatable whether these houses would originally have had electricity when they were built in 1902, as this was the period of transition between gas and electricity. It was not until after the First World War that electricity began to be introduced to existing homes. However, from 1890 some new homes (although usually larger ones than this one, or those in urban areas) began to be built with an electricity supply; I suspect that this house may have originally still had gas. The transition from gas lighting to electricity meant that, in general, homes were lighter, and a large aspect of the interior design of Edwardian homes was about making them feel lighter and more open, in contrast to dark, Victorian ones.

BRADWELL ROAD (1902)

When the two houses were built, they were known collectively as Oak Cottages. Obviously, they did not exist, or were in the process of being built, during the 1901 census. A coronation plaque on the wall suggests that they had to have been built around August 1902 (the coronation of Edward VII and Alexandra took place on 9 August) and the 1901 census had taken place on 1 April 1901 (16 months earlier). By the time of the next census (1911), the two houses had been occupied for approximately eight and a half years. Sadly, the 1911 census makes no differentiation between the two halves of the semi-detached house, both of them being given the same address, 'Oak Cottages'. In 1911, one house was occupied by a widow, Maude Cresswell, and her three young children. Maude was headteacher at the Loughton village school, but when it closed in 1915 (because male teachers had left to fight in the First World War), she joined the staff at Shenley School in the neighbouring village.[4] The other house was occupied by Charles and Clara Cox and their four young children (plus another child boarder). Charles was a carriage fitter for the L&NWR (London and North Western Railway) Carriage Works, three miles away in Wolverton. Therefore, the first residents of the pair of houses would have been lower middle class or upper working class/ skilled working class.

Although the census failed to distinguish between the two houses, it was almost certainly the Cox family who had lived in our house. In 1936 one of the daughters of the family, Jessie Cox, began running a post office from the front room of the house. According to a nonagenarian resident of the village, Jess Cox ran the post office from this house throughout the war and for a period of time afterwards.[5] The fact of the front room being a post office during the war would explain one very strange aspect about the layout of the house, which is a pair of French windows that connect the living room to the garden. These doors never made any sense to me at all, especially since they were so close to the front door. However, if these doors had been put in when the front room was being used as a post office, it would make perfect sense, since the public would have been able to enter directly into the post office/shop part of the house without having to invade the privacy of the rest of the house.

The next event to really affect the two houses, after the war, was their eventual absorption into Milton Keynes (coincidentally, the New Town Movement had its origins in the Garden City movement

125

LIVING IN HOUSES

contemporaneous with the construction of this house). Letchworth, the first Garden City, was founded in 1903. The new towns were intended to help alleviate the desperate housing shortages that came after the Second World War and were made possible through the New Towns Act of 1946. The first new town was Stevenage which was designated a new town that same year. In contrast, Milton Keynes was one of the last new towns, designated as such in 1967, at which stage the two Bradwell Road houses had already stood there for 65 years.

Milton Keynes is famous for its grid road network, its roundabouts and concrete cows. However, when the grid was laid out, it sensitively incorporated the existing towns and villages, rather than rigidly running straight grid roads through existing settlements. Milton Keynes neighbourhoods are defined as 'Grid Squares', namely, the leftover areas between the grid roads (which are designated 'H' roads for those running north-west to south-east and 'V' roads for those running south-west to

6.5 Front elevation of the Bradwell Road semi-detached houses

BRADWELL ROAD (1902)

north-east: horizontal and vertical). Wherever possible, the existing villages and hamlets were placed into a single Grid Square, and so Loughton is now bounded by Portway (H5) to the north, Childs Way (H6) to the south, Watling Street (V4) to the west, and the A5 trunk road to the east. Loughton is one of the most central of the original villages and is located in close proximity to the central railway station, making it popular with commuters. Nevertheless, the village has managed to retain its original character and, visually, the original village has been shielded from most of the infrastructure of the new town.

Layout: The House Plan

Being one half of a pair of semi-detached houses, each half is a perfectly symmetrical mirror image of the other. The symmetry of the facade, therefore, runs across the whole building rather than the one house. Ordinarily the main entrance would be facing forwards, oriented towards the street, but in the case of these two houses, their entrances are at an angle, tucked into the corner formed between the main section of the house and the kitchens, set to one side. There is a small wooden corner-porch above the doorway, the hooded porch having been brought back into fashion by the Edwardians. This one is a particularly interesting feature of the house, as it was described in detail in the architect's specification, which included a little sketch showing the detail of the porch construction (Fig.6.6).

Entering the front door, there is a very small entrance hall (far more Victorian than Edwardian, when halls generally became more spacious) leading to the staircase immediately in front of the entrance and with two reception rooms placed either side of it. To the immediate right of the hallway is the front reception room which was likely to have been the original parlour, or the 'best' room for receiving guests. Although the smaller of the two reception rooms, this was probably the 'best' room as it had a tiled fireplace (rather than a cast-iron one) and a wooden floor (rather than a tiled one); and the top lights of the casement windows are made of coloured glass. Another pair of doors, French windows, connect this room to the garden (see the section on the history of the house for a discussion of the significance of these doors), but we never

Porch

champered wall plates of 3/4" beaded facia, having 2 sets of wood brackets 3" thick as shown with champered edges & wall pieces, other parts as before specified, to be boarded under rafters with 5/8" matchboarding.

Doors

The front entrance doors to have 6 panels 1¾" bolection moulded, hung with 4" butts to 5½" × 2½" rabated & beaded frames, & moulded transome doors 2'-9" × 6'-9", with 1½" fixed fanlight above, furnished with 9" draw back locks, 9" bolt on bottom, china knobs, & combined "Letters & knocker" pc 2/6 bronzed.

The doors to sculleries & closets 1" ledged, braced hung to 5½" × 2½" rabated & champered frames, with stout 18 TEE hings, substantial Norfolk latch furniture, 8" stock lock on scullery 2-9" bolts & 1 small bolt on closet door which shall be 2' × 3" wide hung short. Scullery door to be 2'-6" wide × 6'-8" high.

All the doors inside to be 1½" four panelled double moulded 2'-6" × 6'-6" hung to 1½" rabated jambs with 2 — 3½" butts, & furnished with 6" rim locks & furniture of brass of a substantial character.

Pantry

Perforated zinc 6" high over pantry door for ventilation & framed for same. These doors 1½" single moulded hung & with 4" catch only.

6.6 Extract from the architect's specification showing the design for a porch

(right)

6.7 Plan of the Bradwell Road house

used them, as they were so close to the front door. The parlour was also the room with the bay window; in 1894 an amendment to the Building Act meant that windows no longer needed to be recessed behind a brick reveal, and this became the impetus for bay windows. Canted bay windows, with a straight front and angled sides, became particularly fashionable after this date. In contrast to the parlour, the room to the left of the hall, and to the rear of the house – with its cast-iron fireplace and flush, plain windows – was most likely the family's living room (presently the dining room).

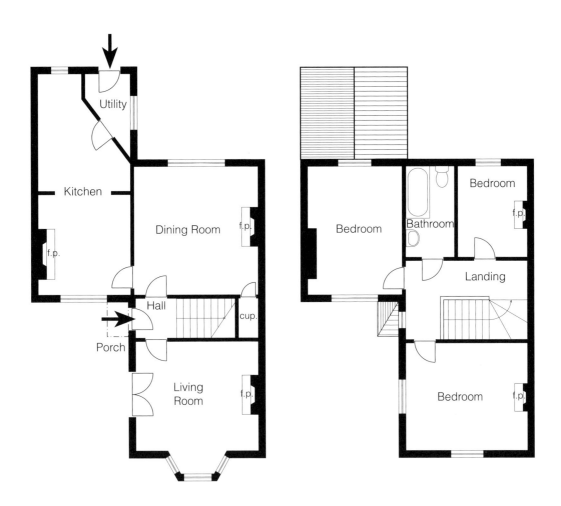

LIVING IN HOUSES

Leading off the living room is, and was, the kitchen. Since the Georgian and early Victorian eras, basements housing the kitchen and service rooms had entirely disappeared and as a consequence, during the Edwardian era, these rooms tended to be placed to the side of the house. This evolution in the plan exactly reflects the layout of this house, with the two reception rooms placed in the main part of the house, with the kitchen off to one side. Originally, in this house, these service rooms were likely to have consisted of a kitchen, with a single-storey scullery (for washing as a separate activity from cooking) located to the rear of the kitchen, and most likely a water closet placed at the very back of the rear extension and only reached from the outside. Today the kitchen and scullery room have been combined into a single, large kitchen and the room for the water closet is a utility/boot room. The living room, kitchen, scullery and water closet were all tiled in terracotta quarry tiles, which were a particularly common feature at the time. In the original architect's specification, now in possession of the current owners, the architect instructs the builder to: 'Pave the sculleries, kitchens and pantries, closets, lobbies and bed room hearths with Stanley red 6" × 6" quarries, seconds, for @ 32/6 pence (32 shillings and 6 pence) per 1000.'[6]

Upstairs were three bedrooms, and I am doubtful about whether the current bathroom was originally a bathroom or not, since it has no outside window. In the Edwardian era, bathrooms were beginning to become standard in medium to large houses, but in smaller houses such as this one, people typically continued to follow the Victorian habit of using a tin bath in the scullery for bathing. The upper floor, therefore, was just for sleeping purposes.

Materials

One of the most interesting building materials to feature in this house is terracotta which was used for various decorative details. After the construction of the Natural History Museum of London (1879–1880), terracotta became increasingly fashionable, which resulted in a wave of mass-produced architectural terracotta products, often selected by the architect/builder from extensive catalogues. The combination of red brick with terracotta details became a widely used combination for

6.8 A selection of terracotta features of the house. Top, moulded string course bricks; bottom left, Edward VII's coronation plaque; bottom right, terracotta roof finial (not to scale)

houses as well as commercial buildings such as schools, libraries and churches,[7] and became most popular from the 1880s.[8]

In this particular house, terracotta components are found in: its decorative moulded stretcher bricks/string courses and cornice; the quarry tiles throughout the ground floor; the window sill shaped bricks; the roof ridge tiles and striking roof ball finials; and, most spectacularly, in a commemorative plaque in honour of the coronation of Edward VII on 9 August 1902 (I will return to this). In architecture, a string course is a decorative horizontal band inserted into an external wall, typically replacing one, or more, brick (or stone) courses. Sometimes a string course consists simply of differently coloured, but otherwise plain bricks, and alternatively it can be quite decorative. String courses are typically used to differentiate different storeys in a building and/ or are often placed along the tops of windows; they are used in all of these ways in this house. The terracotta, string course bricks used in this house are the same size as standard bricks, but their longest side features a decorative relief pattern. Three types are used in this house: one is a fancier, four-petalled flower pattern; another consists of a

LIVING IN HOUSES

pair of roundels (or raised discs) which, when placed in a row, form a continuous run of dots; and a third, a shaped brick, forms the cornice at the very top of the wall, where it meets the roof eaves (Fig.6.8).[9]

The market for 'stock' terracotta (standard pieces selected from a catalogue) peaked around 1890, and by the turn of the century – when these houses were built – demand had fallen dramatically,[10] so it is particularly interesting that such products were used so extensively in this house. Terracotta plaques and tiles were, however, quite a feature of Edwardian homes, and this house's commemorative plaque is a particularly fine example of decorative terracotta ware. I was curious about who might have been the manufacturer of the plaque. Quite unusually, a copy of the original architect's specification is still in possession of the current owners and this document reveals that all of the other terracotta items mentioned above were supplied by the firm Stanley Brothers in Nuneaton; it does not, however, mention the commemorative plaque (perhaps it was an afterthought). One speciality of Stanley Brothers was terracotta plaques of Queen Victoria, produced to mark her Golden Jubilee in 1887 and her Diamond Jubilee in 1897.[11] These jubilee plaques can be found all over the country, but mostly in southern and central England and particularly in the county of Leicestershire. A study of Leicester's plaques was undertaken in 1999 by Arthur Sadler who discovered that there were no existing records or moulds of any of the plaques in the Stanley Brothers' archives, and therefore it is perfectly possible that they may have also made the Edward VII plaque as well.[12] The Victoria plaques are 24" × 24" whereas the Edward plaque is smaller: approximately 18" × 18". Sadler found a salvaged plaque, which he was able to examine closely and describes as being: '3 ½" thick. The sides are roughly scored, presumably to improve bonding, and the back has four holes approximately 10 ½" square by 1 ⅜" deep, to reduce the bulk and to assist drying before firing and to assist bonding. To assist bonding there are also 1" holes in the outside walls of the recesses to take wood or metal plugs which would fit into the plaque for extra security.'[13] Sadler concluded his article by observing that it is not known how long Stanley Brothers were manufacturing such plaques or how many were made, and therefore he makes a plea for any surviving examples to be 'collected' and documented. Sadly, the only other example I have found of an Edward VII plaque is on a

6.9 Advertisement for Stanley Brothers, Midland Tile Works, Nuneaton, from *The Building News*, 12 December 1879

building in the Beamish Museum in County Durham, so I can only presume that these were far rarer.

An alternative theory is that this plaque was manufactured in the village of Ruabon in north Wales. The terracotta made from Ruabon marlstone had a reputation for having a particularly strong, deep red colour, and the colour of this plaque – along with its similarity to other pieces of decorative terracotta, of known provenance[14] – suggests that it was equally possible that the plaque was made by J.C. Edwards of Ruabon. J.C. Edwards was once the largest manufacturer of terracotta in the world,[15] but despite this plaque's visual similarity to some of Edwards' designs, I suspect that in 1902 the builder of our house was thumbing through the Stanley Brothers' catalogue[16] to place an order for the various terracotta components specified by the architect, when he noticed the coronation plaque for sale and, on impulse, ordered one.

The Influence and Inspiration of the Edwardian Semi-detached House

The influence of the Edwardian semi-detached home has been, and is still, immense; John Burnett claimed that the suburban semi was 'the most characteristic expression of English domestic architecture'.[17] In Pamela Lofthouse's doctoral thesis on the semi-detached house, she claims that the first recorded instance of the word 'semi-detached' was from an advertisement in *The Times* for a 'semi-detached gentleman's residence' for rent in 1842.[18] The semi-detached house (known colloquially as a 'semi') is the most common dwelling type in England:[19] according to the government's most recent housing stock survey,[20] there were 6,191,449 semi-detached houses in England in 2019, which accounts for just over a quarter of all houses.

LIVING IN HOUSES

Although not invented by the Edwardians – since examples of 'joined' pairs of houses can be found being built in almost every previous era (just not at sufficient volume to be noteworthy) – it is the Edwardian era that is most responsible for popularising the semi-detached house, leading to a wave of semi-detached house construction during the period between the wars. Prior to the Edwardians, during the Victorian era, plans for 'double cottages for workers' formed a large proportion of the houses proposed by the model dwellings movement (see Chapter 7), and in the 1870s and 1880s, the new suburb of Bedford Park in west London included various semi-detached houses which attracted a number of middle-class intellectuals/creatives. But it was really through the designs for garden villages that the semi-detached house became more familiar to the wider public. The architect Raymond Unwin must therefore be acknowledged for his role in the evolution of the semi. In 1902, the same year that this house was built, Raymond Unwin and his partner, Barry Parker, designed the village of New Earswick for the Joseph Rowntree Village Trust, which included a large number of semi-detached houses. The following year they became involved in the planning and design of houses for the first Garden City, Letchworth. Along with other architects (Mackay Hugh Baillie Scott, Allen Foxley and Courtenay Melville Crickmer), Parker and Unwin designed a number of semi-detached house types for Letchworth,[21] which elicited considerable public interest, and the experiment that was Letchworth was repeated elsewhere (leading eventually, it could be argued, to Milton Keynes).

What has been the long-term legacy of the semi-detached house? Given the sheer numbers of them in the housing stock, the majority of people in England[22] will have either lived in a 'semi' at some stage in their life or had a relative who did. When people's housing preferences are surveyed, a three-bedroom, semi-detached house is still the type of house that most people aspire to live in. And three-bedroom semis are still being produced in significant quantity by current private housing developers.

Architects too are still keen to dabble in this house type, ever seeking ways to update the semi-detached house for the 21st century. Some interesting examples of modern reinterpretations of the semi-detached house can be found in the Officers Field[23] development in Weymouth by HTA Design, which includes a variety of terraced, semi-detached and detached types. Another noteworthy example of modern semi-detached houses can be found in Derwenthorpe in Osbaldwick,[24] York, by the architects Studio Partington, also for the Joseph Rowntree Housing Trust (JRHT). This mixed development consists of a variety of terraced, semi-detached and detached houses. I think it is fair to say that the semi-detached house, as a house type, still has a lot to commend it – but looking to the future, with a greater demand for sustainable buildings and shrinking household sizes, perhaps the era of the semi-detached house is finally coming to an end as it is replaced by smaller and more energy-efficient flats and terraced houses.

Personal Lessons Learnt for Architectural Practice

This is going to sound like a somewhat strange lesson to have learnt as an architect: I must confess that when we first moved into this house, one of its features that I was somewhere between 'indifferent to' and 'disparaging of', was the series of small stained-glass windows in the front reception room (formerly the parlour). Admittedly, they were extremely simple and non-fussy – no more than single panes of textured, golden-yellow coloured glass placed at the very top of the casement windows. I would not say that I underwent a Damascene conversion, but rather that living in this house prompted a gradual warming to the presence of the coloured glass.

The parlour windows faced north-west, and I began to notice the way in which the low evening sunlight shone directly through the yellow panes, filling the room with a diffuse golden light, and I began to love the precise moment in the early evenings when this happened. And so, eventually, I had to spend some time examining my own prejudices against stained glass. I think that the associations that I had with stained glass in houses were that it was rather twee and sentimental, and certainly not architecturally 'cool'. I had certainly failed to realise the sheer visual delight of it. Now, more than a decade after leaving the Bradwell Road house, I find myself living in another house with stained-glass elements (the Regency villa from Chapter 4), and I take unalloyed delight in them. As a consequence, I have also begun to become interested in contemporary architecture that uses coloured or stained glass.

7
Haberdasher Street (1912)
The Story of Model Dwellings for Workers

7.1   Sketch drawing of Haberdasher Street

HABERDASHER STREET (1912)

Introduction: My Lived Experience of this Home

The flat in Haberdasher Street was the first 'proper' flat that I lived in after graduating from university. The sheer novelty of having my own front door, behind which lay a series of entirely separate (if tiny) rooms – my *own* kitchen, my *own* bathroom, my *own* living room and so on – was such an unadulterated delight.

I have scant memory of house-hunting. I had been living in a studio flat in Muswell Hill towards the end of my final year of university, and was looking for somewhere more central to rent. Haberdasher Street just happened to be about the right size, for the right price and, the icing on the cake, it was located in London Transport Zone 1. I recall the first time that I walked to the flat from Old Street underground station: having walked along East Road, which felt exceedingly 'inner-city-ish', I turned the corner and remember experiencing the surprise of encountering Haberdasher Street for the first time. The delight of Haberdasher Street lies not in any single building, but in the effect of the homogenous blocks and the overall streetscape, with its mature trees and the long line of buildings facing each other and slightly set back behind iron railings. In the case of this home, I fell in love with the street first and the flat second.

The flat I moved into was a top-floor flat on the north side of the street. The living room was at the front of the house and had stripped wooden floors and the original, small, cast-iron fireplace, with alcoves either side of the chimneybreast which I immediately filled with books. The fireplace had a metallic, gun-metal patina, was surprisingly elegant in its proportions and was decorated with a couple of neo-classical motifs – a laurel wreath and an 'urn and swag' motif (or a low squat vase with a garland hanging from it). The kitchen was just large enough to accommodate a table, which could, with a bit of a squeeze, seat four people. It had the tiniest and most perfunctory and utilitarian of bathrooms I have ever had and a bedroom which was just not quite large enough to fit both a double bed and a separate wardrobe (I improvised a series of high-level hanging rails fixed to the walls, which meant that my clothes hung partially over the bed). To the rear of the flat was a roof terrace that, with hindsight, I am surprised I did not use more, but at the time it felt far more like an unloved, asphalted flat roof than an actual 'terrace' intended for sitting on.

(overleaf)

7.2 Haberdasher Street streetscape

LIVING IN HOUSES

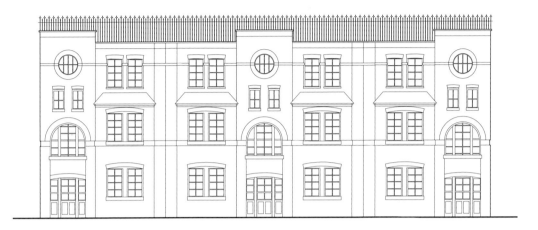

Each group of six flats was arranged around a single staircase, and in one of the ground-floor flats of our block lived an elderly gentleman who would often emerge from his flat just as I was arriving/leaving home, and we would always stop and chat for a bit. He told me stories of how the flats had originally been designed for single 'bobbies' (policemen), and how he had lived there all of his life.

The area surrounding Haberdasher Street, known as Hoxton, still felt scruffy and a bit down-at-heel in the early 1990s (I moved in the summer of 1991). What I didn't know at the time was that the whole area was poised to become probably the coolest place in the country just a couple of years later – according to a *Guardian* article, 'Hoxton was invented in 1993.'[1] I remember visiting friends working for some of the new media start-ups in the late 1990s and barely recognising just how hip and trendy it had all become. 'By the end of the '90s, Hoxton had spawned an entire lifestyle . . . As the groovy district du jour, Hoxton had come to represent the cliff face of the cutting edge.'[2]

7.3 Street elevation of a section of the Haberdasher Street terraces

(right)

7.4 Plan of the Haberdasher Street flat

History of Haberdasher Street and the Model Dwellings Movement

This is a history in two parts, the first part being the history of the Haberdasher Street flats, the second being concerned with the Victorian

140

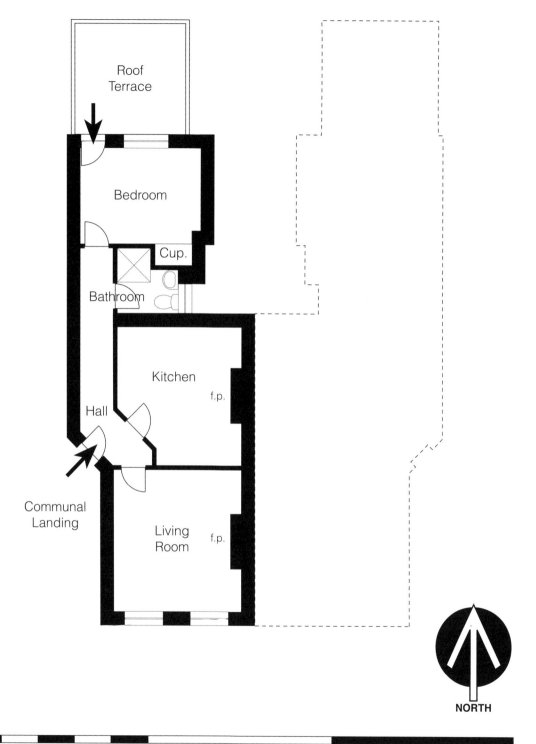

LIVING IN HOUSES

model dwellings movement, which was clearly an influence on the Haberdasher Street flats, despite them being late Edwardian/pre-First World War rather than Victorian.

The name of Haberdasher Street is a bit of a giveaway as to its origins. It was not called Haberdasher Street originally: earlier maps indicate it being called Singleton Street, a street connecting East Road at one end and Pitfield Street at the other. However, a large area of Hoxton was owned by the Worshipful Company of Haberdashers; they were the owners of the Singleton Street site, and it was the Haberdashers' Company which subsequently commissioned the design and construction of the two rows of flats and in doing so bestowed their name on the entire street. The Worshipful Company of Haberdashers is a livery company in the City of London tracing its origins back to the medieval guilds. The livery companies were responsible for apprenticeships and training, wage and quality control, and the general welfare of their members. As with all livery companies, they specialised in a single trade, and in their case, haberdashery encompassed a wide range of activities, from hat making to the selling of small wares such as ribbons, beads, pins and so on.[3] Today they are mostly known for their charitable activities and strong support for education (most of the City of London's livery companies are now charitable foundations).

What is interesting about the fact that the Worshipful Company of Haberdashers decided to develop these flats is that housing development or provision had never been a core concern for them. By the 1900s, they were focusing primarily on education, having previously set up a number of schools. They also owned land in and around Hoxton[4] – or South Shoreditch as it was more commonly called then – and this became the impetus for the building of the Haberdasher Steet flats. According to Isobel Watson in her study of early flats in Hackney,[5] around 1909, the terraced houses to the east end of Singleton Street had become dilapidated and needed to be demolished. An obvious solution would have been to have sold the land, but at the time the market for development land was deemed poor and it was unlikely that the sale would have generated much income, so the Haberdashers' Company decided to try developing the land themselves, as housing. Someone who later became closely

142

HABERDASHER STREET (1912)

familiar with the Haberdasher Street scheme and the Company in the 1980s, Christopher Maunder Taylor, thought that they simply 'saw an opportunity to improve the revenue return and at the same time provide housing accommodation for people, from what we might now describe as a working class sector of the population'.[6]

The development was initially conceived of as 'industrial dwellings' – as Watson says, 'nominally intended for "the industrious classes", that is to say those engaged in manufacturing; in practice they tended to be taken up by shop-workers, clerks, and police families as well as artisans'.[7] However, since the Haberdashers' Company had, hitherto, been concerned primarily with education, the provision of housing clearly fell outside its stated remit as a charitable organisation, so they needed to secure special permission from the government, via the Board of Education, for the venture. Watson reports on board minutes that indicate how the Haberdashers' Company was forced to admit to the development's speculative nature, although permission was eventually granted.

Naturally, they turned to their official surveyors, the company, Stock Page & Stock, to aid them with this endeavour. The company had been founded around 1825,[8] and in 1840 Henry Stock had joined as an apprentice architect (aged just 15[9]), eventually taking over the practice in 1847. He was later joined by his son, Henry William Stock, and another architect, Robert Page, in 1881.[10] The practice's name was changed to Stock Page & Stock in 1906, which is also the year that they were appointed as official surveyors for the Haberdashers' Livery Company[11] (according to the practice's website, a letterhead from that time describes them as 'Stock Page & Stock, Architects, Surveyors and Industrial Planning Consultants'). However, by the time the construction of Haberdasher Street had begun in 1909, both Henry Stocks had died, and therefore it was undoubtedly Robert Page who was the architect of the Haberdasher Street flats.

The houses were developed in blocks of six flats arranged around a central stair, with 16 blocks of six flats and one block of three, resulting in 99 flats in total. When they were first built, the flats on the north side of the street were leased to the Metropolitan Police.[12] On the north side, numbers 57 to 145 have access to a communal rear courtyard reserved for police constables.

LIVING IN HOUSES

							Police Constables									Sergeants	
65	67	77	79	89	(91)	101	103	113	115	125	127	137	139	145	155	157
61	63	73	75	85	87	97	99	109	111	121	123	133	135	143	151	153
57	59	69	71	81	83	93	95	105	107	117	119	129	131	141	147	149

(NORTH SIDE)

HABERDASHER STREET

50	52	62	64	74	76	90	92	102	104	114	116	126	128	138	140
54	56	66	68	78	80	94	96	106	108	118	120	130	132	142	144
	58		70	82	88	98	100	110	112	122	124	134	136	146	148

(SOUTH SIDE)

Ordinary Tenants

7.5 A diagram showing the arrangement of the flats on either side of the street, indicating which were used by the Metropolitan Police. My flat is indicated by the circle

The current company secretary of Stock Page Stock does not know how long the flats were in use by the Metropolitan Police. However, the date that they ceased using them was likely to have been around the mid-1930s as a consequence of Lord Trenchard's 1932[13] 'Report on the Metropolitan Police' in which the state of police accommodation was decried as being old-fashioned, cramped and generally unfit for purpose. This led to the Metropolitan Police Act of 1933 and the immediate building of a large number of new, modern section houses for the police; my assumption is that any police living in Haberdasher Street at this time were subsequently moved into newly built accommodation. When the police ceased leasing the north side of the street, the Haberdashers' Company simply let them to new tenants on the same basis that the flats on the south side were already being let, with Stock Page & Stock managing them on their behalf. In 1985 tenants were given the opportunity to buy their flats, a deliberate policy (under the, then, Master of the Haberdashers' Company, Harold Quitman) to sell off all their residential properties to generate revenue. Christopher Maunder Taylor – formerly of Stock Page & Stock and who collaborated with Harold Quitman on the process of selling off the flats – explained that: 'the Rent Acts, the Landlord and Tenant Acts and various measures intended to improve housing stock, came onto the Statute Book for this underlying purpose. The downside for a private-rented-sector landlord was that rental income was managed

144

HABERDASHER STREET (1912)

by statutory control provisions and it became increasingly difficult to generate sufficient net revenue from the capital assets.'[14]

It took 13 years to break up and sell off the estate and sales of properties in Hoxton (including the Haberdasher Street flats) raised £2,395,529[15] for the company's charitable concerns. Today, only one flat is still being occupied by the last remaining lifetime tenant. Stock Page Stock now owns the freehold and the Haberdashers' Company no longer retains any interest in the properties.

The first time that I visited Haberdasher Street I was forcibly reminded of Victorian model dwellings,[16] and in particular what was, arguably, the most influential model dwelling of all, designed by the architect Henry Roberts for the Great Exhibition of 1851.[17] During the industrial revolution workers had flocked to the cities, and by the mid-19th century, housing conditions – especially in large cities such as London – were extremely poor. This had become a matter of general public concern (having been brought to the public's attention through the efforts of writers such as Charles Dickens and Henry Mayhew in the 1830s and 1840s,[18] and culminating in Edwin Chadwick's 1842 *Report on the Sanitary Condition of the Labouring Population of Great Britain*), so much so that an organisation was set up: the Society for Improving the Condition of the Labouring Classes. This society was established in 1844 and Queen Victoria's husband, Albert, the Prince Consort, was its President. Henry Roberts was the society's honorary architect, and it was in this capacity that he designed the 1851 model dwelling.[19]

The model dwelling 'exhibit' attracted 250,000 visitors[20] that year, and although some early model dwellings had been built prior to 1851, the influence of this one can be evidenced by the number of model dwellings that were built after it. Peter Malpass, in a paper on the history of housing associations,[21] suggests that over 30 model dwellings companies and charitable trusts were engaged in building homes in London during the second half of the 18th century.[22] In 1875 a statistician named Charles Gatliff wrote a paper for the Statistical Society of London in which he attempted to correlate the rise in model dwellings with a commensurate drop in mortality rates. In order to do this, he undertook a process of tallying and mapping all the model dwellings that had been built by that date. His enquiry resulted in the

LIVING IN HOUSES

following cumulative figures: 6,838 dwellings accommodating a total of 32,435 people. Furthermore, he calculated that over £1.2 million had been spent on constructing them (this would be over £2 billion today).[23] Anthony Wohl, however, suggests that fewer than 40,000 dwellings had been built by 1910.[24]

Of course, some model dwellings were more obviously 'influenced' by Henry Roberts' house (that is to say, reusing his design) than others. Ten years after the Great Exhibition, the Improved Industrial Dwellings Co. Ltd was formed and Matthew Allen's prototype blocks, based directly on Roberts' model, were built between 1864 and 1865. The next builder whose work clearly represented a further refinement of Roberts' model was Joseph Nathan, working for the Four Per Cent[25] Industrial Dwellings Company (in 1952 it became the Industrial Dwellings Society[26]). From Joseph Nathan's first buildings, the Charlotte de Rothschild Dwellings (1886), through to his last, the Navarino Mansions (1903–4), his gradual modification and adaptation of Roberts' model dwelling is clear. The final step, therefore, of drawing a thread of architectural influence between Henry Roberts' work and Robert Page's design for Haberdasher Street in 1906 is not a great one, chronologically.

Although it is easy to think of the model dwellings movement as being purely a Victorian phenomenon, many of the model dwellings companies continued to build until the early 20th century. Companies who were still building into the early 1900s – at the same time that the Haberdasher Street flats were being built – include the East End Dwellings Company, the Four Per Cent Industrial Dwellings Company, the Improved Industrial Dwellings Company and the Peabody Trust. Peter Malpass suggests that perceived criticisms of the model dwellings movement (namely that they did not build at sufficient volume, that they often neglected to focus on the very poorest levels of society and that some of their designs were just a bit too utilitarian and 'grim') have resulted in a historical neglect of their work between 1890 and 1910. Malpass is clear that the model dwellings movement was active up to and even beyond the First World War. He explains: 'Closer examination of the years up to the outbreak of the First World War shows that in fact the voluntary organisations enjoyed a period of growth and innovation', and he goes on to observe that some model

HABERDASHER STREET (1912)

dwellings companies 'survived for a lot longer than the literature has tended to imply'.[27] I therefore think that it is entirely appropriate to view the Haberdasher Street flats in the context of them representing one of the very last-to-be-built examples of the philanthropic model dwellings movement, at the very cusp of the transition to local authority council house construction.

Finally, I will return to my first observation, that when living there, I was struck by similarities between Henry Roberts' model dwelling and the design of the Haberdasher Street block. The similarities between the two include the use of contrasting red and buff-coloured bricks (or polychromatic brickwork – see pp 150–51 for a discussion of this): in Haberdasher Street, contrasting bricks are used for the window and doorway arches as well as in horizontal bands of contrasting bricks, which precisely mimics the design of Roberts' model dwelling. The only difference is that the Haberdasher Street flats do not have contrasting brick quoins which Roberts' building features (since the Haberdasher Street blocks are repeated in a terrace, they have no 'corners' to accommodate quoins except at the very ends of the rows).

Both block designs are organised around a central stair, which in the original Roberts design was fully external but in Haberdasher Street has been transformed into an interior staircase (this was a typical refinement of the original Roberts model, used often in other later model dwellings developments). Compositionally, the stairway section of the facade in both buildings is represented as a sequence (from ground to roof level) of a rectangular door set into a two-storey brick arch with a circular motif above it (although what in Roberts' facade is a decorative rondel has been transformed into a circular window in Haberdasher Street). In both buildings the central archway and stair are recessed behind the line of the main facade. In Roberts' building this is because the stairwell space is an exterior space entered through a recessed void; in Haberdasher Street this is achieved slightly differently as the ground and first-floor windows protrude beyond the line of the main facade, creating a sense that the archway and main entrance are recessed. (See Fig.7.6 which illustrates the transformation of Henry Roberts' model dwelling into a Haberdasher Street block.)

LIVING IN HOUSES

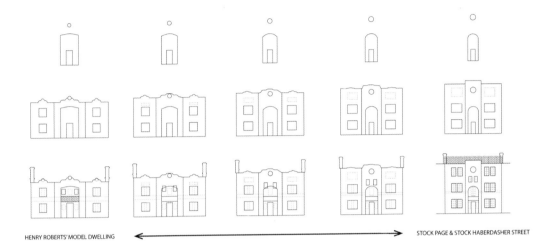

HENRY ROBERTS' MODEL DWELLING STOCK PAGE & STOCK HABERDASHER STREET

Layout: Typical House Plans

Like many of the previous model dwellings, including the Roberts house, the Haberdasher Street plans were designed to be fully modular: they could be stacked both vertically and horizontally. In Haberdasher Street, each block of six flats, arranged around a stair, can be clearly repeated, horizontally, forming the next set of six flats and so on, resulting in a long, terrace-like effect. Each terrace of merged blocks is then repeated on the opposite side of the road.

Returning to the level of the block, in the case of Haberdasher Street there is a perfect symmetry of layouts on either side of the stairway, with each flat in the pair being an exact mirror image of the other. Generally, the ground-floor and second-floor flats were the largest, having two bedrooms, while the third-floor flats (like the one I lived in) contained only a single bedroom (hence having a roof terrace occupying the space of the additional room in the flats below). To enter from the street, you must first pass through the communal front door and into a shared lobby, where the doors to the first two ground-floor flats are positioned immediately either side and the staircase is immediately in front; subsequent flats are accessed via the stairs. From the upper-floor landings, entrance to each flat is via the front door at a 45° angle, and the long corridor that links the rooms towards

7.6 The transformation of Henry Roberts' 1851 model dwelling into a Haberdasher Street block. Top row: transformation of the stairway section of facade; middle row: transformation of the block massing; bottom row: detailed transformation of facades

HABERDASHER STREET (1912)

the rear of the flats to the front room is forced to make a slight 45°
'wiggle' to accommodate this. The flats are sufficiently narrow that
the layout of each flat is simply a sequence of rooms from front to
back – in the case of my flat, the living room was at the front, followed
by the kitchen, then the bathroom, with the bedroom and terrace at
the back, in that order.

There is one other, really fascinating, feature of the Haberdasher
Street flats and this is hinted at by the elevation: looking down the
length of the street, you can see that the stone parapet at the roofline
supports cast-iron railings running along the entire terrace. This is
because the roof is flat since it was designed to facilitate clothes drying.
If you continue up the stairs to the very top of the staircase, you arrive
at a door which permits access to this communal roof, where clothes
lines were originally provided. According to architect and current
resident Steven Smith, the drying areas on the roof terrace were just
part of a complex system for drying clothes. The ground- and first-
floor flats had access to a rear, communal courtyard (one on each side
of the street), which also contained washing lines. In addition to this,
the first-floor flats had 'a system of clotheslines attached to pulley
wheels allowing wet clothes to be attached to a line from a window
and then winched out across the yard'.[28] And finally, the upper-floor
flats, such as mine, also had a washing line available on their rear
terrace. Such a superabundance of clothes drying facilities seems
quite strange now in our era of tumble dryers, but perhaps we will
return to this as we all strive to be more environmentally conscious
in the future.

What I have found most fascinating about looking at the current
Haberdasher Street flats is just how varied they have become. Since
they were sold to the tenants in 1985 they have been constantly altered
and adapted by new generations of owners; this is partially due to the
fact that the buildings were never listed (which, I confess, surprises
me). Indeed, some adjacent pairs of flats have even been combined
into one (or even combined and then de-coupled again). So, in
the space of just over 35 years, they have changed from all having
precisely the same layout and fixtures, to there being no standard
layout at all – they are far, far more individual now than they were
originally intended to be.

LIVING IN HOUSES

Materials

I have already commented on the fact that both Henry Roberts' original model dwelling and the Haberdasher Street flats share a similar, material palette achieved by combining contrasting red and London (buff-coloured) stock bricks. Where did this interest in combining bricks of different colours in the same building – or 'constructional polychromy' – originate from? It is often said that architectural polychromy was a mid-to-late Victorian trend,[29] but in Neil Jackson's paper on the topic, he suggests that it has its origins in the early 19th century, when architects, visiting Italy as part of their Grand Tours[30] (see Chapter 3) were inspired by the use of coloured banding – or 'courses' – in medieval Italian churches. The first Victorian architect to experiment with such polychromatic brickwork was James Wild who used it in his design for Christ Church in Streatham (1840–42), about which John Ruskin, the artist, writer and art-critic, commented: 'It affords . . . a means of obtaining some idea of the variety of effects which are possible with no other material than brick.'[31] However, the more influential early example of polychromatic brickwork was William Butterfield's later masterpiece, All Saints' Church, Margaret Street, which was built between 1850 and 1852 (and opened in 1859). Butterfield's church is an exuberant celebration of the sheer variety of colours that can be achieved using different building materials, and his brickwork is no less of an experiment with how far one can push the possibilities of different brick colours. Today, it still has the power to surprise with its vibrancy of colour.

The person who was most influential in encouraging architects to use colour in architecture (and ideally through the natural[32] colours of materials, rather than through painted surfaces or decoration) was John Ruskin. In *The Seven Lamps of Architecture,* first published in 1849, he states: 'I cannot . . . consider architecture as in anywise perfect without colour.' Later, in his 1851 book, *The Stones of Venice* (the same year that Henry Roberts' model dwelling was opened to the public), Ruskin expounds at length on the virtues of polychromy; and where Ruskin pronounced, others followed rapidly. Anuradha Chatterjee suggests that he was one of the main advocates of polychromy in architecture.[33]

One example of the change in attitude can be found in a book written by George Street, first published in 1855, as 'a simple narrative

150

HABERDASHER STREET (1912)

of a tour undertaken'[34] through northern Italy. Street was particularly fascinated by the local builders' use of brick and marble, and in his conclusions to the book, he has much to say on how British architects should be approaching the use of brick in their buildings. First, he addresses the question of whether brick should be used at all and describes people's attitudes on brick being a 'common' building material as nothing more than 'ignorant prejudice', stating that 'what now mainly remains to be done is to shew how it may most effectively be used'. Street also has much to say on the colour of brick: 'One word only as to [brick's] colour, for I think that we ought as much as possible to insist upon this being taken into consideration . . .'. He goes on to say:

> At the present day there is, I think, absolutely no one point in which we fail so much, and about which the world in general has so little feeling, as that of colour. Our buildings are, in nine cases out of ten, cold, colourless, insipid, academical studies, and our people have no conception of the necessity of obtaining rich colour, and no sufficient love for it when successfully obtained. The task and duty of architects at the present day is mainly that of awakening and then satisfying this feeling; and one of the best and most ready vehicles for doing this exists, no doubt, in the rich-coloured brick so easily manufactured in this country, which, if properly used, may become so effective and admirable a material.[35]

If this was the mindset of architects in the mid-19th century, it is no surprise that the use of polychromatic bricks became prevalent between 1860 and 1900, so much so that it can be considered one of the defining characteristics of Victorian buildings. This is also the reason why the Haberdasher Street flats are often mistakenly identified as being Victorian,[36] rather than Edwardian/pre-First World War.

The Influence and Inspiration of Victorian Model Dwellings

The long-lasting influence of the model dwellings movement in general – and of the Haberdasher Street flats purely by association – lies in two

151

LIVING IN HOUSES

areas: first, in the history of social housing, and second, in the spatial layout of modern houses – and I will address each of these in turn.

The period of the model dwellings movement lasted from the mid-19th century up until the First World War. As mentioned above, the movement was not without its critics. One criticism is that there were simply never enough model dwellings built to make any difference to the living conditions of the poor (compare Wohl's estimation of 40,000 model dwellings built by 1910 – over, approximately, a 60-year period – with the estimated 89,000 council houses built by the London County Council (LCC) between the wars; LCC's council houses were being built at nearly seven times the rate of construction of model dwellings). The counter-argument is that the model dwelling companies, nevertheless, built a sufficient number of them to demonstrate the concept that affordable housing could be built efficiently and even profitably, and as such effectively paved the way for the later construction of council houses.

Another criticism is that despite the clearly articulated aims of the various model dwelling companies to be focused on the very poorest of society, quite often their tenants were drawn from the relatively affluent, salaried working class – the police being a good example – and even, at times, almost bordering on being middle class. It would, therefore, be fair to say that they can be deemed to have failed in their original objectives.

The final criticism that can be levelled at the model dwellings companies regards the scale and density of their developments: they have been criticised for being over-developed and their designs being somewhat 'grim'. Regarding the Haberdasher Street flats, I personally think that they are anything but grim; rather they serve as an excellent example of what can be achieved at a relatively high density, but without compromising either the public space of the street or the semi-public/private areas provided by the communal courtyards at the rear and roof spaces. I believe that Robert Page designed an exemplary housing scheme for the Haberdashers' Company and it is a pity that it has not received more attention from architectural historians. Despite these criticisms, a strong argument can be made that the model dwellings acted as both the precursor to council house building (the newly established LCC began to build its first council estates in 1900[37]), in addition to the private companies building the model dwellings being

HABERDASHER STREET (1912)

the true antecedents of our modern housing associations. This can be considered to be one of their long-term legacies.

There is another influence of the model dwellings that has become so utterly pervasive as to have an effect on *all* subsequent houses, not just social housing. The second way in which we are still experiencing the influence of the model dwellings is through the layout and arrangement of rooms in our modern homes today. Robin Evans, in 'Rookeries[38] and Model Dwellings', discusses the morality of the model dwellings: his theory is that the Victorians effectively fused the concepts of morality and space. While it was clear that Victorian slums were unhealthy environments (and hence there was a justified fear of disease spreading from the slums to adjacent areas), they also had a reputation for being, allegedly, hotbeds of criminality and prostitution. So not only did the Victorians fear the spread of infection in a literal sense but also as a metaphorical, moral contagion: a sense that, somehow, corruption might leak from the slums and infect other parts of the city. It is easy to see how such ideas of literal and metaphorical contagion can become easily intertwined. This impression that morality had a spatial dimension also had a direct effect on Victorian ideas about how houses should be internally organised, in particular, the belief that various groups of people, functions or activities should be kept strictly segregated. For example, it was considered important for the correct social and moral development of children that siblings of different genders should have their own rooms and, therefore, in most houses, three bedrooms became the minimum requirement: one for the parents, one for any son/s and one for any daughter/s. Associated with this is the idea that the parental bedroom should be strictly private, and anything that might take place in this room, behind closed doors, should be kept hidden from the children. Families should also be separated from other families through a literal merging of family boundaries with house boundaries. (This was the opposite of the spatial arrangement of rooms in the 'rookeries' where multiple families consisting of all genders and generations could be found co-inhabiting a single room.) This notion of spatial separation – of keeping cooking and eating, washing and personal cleansing, toilets/waste and sexual activity far apart and clearly delineated – resulted in the spatially segregated, functional rooms that still form the basis for our housing layouts today.

LIVING IN HOUSES

Personal Lessons Learnt for Architectural Practice

I think, for me, the main lesson that I learnt as an architect from living in Haberdasher Street concerns my – then – under-utilisation of the roof terrace space. When I moved into Haberdasher Street, it was only a few years after the tenants had been given the opportunity to buy their flats and, at that stage, very few of the upper-floor flat roofs were being used as external seating areas or 'outdoor rooms'.

I have since returned to the street and been particularly struck by the rear view of the upper-level flats. Furthermore, having examined recent aerial photographs and estate agents' listings and videos, it is clear that almost every available flat roof has now been converted into a garden terrace. Many owners have ensured their privacy by adding fences, trellises or privacy screens constructed of wicker, thatch or reed. Again, from photographs, it is possible to see how the garden terraces are full of pot plants and chairs. It is truly wonderful to see every square metre of outdoor space being made use of.

As well as the upper-level garden terraces, some residents have begun to make use of the small 'area' at the front of the buildings, the thin strip of 'nothingness' wedged between the front railings and the front brick wall of the building. Many contain little more than bicycles locked to the railings, but a few now contain planters and even the occasional bistro table and chairs. The third area of outdoor space is the large communal courtyard behind the houses, to which the ground-floor flats have direct access and the first-floor flats have access via a metal stair. When I was there, I never saw anyone in this space – it was entirely empty. Now it is full of plants in containers and tables, chairs and benches spread out along the full length of the space, as a communal garden to be enjoyed.

For many years now, psychologists have conducted research into the restorative effect of greenery and vegetation, and the recent pandemic has been a reminder to us all of the importance of exterior spaces. Particularly in an inner-city neighbourhood such as Hoxton, any available outdoor space – no matter how small – is precious and should be utilised to the full. My task, as an architect, is not to forget this lesson.

(right)

7.7 The flat roofs transformed into garden terraces

(below)

7.8 The current roof terrace of my old flat, now a riot of lush greenery

8

The Gloucester Grove (1977) and North Peckham Estates

The Story of a London 'Sink Estate'

Introduction: My Lived Experience of this Home

Before anything else, I should clarify the difference between the Gloucester Grove Estate and the North Peckham Estate, since they frequently get mixed up (and I am perpetuating this habit by including both names in the chapter title). Technically, the two estates were separate – but adjacent – local authority housing estates in North Peckham in the London Borough of Southwark. The North Peckham Estate was the larger of the two, both in extent and in the number of dwellings, with the Gloucester Grove Estate occupying a strip of land sandwiched between the North Peckham Estate and Burgess Park. But despite having different appearances, arrangements of blocks, architects (one was built by the Greater London Council, the other by the London Borough of Southwark), completion dates, and so on, the Gloucester Grove Estate was habitually lumped under the umbrella name of the North Peckham Estate. In the rest of this chapter, I will attempt not to replicate this error, and will be careful to ensure that each estate is referred to by its correct name.

(left)

8.1 Sketch drawing of part of the Gloucester Grove Estate

This section is not so much about *my* lived experience as *our* (and, to be honest, more my husband's) lived experiences. When my husband and I started dating, he was living in a flat on the Gloucester Grove Estate (for which his nickname was, endearingly, 'The Fortress'): he lived there between 1987 and 1997. From the moment we got together we were pretty much inseparable – I cannot recall us spending a single night apart. Since I already owned my house in Camden, north London (see Chapter 9) and he had his flat in south London, we rapidly developed the habit of simply dividing our time equally between the

(overleaf)

8.2 A view of one of the remaining eight blocks

LIVING IN HOUSES

two properties and spending part of each week at each other's place. After we had been together for a little over a year, my husband received a letter from Southwark Council informing him that he needed to vacate the property because it was going to be demolished. He was given various options to apply to be re-housed locally, but in the end, we just accepted this as the nudge we needed and without much further ado, we moved his things to Camden. We never saw his block, Withington Court, again. It would be fair to say that I do not think either of us gave it a second thought until it suddenly reappeared in the headline news, due to the tragic death of a young boy, Damilola Taylor, in November 2000, at which point the estate was already part way through the process of being demolished. But I will return to this later.

Given I spent the better part of a year, more or less, living on the Gloucester Grove Estate, did I realise that it was considered to be 'one of the toughest in Europe'?[1] As strange as it sounds, I did not. First, I did not have a vast experience of inner-city housing estates; after all, growing up in a tiny village in Leicestershire meant that they were entirely disconnected from my childhood. After moving to London, I recall attending a couple of parties in friends' council flats, but that was pretty much it. As an architecture student I studied a couple of estates as topics for essays or as possible sites for architectural design projects, but studying somewhere is very different from really spending time in a place, and so my first close-up and prolonged experience of any local authority housing was the Gloucester Grove Estate. And, not knowing its reputation, I simply accepted what I saw, at face value – and what I saw was, actually, not too bad. Second, I never really walked around the estate on my own or after dark. This was not for reasons of caution; it was just that we were a couple, it was early on in our relationship and so we tended to be together most of the time. Most of my experience of the estate consisted of the walk from the bus stop to the flat (and vice versa), the main entrance and its immediate communal areas, the lift, the corridor leading to our flat and the flat itself. Withington Court was an eight-storey slab-block, facing Burgess Park – hence it was on the very edge of the estate – and so there was never any need to venture deep into the estate to reach our flat, so I had no particular reason to walk around the estate. Third, my other main source of knowledge of the estate came from watching life unfolding on the estate from our seventh-storey[2] balcony, which overlooked the children's cycle/skate park. I never observed anything that gave me any cause for concern or made me feel unsafe; indeed, from that vantage point, it looked fairly 'normal' and quite far from being the dysfunctional place later portrayed in the media.

The flat itself was rather impressive, having large, spacious rooms with lots of in-built storage; it was white-walled, linoleum-floored and sparsely furnished. It felt modern, bohemian and, due to the large, brightly coloured canvasses on the walls (my husband's own work), a bit like an art gallery. Both the living room and the kitchen had balconies, although when I was there the smaller kitchen-balcony had pigeons nesting in it, which my (now) husband had been too soft-hearted to evict, so as a consequence this balcony was rendered completely unusable. From an architectural perspective, what was most intriguing was that the flat was split-level (known as a scissor flat; see p.174), and so the living and dining rooms faced the middle of the estate but the two bedrooms overlooked Burgess Park, and from the top floor, the view across the park – with the burgeoning skyline of the City of London[3] on the horizon – was simply stunning. All in all, I found it a generous, well-designed, light and spacious flat that I enjoyed spending time in.

History of the Gloucester Grove Estate

If you look at a map of the Gloucester Grove Estate in the mid-20th century, it looks just like any other part of London, a densely packed jumble of terraced housing with a small patch of more gracious, semi-detached villas, located towards the east end of a long, irregular road called Gloucester Grove (the estate's namesake). The longest terrace was St George's Road (now St George's Way), which ran parallel to the Grand Surrey Canal, and many of the gardens in St George's Road backed onto the canal's wharves. The Grand Surrey Canal connected Camberwell to the Surrey Commercial Docks at Rotherhithe (now Surrey Quays) and was closed in 1970, with the section running along the north edge of the Gloucester Grove Estate filled-in in 1974 (at precisely the time that the Gloucester Grove Estate was under

LIVING IN HOUSES

construction). The filled-in canal route was eventually transformed and incorporated into an extensive park, Burgess Park which itself, was a result of the post-war *County of London Plan* by J.H. Forshaw and Patrick Abercrombie,[4] in which a need for green space in this part of Southwark had been identified.

The area had suffered some bombing during the Second World War – for example, two V2 rockets landed on the edge of Burgess Park[5] – but actually, the site of the Gloucester Grove and North Peckham Estates emerged relatively unscathed from the war[6] – certainly, more intact that one might otherwise have guessed. The decision, therefore, to redevelop the area and to raze these houses to the ground was less precipitated by the Luftwaffe, and more by a desire to upgrade the existing poor housing conditions. There is no question that there was an urgent need for new housing after 1945; the government estimated that 750,000 new dwellings were needed, plus a further 500,000 to replace the worst of the slums.[7]

However, Dr Phil Jones from the University of Birmingham suggests that slum clearance was all too often a flimsy excuse for a local authority to show off their modernising credentials: 'Most local authorities . . . preferred the opportunity to thoroughly modernise their towns as a symbol of their power and prestige. Had the resources been available to them, [they] would have continued clearances until virtually the entire stock of Victorian era houses had been demolished.'[8] The architect Tim Tinker, one of the architects of the adjacent North Peckham Estate, put forward another reason for such sweeping redevelopment. He explained that, at the time, local authorities could only secure central government funds to build new housing and not to upgrade existing stock. He explained that 'whole swathes of potentially reasonable terrace housing were sacrificed in the numbers game of upping the densities of places like Peckham to compensate for lowering the densities of places like over-crowded . . . Bermondsey'.[9] Whatever the motivation, following a slew of compulsory purchase orders for the Victorian terraces,[10] two massive housing estates – on a scale rarely, if ever, attempted these days – were built between the late 1960s and mid-1970s: the North Peckham and the Gloucester Grove Estates.

The North Peckham Estate was the first of the two estates to be built. It was begun in the 1960s, completed in March 1973 and was designed

(right)

8.3 One of the remaining ground-floor flats with its own garden

LIVING IN HOUSES

by the London Borough of Southwark's Architects' Department.[11] Tim Tinker confirmed that Southwark's architects' department played no part in the design of the Gloucester Grove Estate, which he recalled as being 'a network of scissor blocks with linking circulation nodules that were very space age'.[12] The Gloucester Grove Estate was built by the Greater London Council's Architects' Department (formerly the London County Council's Architects' Department,[13] having been transformed into the GLC in 1965). This is where tracing the architect becomes a little more difficult as the GLC Architects' Department was, at its height, the largest architects' department in the country, with a staff of 340 architects just in the housing section.[14]

Interestingly, there was an urban myth circulating around the Gloucester Grove Estate that the architect had been so overcome with shame on seeing the outcome of their design that they committed suicide. I saw this story perpetuated in a couple of places – for example, in the Facebook group for former residents of the Gloucester Grove Estate – where one member swore it was true as she remembered her parents reading a newspaper article about it. Another former resident, and poet, Caleb Femi,[15] also makes reference to this in his recent anthology, *Poor*. In his poem, *A Designer Talks of a Home/A Resident Talks of Home (I)*, he writes: 'y'know the architect that designed this estate killed himself.'[16] This is not an uncommon urban legend and has been attributed to many other architects and other council estates. For example, in Lynsey Hanley's book, *Estates: An Intimate History*, she recounts a similar myth about the Hungarian architect Ernő Goldfinger with respect to his famous Trellick Tower building in west London.[17] It is possible to see how such myths might perpetuate, especially when no individual architect is attributed to a project, and as the GLC was such a nebulous and monolithic entity. For this reason, I set out to try and find out, once and for all, who had actually been the architect of the Gloucester Grove Estate.

In reality this proved to be a far harder task than I had originally – and with hindsight, optimistically – thought, despite the fact that the London Metropolitan Archives holds all of the original drawings of the Gloucester Grove Estate and I had been hoping to find an architect's name on one of these. In the end, the only name (apart from a few enigmatic and ultimately unattributable initials) found on any of the

THE GLOUCESTER GROVE ESTATE (1977)

drawings was the signature of Sir Roger Walters, the Chief Architect of the GLC between 1971 and 1978,[18] and he was required to sign off all of the drawings. A number of other writers and researchers far more knowledgeable about the LCC's and GLC's Architects' Departments than I am have commented on the frustrating opaqueness of the GLC's architecture department, including the writer Thaddeus Zupančič who observed that 'annoyingly the GLC themselves were very coy about their employees'.[19] However, I think that there may have been an additional reason why, specifically, the architect of the Gloucester Grove Estate has been so hard to identify.

An article in the *Architects' Journal* from 1975 refers to a scandal about the financial mismanagement of the Gloucester Grove Estate's budget:[20] the cost of the project was already in excess of £15 million (up from an original contract price of £8.3 million[21]) and this was still two years before the estate was completed (in the end, costs would exceed £16 million: the equivalent in today's money is likely to have been over a quarter of £1 billion[22]). An internal inquiry was convened to investigate the overspend and clearly the whole issue was considered to be extremely politically sensitive since an article in *Building Design* noted that: 'Press and public were excluded from a meeting where the request for additional costs is said to have been made.'[23] The subsequent inquiry was headed by an accountant and prominent local government councillor, Serge Lourie. An article in the *Architects' Journal*, commenting on the outcome of Lourie's report, noted that financial risks had been taken by a 'now retired GLC architect'[24] and I had wondered if it was possible that this individual 'took the rap' for the overspend and had accordingly retired, possibly having been promised anonymity by the department.[25]

Fortunately, Serge Lourie's report into the financial mismanagement of the project is available in the London Metropolitan Archives, and this document reveals how the former project architects, all of whom had retired, were 'recalled' to provide evidence. This report – along with letters and internal memoranda which were included as appendices – shows that the architects of the Gloucester Grove Estate were James William Oatley (the former Divisional Architect) and R. Jackson[26] (the former Group Leader), both of whom served under Kenneth Campbell (the former Housing Architect). The other architect's name

LIVING IN HOUSES

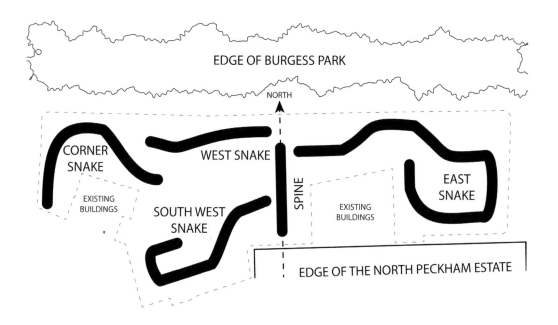

8.4 Diagrammatic layout of the Gloucester Grove Estate

that occurs frequently in memoranda and meeting minutes is Cecil Elson. Therefore, I propose that the architects were Oatley, Jackson and Elson. It should be noted, for the record, that no disciplinary action for misconduct was ever taken by the GLC, as it considered that there were no grounds for doing so.[27]

Moving on from the architects to the buildings: the site for the Gloucester Grove Estate had an existing net area of 28.6 acres, which after deductions for non-housing use left a gross housing area of 27.9 acres. The site was long, with a straight north edge running more or less east to west for nearly half a mile. Its short east and west boundaries were quite orderly, but its southern edge, where the site met the North Peckham Estate, was far more irregular and broken up due to the presence of a number of existing buildings that needed to be retained, including a couple of schools (the Church School and the Gloucester Junior School); hence, the new housing scheme had to somehow fit itself around these.

The eventual layout of the estate, on such an irregular site, was achieved by creating a central, anchoring 'spine' block (the tallest of

THE GLOUCESTER GROVE ESTATE (1977)

all the blocks, at 10 storeys high, and called Winchcombe Court) which was perpendicular to the Burgess Park site boundary. Three snaking lines of connected blocks (slab blocks connected to adjacent blocks via striking, circular, stair/lift towers) were tethered to this central spine. The two distinct 'snakes' that meandered alongside Burgess Park headed off to the east and the west, respectively. The eastern 'snake' eventually met the corner of the site and turned back on itself, almost forming a loop. The third 'snake' of connected blocks left the spine block further down, towards its southern end, and wiggled off in a south-westerly direction. Finally, a small, isolated section of blocks curled up the north west corner of the site, connected only to each other. As the 'snakes' got further away from the central spine, they tended to decrease in height as their blocks became progressively lower (most blocks were six storeys tall).

After approximately four years on the drawing board and planning delays,[28] the construction tender contract was signed in December 1971[29] and building work commenced in February 1972.[30] The estate consisted of 29 blocks, the largest block housing 352 people and the smallest just 16. My husband and, later, I lived in Withington Court (flat number 62), the fourth most populous of the blocks: Withington Court on its own would have housed more people than the entire population of the village of Burton Overy (see Chapter 1).[31] Incidentally, all of the 29 blocks were named after places in the counties of Gloucestershire and South Gloucestershire, in reference to the original Gloucester Grove street that had run through the centre of the site.[32] All the block names included the word 'Court'[33] as a suffix (see Fig.8.5).

In total, there were 1,210 newly built dwellings and 36 refurbished dwellings – making a total of 1,246 altogether – housing approximately 4,378[34] people. It is sobering to think that this was the equivalent to a medium-sized medieval town when it was finished in 1977.[35] I suspect that the GLC was conscious of this, since it went to some length to consider what else was needed to support such a large community, and the estate included: a tenants' meeting hall, shops, two areas for ball games, two toddler play areas, three junior play areas (one of which was a skateboard/BMX park), six older persons' gardens, two older persons' club rooms and an older persons' roof terrace. In addition, an older persons' craft centre, a youth club and a pub

LIVING IN HOUSES

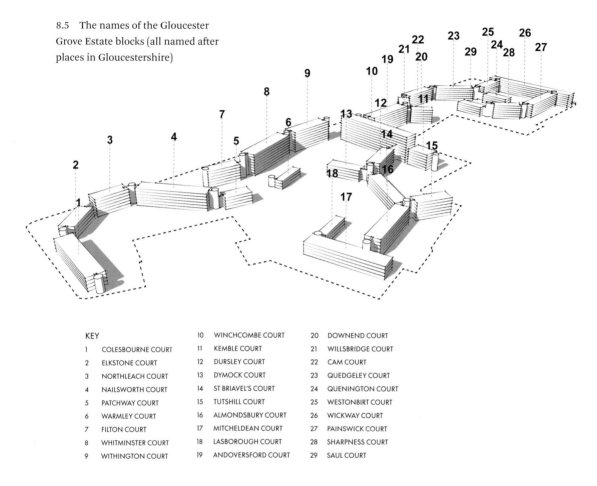

8.5 The names of the Gloucester Grove Estate blocks (all named after places in Gloucestershire)

KEY					
1	COLESBOURNE COURT	10	WINCHCOMBE COURT	20	DOWNEND COURT
2	ELKSTONE COURT	11	KEMBLE COURT	21	WILLSBRIDGE COURT
3	NORTHLEACH COURT	12	DURSLEY COURT	22	CAM COURT
4	NAILSWORTH COURT	13	DYMOCK COURT	23	QUEDGELEY COURT
5	PATCHWAY COURT	14	ST BRIAVEL'S COURT	24	QUENINGTON COURT
6	WARMLEY COURT	15	TUTSHILL COURT	25	WESTONBIRT COURT
7	FILTON COURT	16	ALMONDSBURY COURT	26	WICKWAY COURT
8	WHITMINSTER COURT	17	MITCHELDEAN COURT	27	PAINSWICK COURT
9	WITHINGTON COURT	18	LASBOROUGH COURT	28	SHARPNESS COURT
		19	ANDOVERSFORD COURT	29	SAUL COURT

were all proposed, but I have been unable to find out whether these last proposed buildings were ever built. Interestingly, the poet Caleb Femi, in a recent interview for the *RIBA Journal*, held the view that providing all of these facilities on the estate only made it more insular and inward-looking since the 'only time [he] ever left the estate was to go to church or visit family'.[36]

There is a Facebook group of former residents of the Gloucester Grove Estate and I have collected and analysed all of the comments made by them. What is surprising is – even allowing for a certain nostalgia involved in looking back on an estate which now only

THE GLOUCESTER GROVE ESTATE (1977)

exists, for the most part, in people's memories – how positive most of the comments are (89 per cent of all comments are overwhelmingly upbeat): 'I don't think any estate was as good as Gloucester back in the days. The best memories.' And: 'I still tell our mates how fantastic the homes on Gloucester Grove were. There was so much space and despite its reputation not once did we have problems.' And: 'Those were the days, they should NEVER have knocked it down.' It is clear that there was a lot of genuine affection for the flats, the estate and the strong sense of community. However, the writer John Boughton, in his online blog, 'Municipal Dreams', suggests that 'if there was a honeymoon period [for the Gloucester Grove Estate], it seems to have been a relatively short one'.[37] By my estimations, the honeymoon period lasted approximately four years: 1979 to 1982.

The first concerns appear to have emerged around 1983, according to a Thames Television News feature on how the award-winning[38] estate had started to develop problems, not least with the design of the rubbish chutes (the rubbish chutes became a persistent issue). By 1985, Alice Coleman – at that time a lecturer in the Geography Department of King's College London – was conducting a study on the physical causes of crime and antisocial behaviour on 'problem' estates in the London Boroughs of Tower Hamlets and Southwark, which included the Gloucester Grove Estate. Coleman and her team surveyed the estate, along with many others, tallying different indicators of deprivation (graffiti, vandalism, dog faeces, and so on) and then correlating these with various quantitative data on the design of the estates, such as the number of building storeys, the number of dwellings accessed from a single entrance, the number of overhead walkways and so on. When correlations were produced, she claimed, controversially, that they were causal.[39] What Coleman failed to consider was the statistical likelihood that a deprivation indicator and a design feature might both be correlating with a third, namely social, factor. Her approach was discredited[40] by Bill Hillier,[41] then a Reader at University College London, who pointed out her statistical errors and fallacious assumptions. Others were equally critical,[42] stating that poverty and a general lack of employment, facilities and opportunities were far more important than whether a building was two or four storeys in height or whether its roof was flat or pitched.

LIVING IN HOUSES

Despite determined opposition to Coleman's ideas, a programme of 'improvements' was instigated to the North Peckham and Gloucester Grove Estates, which included closing off some of the internal walkways between blocks[43] and reinstating individual gardens for ground-floor flats. The cost of the Gloucester Grove part of this refurbishment scheme was £1.25 million, led by Rolf Rothermel of Rothermel Cooke Architects,[44] and was undertaken in 1986.[45] However, this intervention seems to have changed very little on the estate as that year complaints had risen once again, and the following year, 1987, there was a report of 70 muggings in one week across the Gloucester Grove and its four neighbouring estates.[46]

By 1989,[47] three years after Alice Coleman's and Rolf Rothermel's 'improvements', the situation on the estate had reached a level of such notoriety that Harriet Harman, Member of Parliament for Camberwell and Peckham, raised it in the House of Commons:

[The] Gloucester Grove Estate was recently described by the national press as a 'no-go' area when the postal workers stopped deliveries in protest at attacks on them. It is not difficult to understand the problems of the estate or to see how they could be remedied. Gloucester Grove could be transformed into a desirable place to live if it was broken down into smaller units. It is too massive with over 1,000 flats. It could be transformed if the access to the flats was altered – at the moment tenants have to go up blind towers to reach the flats – if the refuse system was changed so that it efficiently coped with rubbish instead of efficiently breeding flies and constituting a fire hazard, if it had better transport which means more frequent bus services, if more people on the estate had jobs and if there were better leisure facilities in the area. Most of those factors are vital just to make it a decent place to live either as a pensioner or to bring up a young family.[48]

It is interesting to note how many of Harriet Harman's issues were social ones, not design ones (although there clearly were some design issues as well). These problems eventually prompted a second renewal project, this time undertaken by the London Borough of Southwark's Architects, who, in 1995, wrapped the cylindrical, brick stair towers in

170

THE GLOUCESTER GROVE ESTATE (1977)

glass blocks,[49] attempting to address the combined issues of rubbish chutes and secure access, and for which they subsequently won an RIBA award.[50] Finally, the third and most recent design intervention resulted from the London Borough of Southwark securing Single Regeneration Budget funding for the Gloucester Grove, North Peckham and three other estates (by then known, collectively, as the Five Estates). This final improvement scheme – costing £160 million,[51] by the architects Pollard Thomas and Edwards – was the one that resulted in the partial demolition and refurbishment of the Gloucester Grove Estate, replacing the blocks with more traditional streets and houses, and *almost* returning it to its 20th-century layout. Of the original 29 blocks on the Gloucester Grove Estate, only eight blocks were retained – those to the north-east of the site.

However, it was during this final stage of regeneration/renewal/demolition that problems on the Gloucester Grove Estate once again came to national attention. In November 2000, a young, 10-year old boy, Damilola Taylor, was walking home to his flat on the Gloucester Grove Estate (he lived in St Briavel's Court[52]) when he was attacked and stabbed. He managed to crawl to a nearby stairwell of a block that was in the process of being demolished, but there he lost a lot of blood before dying in an ambulance on the way to hospital. The crime immediately became one of the most notorious murder cases of our generation, one which, quite rightly, shocked the nation. At the time, many of the blocks on both the Gloucester Grove as well as the North Peckham Estates had already been emptied[53] and their residents moved elsewhere. Damilola's death sped up the process, with many residents being rapidly 'decanted'. Twenty years later, one of Damilola's friends, Yinka Bokinni, made a Channel 4 documentary[54] to mark the anniversary of his death. In an accompanying interview, she described how rapidly people had been moved out: 'My best friend . . . moved out five days later. We were "decanted" to different areas . . . We're not wine – we're human beings.'[55]

Even this process of 'decanting' was not without its issues and controversies, therefore: the Gloucester Grove decant (along with its neighbouring four other estates) was studied[56] in depth by an anthropologist, Luna Glucksberg, who conducted a series of interviews, one of which was with a retired housing officer from Southwark Council.

LIVING IN HOUSES

The interviewee described how 2,000 former households across the Five Estates had been moved out and subsequently disappeared completely (we were evidently one of these). The reasons behind these 2,000 missing households are complex,[57] but part of the reason was that one-bedroom flats were being replaced by larger family homes, making it impossible for certain people – that is, single people or young couples – to return. Part of the aim of the regeneration had been to achieve lower densities and a more diverse tenancy, mixing social and private rental with home ownership, but this process has been described as 'social cleansing' by many critics.[58] Today the former estate is all but unrecognisable, with some of the privately owned flats in the eight remaining Gloucester Grove blocks even selling for between £300,000 and £400,000, as of the writing of this chapter.

Layout: Typical House Plans and Split-level Sections

I have already mentioned that our flat was quite spacious, but examining the GLC's data of blocks and flat types, all of the 72 flats in Withington Court (our block) were intended as four-person maisonettes (presumably one double bedroom for parents and a second bedroom for two children), and since my husband had been living there alone, it was certainly large for one.[59] You approached the flat down a long, windowless corridor, with doors on either side. Interestingly enough, there were two sets of doors per flat: the 'normal' front door, and a smaller, trapezoidal-shaped door (the top of the door was steeply angled because it had to fit beneath the internal staircase). These were originally intended as pram stores, the idea being that a resident need not clutter their own hallway with a pram but could leave it in the corridor outside, secure in their own pram store. Sadly, we never got to look inside our 'pram store' (they would have been good for small/folding bikes as well) as it was locked and, from my husband's perspective, always had been. Indeed, they all appear to have been locked, because there was no sign that any of them were used in the manner intended. The front doors were also slightly staggered to afford residents some privacy, so that you could not look accidentally into someone else's flat, and vice versa, if you were both leaving/arriving at the same time.

THE GLOUCESTER GROVE ESTATE (1977)

8.6 Photograph of Withington Court adjoining Winchcombe Court (visible to the far left), taken on 7 October 1989 (when my husband was living there). Number 62 is shown outlined in black.

The flat was entered via a reasonably sized hall, which included a large cupboard for bags and coats and a second cupboard for the boiler. The kitchen and living room led off the hall. The kitchen was large enough for a dining table and had a small balcony at one end, which was generous enough to sit in (if you didn't have pigeons nesting there). Being a maisonette, it was necessary to go upstairs to reach the bedrooms. Effectively, going upstairs meant switching from one side of the block to the other (the living room and kitchen faced south, but the bedrooms on the floor above faced north). The two bedrooms were

LIVING IN HOUSES

almost identical in size and shared a long double balcony. This was the balcony with the amazing views over Burgess Park and the City of London beyond.

This strange arrangement of rooms and levels meant that the downstairs of flat number 62 was situated beneath the bedrooms of number 61, but the upper floor of number 62 sat above the living room and kitchen of number 61. If this sounds confusing, make two scissor shapes with your index and middle fingers (exactly as if you are playing the game 'rock paper scissors') and then place the index finger of one hand above the index finger of the other hand, and then reverse this for the middle fingers. This ingenious mechanism was indeed known as a 'scissor block'. The scissor block effectively managed to achieve a number of things: first, it meant that flats could consist of two storeys (in other words, be *maisonettes*), rather than being on just one storey, and hence be more familiar to those who had hitherto lived in more traditional houses; second, it meant that flats could be double-aspect, looking out towards both the front and the back of the block, again something more associated with traditional houses than flats (and useful if you want to keep an eye on children in the playground); third, it was a highly efficient use of space, since there only needed to be a corridor *every other floor*, and the space on the intervening floor (which would otherwise have been lost to yet another corridor) actually became useable space – in the case of the Withington Court flats, this space above the corridor was the upper landing/bathroom/WC area.

Of course, not all the flats were maisonettes like this one: there was quite a variety of flats on the estate. There were 277 older person, two-bedroom flats; there were two-, three-, four-, five- and six-person dwellings, both flats and two- (or more) storey maisonettes. Some had gardens, some balconies and some roof terraces, and almost all had some form of outdoor space, however small. Had the Gloucester Grove Estate been located north of the river and housed a less disadvantaged community, I suspect that it too could have become a Brutalist/modernist icon in the same way that some of the other LCC/GLC housing schemes – such as Ernő Goldfinger's Trellick Tower, Alison and Peter Smithson's Robin Hood Gardens (now demolished) or Roger Walters' Perronet House – have become.

(right)

8.7 Plan of the Gloucester Grove Estate scissor flat

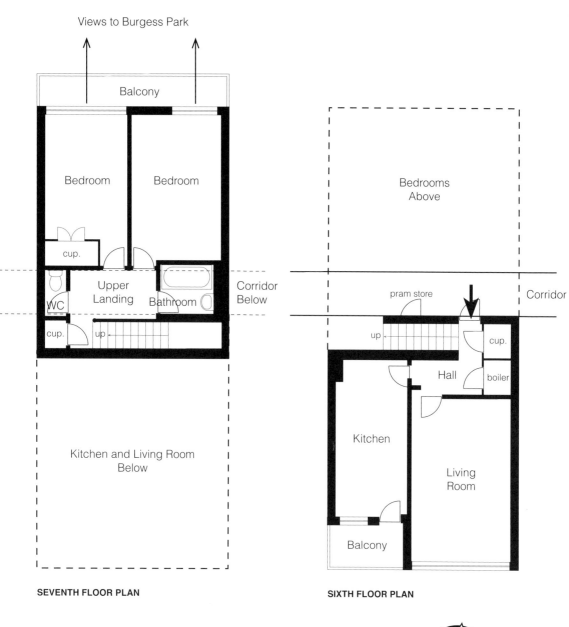

SEVENTH FLOOR PLAN

SIXTH FLOOR PLAN

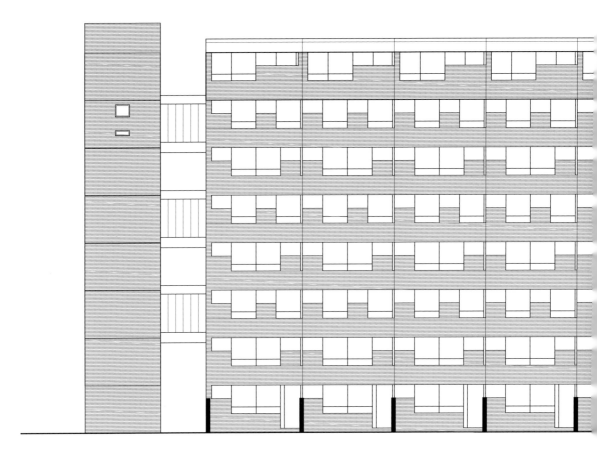

8.8 Elevation of a Gloucester Grove block and lift/stair tower

Table 8.1 Block names, heights and number/types of dwellings

BLOCK NAME	NO. OF STOREYS	TOTAL NO. OF DWELLINGS	PERSONS (BED SPACES)	HABITABLE ROOMS
Almondsbury Court	6	42	196	182
Andoversford Court	8	88	352	264
Cam Court	6	36	168	156
Colesbourne Court	4	48	96	96
Downend Court	6	18	84	78
Dursley Court	6	30	140	130
Dymock Court	4	16	80	72
Elkstone Court	4	16	80	72
Filton Court	6	24	112	104
Kemble Court	6	16	64	48
Lasborough Court	3	8	16	16
Mitcheldean Court	3	42	84	84
Nailsworth Court	6	48	224	208
Northleach Court	6	24	112	104
Painswick Court	6	48	224	208
Patchway Court	4	12	60	54
Quedgeley Court	6	36	168	156
Quenington Court	4	32	64	64
Saul Court	4	32	64	64
Sharpness Court	6	24	112	104
St Briavel's Court	6	42	196	182
Tutshill Court	6	24	112	104
Warmley Court	3	12	24	24
Westonbirt Court	6	30	140	130
Whitminster Court	8	88	352	264
Wickway Court	6	118	236	236
Willsbridge Court	6	24	112	104
Winchcombe Court	10	160	320	320
Withington Court	8	72	288	216
TOTAL		1,210	4,280	3,844

THE GLOUCESTER GROVE ESTATE (1977)

Materials

What is interesting about the construction of the Gloucester Grove Estate is that clearly the GLC had originally intended to use more traditional methods of construction. However, due to high inflation rates in the early to mid-1970s and a shortage of bricks and bricklayers, construction costs rose unacceptably, and one remedy[60] that their contractor, M.J. Gleeson, proposed was to switch to their own system (of offsite, pre-fabricated components) known as the GLE System. The GLE System was a heavy, medium-to-high rise system that used battery-cast panels for both party and cross walls. In situ floors and roofs were cast with smooth soffits on mobile shuttering and incorporated a quilt under the screed in party situations. Unlike many competing heavy systems, the cladding was not usually formed of pre-cast structural panels, but typically consisted of traditionally built cavity brick and block walls, or even timber. In the case of the Gloucester Grove Estate, its outer walls were vernacular London stock brick, a soft, buff yellow-coloured brick. The 1960s panel-based systems were notoriously beset with problems,[61] which even included external wall panels falling off buildings because they had been inadequately tied back to the structural frame. By the 1970s, GLC architects would have been only too aware of such past failings,[62] and perhaps restricting the 'system' components to floors and internal walls, while using traditional methods externally, seemed a good compromise between expediency, cost and quality. According to the non-standard house construction website,[63] 3,237 houses were built using the GLE System. Since 1,100[64] of the 1,210 Gloucester Grove Estate flats were built using this system, this means that over one third of all dwellings that used the GLE System were on this one estate.

Personal Lessons Learnt for Architectural Practice

The key thing that I learnt, as an architect, from my time spent on the Gloucester Grove Estate was the importance of experiencing things for yourself. Had I simply relied on second-hand accounts of the estate, I probably would never have dared set foot there myself. As it

LIVING IN HOUSES

was, there was a lot to be impressed by: the build quality of the flats seemed good; we never heard any noise from our neighbours (good acoustics); the flat was warm and easy to heat; a lot of thought had gone into the landscaping around the estate – we looked out over a BMX/skateboard park of delightfully undulating tracks on top of little grassy hillocks (I later found out this was the work of the artist Brian Yale[65]); and the scissor flats were a lesson, in and of themselves, in architectural 'Tetris'.[66]

Indeed, there was a lot to like. But there were also clearly things that did not work so well: the long, dark corridors that had no windows to the outside (frequently mentioned by former residents as one of the aspects they did not like); the tall rubbish chutes that meant rubbish hurtled down to the ground at a high velocity (assuming the rubbish bags did not get stuck halfway), landing in the perpetually overflowing, fly-attracting, industrial wheelie bins at the base of the towers; the fact that a single lift sometimes served as many as 88 flats (no wonder they were so often out of service). How can an architect know or anticipate any of these things without either listening to residents or experiencing it for themselves? I believe that every architecture student should spend some time living in social housing. This should be as important a part of architectural education as learning how to detail a building. The GLC architects who designed the Gloucester Grove Estate clearly had high aspirations (consider the long list of additional facilities that they tried to incorporate into the estate), but somehow their lofty goals fell short of reality. Perhaps if they had spent time experiencing other estates prior to building the Gloucester Grove Estate, they might have done some things differently.

In Lynsey Hanley's book, *Estates*, she describes the process of the regeneration of the estate in which she was living at the time that she was writing the book. She describes walking around the estate with the team of architects and planners, and wrote: 'that evening's walk was the first time that they had witnessed what made the estate so difficult to live on in the presence of the people who lived on it'.[67] She goes on to stress how such first-hand experiences and conversations with residents are precisely what should have happened at the peak of council house building, and that prospective tenants should have

THE GLOUCESTER GROVE ESTATE (1977)

been consulted about where and how they wanted to live. This is echoed by Caleb Femi, the poet who used to live in Winchcombe Court on the Gloucester Grove Estate, who believes that architects should have 'a focus on responsibility for the lives of others'.[68] Therefore, the lessons I learnt from the Gloucester Grove Estate were of the power of personally experiencing a place, and, by extension, the importance of involving communities (namely, those who know a place best) in any design process.

9

Elm Village (1984)

The Story of the First Mixed Tenure (Fair Rent, Shared Ownership and Cost Sale) Estate

9.1   Sketch drawing of the Elm Village house

ELM VILLAGE (1984)

Introduction: My Lived Experience of this Home

I lived in Blakeney Close, Elm Village, for longer than I have lived anywhere else as an adult: from 1994 to 2005, 11 years in total. As a consequence of the number of years I spent living there, and the age that I was (mid-twenties to mid-thirties), Blakeney Close in Elm Village, Camden, became the backdrop to some of my most significant life changes. When I first moved in, I was working as an assistant architect at Sheppard Robson Architects in Camden. Later, I returned to study to pursue a master's course, followed by a PhD at UCL, and by the time I left this house, I was working again as a full-time lecturer at the same university. I also married while living in this house and had my first child here. We eventually left when I was heavily pregnant with my second child (we moved to Bradwell Road in Milton Keynes, see Chapter 6). And so, this house has accommodated me single/married, working/studying and childless/pregnant/a mother. In other words, it bore witness to all of the most transitional pivot points of my life.

I had actually been well acquainted with the neighbourhood, known as Elm Village, because during my undergraduate years I lived there for a summer in a flat belonging to a fellow undergraduate, while they were abroad. During this summer, I had walked around the neighbourhood and become fairly well acquainted with it. Even then, in 1994, houses in Elm Village were rarely sold (and even less so now). At the time, I was working on Parkway in Camden, a street that used to contain a lot of estate agents. One day, as I walked to work, I noticed the listing for this house in one of the estate agents' windows. I remember being surprised at how low the price appeared to be, given that it was an entire two-storey house with a small front and back garden in Camden, so naturally I enquired about it. The reason it seemed surprisingly cheap was that it was a shared ownership property, so the price was actually 50 per cent of its full value, the other half being owned by a housing association. Somewhat to my surprise, I easily met the housing association's eligibility requirements[1] and that is how I ended up living in the Elm Village house, owning half of it and paying rent on the other half. At this time, shared ownership was very unusual (see p.192 for a more detailed discussion of this); when Elm Village was built in 1984, it was the first mixed-tenure, housing association scheme to include

LIVING IN HOUSES

shared ownership. Ten years later, when I bought the house, the estate was still a rare model of shared home ownership.

Elm Village was, and still is, a delightful place and Blakeney Close (where I lived) consisted of just a short terrace of eight small houses. There were parking spaces to the front of the terrace, but at a lower level than the front gardens, designed to minimise the visual impact of the cars. The small front garden was big enough for a few plants (or, in my case, a secure cycle shed). Equally, it had a small wooden conservatory and a garden to the rear, whose back gate led to a pedestrian path running between the backs of our houses and those of an adjacent terrace.

Did I like the architecture? If I am honest, I found the estate intriguing or even puzzling as much as anything – it was a small neighbourhood (in terms of its area) and yet its layout was spatially complex. It felt like a markedly different place to the rest of Camden, yet it was just a few minutes' walk from Camden underground station. It was undoubtedly modern, yet featured urban design elements more reminiscent of Georgian London – terraces, mews, crescents, and so on, but on a far, far smaller scale than the originals. Its name was no misnomer: it did feel a bit 'village-y', but was located in the middle of Camden Town, in the middle of London (a village, in a town, in a city). The buildings had either Neo-Georgian or postmodern features

9.2 Elevation of part of an Elm Village terrace

ELM VILLAGE (1984)

(depending on how you wish to classify them), and yet this was not the colourful, witty and brash postmodernism that, even by that time, was being treated with some degree of scepticism by the architecture profession. Was it out-and-out postmodernism or possibly just postmodernism-light? Or was it, rather, a deeply reverential homage to Georgian London, namely Neo-Georgian (see Chapter 3)? Stylistically, therefore, it was – to me at least – quite the paradox. My interest was sufficiently piqued that I ended up writing my master's thesis about Elm Village and invited the architect, Peter Mishcon, to visit and be interviewed by me, which he very generously did. This, therefore, is the second time that I find myself writing about Elm Village (and the second time I am indebted to Peter).

What did I think about the house itself? Externally, it fitted effortlessly into the rest of the estate (being both similar and dissimilar to the other houses in Elm Village, deliberate variety being one of the estate's defining characteristics). Inside, it was a quintessential small house, and the best thing that can be said about it – and this is not an adjective I would normally use in relation to architecture – was that internally it was 'bland'. There are, after all, only so many ways of packing a prescribed number/types of rooms into a very small footprint space. But is bland so bad? After all, it gave the residents an opportunity to turn it into their own space – to put their own mark on it. And this I tried to do: one of the first things that I did was to (almost) completely remove all internal walls on the ground floor, making it open plan. Another change I made was to install an array of solar-powered, evacuated tubes onto the roof for water heating. This was amazing, as it meant that even in the middle of winter nearly all our hot water was heated by the sun, and it also meant that during the period of time I was a doctoral student, my energy bills were exceptionally low.[2] In short, Blakeney Close, Elm Village was exactly the perfect 'starter home' for me at that stage in my life.[3]

History of Elm Village and a Brief History of Housing Associations

Elm Village can trace its origins back to the mid-1970s when the London Borough of Camden produced a planning document called

LIVING IN HOUSES

the 'Plan for Camden', which was the borough's written statement of its intended land-use policies for the next 10 to 15 years. Consultation on the plan began in 1974 and included numerous public meetings intended to encourage local organisations and individuals to submit their ideas on the future planning of the borough.[4] Nearly a thousand residents attended these meetings, and according to an analysis of the public participation process, affordable and good-quality housing provision was ranked as being the highest of concerns.[5] A draft plan was subsequently produced in 1976, and after further consultation and modifications, the plan[6] eventually came into effect in 1979.[7]

Through this extensive and lengthy process, some parts of the borough were identified as being areas of greatest need and hence warranted special action area plans – and one such special action area was the land surrounding King's Cross station, part of which later became the site of Elm Village. Specifically, the land on which Elm Village was built had originally been part of the King's Cross and St Pancras station railway lands. In the 1870s it was the goods depot for the Midland Railway, by the 1890s it had become a coal depot, and by the 1960s it was St Pancras station's freight depot.

In 1976, Camden Council purchased the site from British Rail specifically for the purposes of building new homes (as per the – then draft – 'Plan for Camden'). However, by 1980 the land still remained vacant and it was becoming increasingly clear that the council was in no financial position to be able to develop the site itself. Camden Council then took the difficult decision to invite bids for the purchase and development of the land. This decision was somewhat controversial at the time as the council specifically had a policy *not* to sell off any land with potential for housing construction, but it obviously took the pragmatic decision that it was better for houses to be built on the land, regardless of who did the building, than for it to remain empty. Furthermore, the fact that the land was not being sold to a private developer purely for the purposes of making a profit also clearly helped to alleviate some of the concerns.[8] The winner of the bid for the purchase and development of the land was a public/private partnership (unusual for the time) between a housing association – the United Kingdom Housing Trust (UKHT)[9] and their consultant, Alan Edgar – and the Halifax and Nationwide building societies. Before

(right)

9.3 Aerial photograph of Elm Village under construction, courtesy of the architect, Peter Mishcon. Blakeney Close is the terrace of eight houses in the foreground of this photograph and my house is the third from the left (the first one with the completed roof, next to the two houses without roof-tiles)

(below)

9.4 Map showing the location of the Elm Village development in grey and the location of my house, as a small rectangle in the middle, superimposed over the 1890 Ordnance Survey map of the railway lands

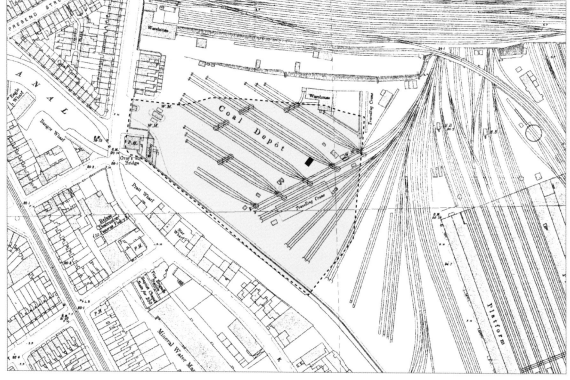

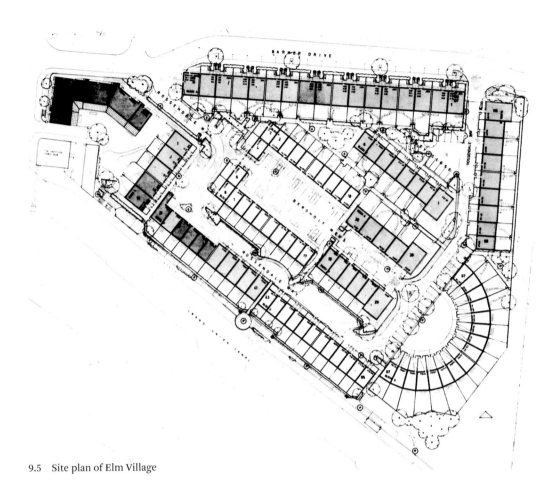

9.5 Site plan of Elm Village

Table 9.1 Social housing type, number of dwellings and density of the Haberdasher Street, Gloucester Grove and Elm Village estates

LOCATION	SOCIAL HOUSING TYPE	DWELLINGS	AREA/ HECTARES	DENSITY/DWELLINGS PER HECTARE (DPH)
Haberdasher Street	Model dwellings/ philanthropic housing	99	0.5	198
Gloucester Grove Estate	Local authority council housing	1,246	11.3	110
Elm Village	Housing association	162	1.7	95

ELM VILLAGE (1984)

preparing UKHT's bid, the architects, Peter Mishcon and Associates – who had already worked with the director of UKHT, Stephen Thake, on a previous scheme – were selected to design UKHT's entry,[10] which became Camden's preferred design, and the council accepted UKHT's bid in March 1982.[11] The project commenced on site in October 1982, and within a year the first residents were moving in (this astonishing speed was achieved through timber-frame construction methods, and Elm Village was the first UK, large-scale housing scheme to use this). By July 1984, 60 per cent of the homes had been completed and were occupied, and the scheme was fully completed in September 1984. It subsequently won the Housing Centre Trust Golden Jubilee Award for 'outstanding housing achievement'.

The original site area was 4.2 acres (1.7 hectares), and the design consisted of 61 flats and 89 houses (150[12] dwellings), followed by an additional 12 flats on the corner of St Pancras Way. Just to put this in context of other estates in this book, this is a 64 per cent increase on the number of flats in Haberdasher Street (Chapter 7), but only 13 per cent of the total dwellings of the Gloucester Grove Estate (Chapter 8). In terms of density, Elm Village was, and still is, remarkably dense, being 95 dwellings per hectare – approximately double the average density for Camden, which in 2019 was 48.5 dwellings per hectare[13] (see Table 9.1 for a comparison of the densities of the three schemes). All three schemes would be considered high density today; what is rather surprising is that Elm Village – while feeling quite spacious and verdant, and being only two storeys high – is in fact, almost as dense as the Gloucester Grove Estate, some of whose blocks were 10 storeys high. Surprisingly, Haberdasher Street is the densest development of all, demonstrating just what pleasant housing schemes can be achieved at relatively high densities.

Part of the aim of the architects was to design a housing scheme that did not feel like an 'estate'. And, indeed, I think that they clearly succeeded in this. In an article on Elm Village for the *Financial Times*,[14] the writer and broadcaster Gillian Darley commented enthusiastically that 'you would never guess you were standing on an "estate"'. This was partially due to the fact that the different tenures were so mixed up, on site, that it was not possible to tell from the outside which were cost sale, shared ownership or fair rent properties. It was also

189

9.6 A view of the estate today with its matured landscaping

LIVING IN HOUSES

partially due to the architect deciding to design the flats and houses with a deliberate 'variety on a common theme'[15] by introducing a mixture of materials, components and detailing. And finally, I think that this was also due to the high attention paid to the hard and soft landscaping,[16] something that is so often an afterthought, especially on social housing estates. It is wonderful to walk around Elm Village today and see how the architecture has blended with its well-tended and matured planting (see Fig.9.6).

Part of the intention behind the scheme was to create a wide social mix, and hence sense of community, by providing a large range of flat and housing types, and the UKHT proudly declared, at the time, that 'the last ounce of social value has been wrung from the limited public money spent'.[17] Dwellings in Elm Village ranged from one-person flats to eight-person houses and were originally divided into three types: cost sale (31 per cent), shared ownership (52 per cent) and fair rent (17 per cent).[18] The incorporation of shared ownership into its tenure mix was one way in which Elm Village was highly unusual for its time (but is something that would be considered almost commonplace now). According to government statistics, in 1980 there were 21,423,000 dwellings[19] in the UK, and according to a 1980 report produced by the Housing Association, at the same time only 36,306 dwellings in the UK were occupied through a co-ownership tenure. Shared ownership in 1980, therefore, constituted just over 0.1 per cent of all British houses. This is the context in which Elm Village was being designed, so to say that the Elm Village's co-ownership scheme was unusually radical and trailblazing is not an understatement. However, it was possible, for those owning shared ownership properties, to buy another proportion at any point (a process known as staircasing), and even when I was living there in the mid-1990s – 10 years after the Elm Village houses and flats had been built – almost all of the original shared ownership property owners had exercised this right to buy some or all of the remainder portion of their homes. The house that I lived in, in Blakeney Close, had been one of the very few remaining shared ownership houses, and I imagine that almost all of the 83 per cent non-rented properties are probably now owned outright; see Table 9.2 which shows the estate's original mix of dwelling sizes and types of tenure.

ELM VILLAGE (1984)

The story of Elm Village, therefore, fittingly picks up a narrative thread running through the second half of this book that started with the construction of Haberdasher Street (both influencing, and being contemporaneous with, the first council house building) and ran through the construction of the Gloucester Grove Estate (representing the peak of the wave of post-Second World War local authority construction). This thread is picked up again by the 1980 Housing Act, the resultant decline of council houses and the contemporaneous sell-off of Haberdasher Street to its residents, and it leads us to the construction of Elm Village by a housing association. To put it simply, first came the model dwellings and philanthropic housing, then the rise and fall of council houses, and finally we arrive at the current dominance of modern housing associations as being the largest provider of social housing in the UK. This evolution of social housing

Table 9.2 Schedule of dwelling sizes and types of tenure[20]

TYPE	COST SALE	SHARED OWNERSHIP	FAIR RENT	TOTAL DWELLINGS	TOTAL PERSONS
1 bed flat	0	51	14 (inc. 2 wheelchair)	65	130
2 bed flat	0	0	4 (inc. 2 mobility)	4	8
3 bed flat	0	0	4 (inc. 2 wheelchair)	4	12
2 bed, 3 person house	50	0	4	54	162
3 bed, 4 person house	0	10	0	10	40
3 bed, 5 person house	0	10	1 (manager)	11	55
4 bed, 6 person house	0	10	0	10	60
6 bed, 8 person house (wheelchair)	0	4	0	4	32
Total	50 (31%)	85 (52%)	27 (17%)	162	499 persons

LIVING IN HOUSES

is told in these last three chapters, in microcosm, via Haberdasher Street, the Gloucester Grove Estate and Elm Village.

What is a housing association and when did they start? Sadly, there is no simple definition. Peter Malpass, an academic who has written extensively on social housing, suggests that: 'The housing associations ... category is perhaps the most artificial and diverse, in the sense that it embraces a wide range of quite different organisations, varying from ancient almshouses trusts and Victorian charitable foundations to self-build co-ops and former local authority housing departments.'[21] If he cannot give a single definition, Malpass is quite clear that the history of housing associations can be thought of as forming specific waves. The first wave covers the period up until, and just after, the First World War and would include the Victorian model dwellings companies and other philanthropic housing schemes (such as Haberdasher Street). The second wave began in the 1930s when the National Federation of Housing Societies was formed, with 75 societies constituting its initial membership. These housing societies scarcely differed from the first wave of social housing providers in that their business model was still based on raising capital from shareholders and investors. This second wave housing association movement grew after the Second World War and thrived well into the 1950s; however, their influence never became particularly widespread because of government policies promoting local authorities as the main providers of social housing and, furthermore, ensuring that there were strict rent controls on housing associations which lasted until 1954.

The third wave of housing associations occurred in the 1960s. According to Malpass, the Housing Act of 1961 provided a construction fund of £28 million to be lent to housing associations and administered by the National Federation of Housing Societies. This was soon followed by an additional £100 million of government money in 1964. Further fuelling this third wave of construction in the 1960s, such government-initiated activity was augmented by the formation of a number of independent organisations, often with connections to the church, such as the British Churches Housing Trust (1964) and Shelter (1966). However, despite the synergy of these initiatives, by 1969 the vast majority of social housing was still being provided by local authorities, and any housing association provision was relatively

ELM VILLAGE (1984)

minor.[22] The biggest change happened in 1987, arguably leading to the fourth and current wave of housing associations, when the Conservative government brought an end to new building[23] by local authorities, and then further legislation enabled housing associations to become the main builders of new homes at 'affordable' rents as well as being the fastest growing component of the British housing system.[24] Malpass adds that, now: 'Housing associations have become key instruments of government housing policy, and as a result they are extensively regulated, their development activity remains heavily dependent upon grant aid, which is distributed largely on the basis of housing strategies formulated by the local authorities.'[25] Being built in the early 1980s, Elm Village can be seen as being right on the cusp of this present wave, and was an influential example of what was possible to achieve through public and private cooperation.

In summary, Elm Village was radical for its public–private model of construction by a housing association (pre-empting the current dominance of housing associations as providers of new homes), its diverse mix of tenure and inclusion of shared ownership in its tenure-mix, its use of timber construction (see p.203 on its legacy), its tenure-blind design policy, its deliberately designed variety of houses and its high-quality landscaping. Was it successful? In an article written for the *Camden Journal* at the time, Bob Latham, the then Chairman of Camden's private housing committee, remarked that: 'The success of the project can only be judged by the test of time.' Well, when Elm Village was first built, the UKHT had over 700 applications[26] from prospective tenants, so from the beginning, it was clearly popular with would-be residents. Today, there is a strong sense of community evidenced through the Elm Village Tenants and Residents Association – of which more than half of households are members[27] – and stability of residents (houses rarely become available for sale). One of the longest-residing occupants confirms this: 'We loved the look of the estate and of the houses [and] it was easy to get to know people . . . We quickly formed a residents' association, to which I still belong today . . . There's been a great sense of community even though people have moved on, a community has remained.'[28] I therefore believe that Latham's test of time has been well and truly passed.

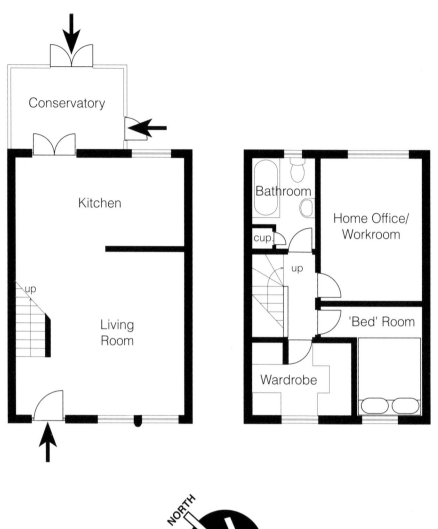

9.7 Plan of 3 Blakeney Close, with my modifications, *c*.1997

ELM VILLAGE (1984)

Layout: Typical House Plans and the Urban Layout

There are no typical flat/house plans for Elm Village; as mentioned in the previous section, the accommodation varied from one-person flats to eight-person houses. Number 3 Blakeney Close was a simple, two-storey, three-bedroom, terraced house with a boxy, square-proportioned, front elevation. When I moved in, there was a tiny hallway, with a door to the right leading to the living room. In turn, the living room led into the kitchen-diner at the back of the house, and also to a small storage space under the stairs. Beyond the kitchen was a wooden conservatory (built by the previous owners) and the back garden. However, one of the first things I did was to remove nearly all the ground-floor walls, leaving just a stub of kitchen walls – useful for hanging kitchen wall units – but making it, to all intents and purposes, an open plan ground floor.

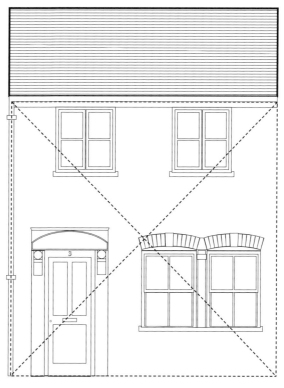

9.8 Elevation of 3 Blakeney Close showing its non-Georgian, square (rather than rectangular) proportions

SQUARE PROPORTION

LIVING IN HOUSES

Upstairs there were three bedrooms, and two of these were extremely small – what would have been called 'box rooms' in previous generations. Over 11 years of living there, the uses of the upstairs rooms changed frequently – I had a number of friends staying in my spare room, at various times, in the early years, and towards the end, one room became my son's bedroom – but after my husband moved in, we made the most drastic, functional change of all. I worked out that one of the smallest bedrooms was actually the exact size of my double bed. It took some dextrous manhandling to get it in, but once we did, we had, effectively, a 'wall-to-wall' bed (forget wall-to-wall carpets – wall-to-wall beds really are the way to go). And what fun it was: I have such pleasant memories of lazy Sunday mornings spent reading the papers (clearly this was pre-children!), each of us sociably propped up against opposite walls for easy conversation, something that is far more companionable than two people sitting and facing in the same direction. Admittedly, it rendered changing the bed linen and making the bed a bit trickier, but it was well worth the sacrifice. This room went from being a small, nondescript spare room to easily being my favourite room in the house. As a result, we had to make the other smallest bedroom into a walk-in wardrobe and storage room. This left (what was intended to be) the large double bedroom to become our home office. Since my husband was working from home a lot and I was, then, studying full-time for a PhD, we really needed a good quality space in which to work that was big enough for us both, without getting on top of each other (a move that actually feels quite prescient of the more recent pandemic-induced changes in patterns of home-working).

I have mentioned that the house was small – clearly, if one of the bedrooms was actually the size of a double bed it *had* to be small. However, it was only through writing this book and drawing up all the plans of the different houses that I came to realise that by placing both floors of my Blakeney Close house side by side, the resultant space would almost fit into the master bedroom of the Priestpopple House[29] (Chapter 2). It is even more sobering to think that standard house sizes have, on average, decreased by a further 9 per cent since the 1980s, when Elm Village was built,[30] and (master) bedrooms are on average 3 per cent smaller.[31]

(right)

9.9   Current exterior of the house

LIVING IN HOUSES

Materials

One aspect of the construction of Elm Village that is worth mentioning is its postmodernist detailing. I have already discussed, in the introduction to this chapter, how there is a fine line between whether the neo-classical features of Elm Village are simply Neo-Georgian, or whether they are examples of postmodernist architecture. By looking at the elevation of Blakeney Close, we can easily pick out features that would have been just as familiar to the Georgian builder/architect (see Chapter 2) – pilasters, corbels, pediments, arches and sash windows – as they were to Elm Village's architect, Peter Mishcon, 200 years later.

It is worth noting, however, that while postmodernism in architecture was a very short-lived movement lasting, roughly speaking, from the late 1970s to the late 1980s (in Terry Farrell's recent book that revisits and reflects on postmodernism, he suggests that: 'The stylistic phenomenon that was briefly perceived in design and architecture in the 1980s, generally called "PoMo", was a tangential blip'), Elm Village was built at the very peak of its flourishing. Without defining exactly what postmodernism was, Terry Farrell suggests that it was characterised by 'expression, wilfulness and whimsy', in direct contrast to the 'heroic, iconic architecture' of modernism. I find it surprising, given the construction date of the scheme, that the design of Elm Village would not have been influenced by the postmodernist zeitgeist that was so prevalent at the time. Elm Village is, indeed, a short walk

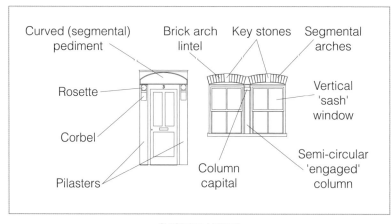

9.10 Classical motifs found in the elevation of the Blakeney Close house

ELM VILLAGE (1984)

(just over 500 metres as the crow flies) along the canal from Terry Farrell's TV-am building in Camden, arguably one of the UK's most recognisable postmodernist buildings. This was a building that was completed in August 1981, midway between Elm Village's project start date and its commencement on site. Therefore, not only was it scarcely possible that the architects would have been unaware of their scheme's significant architectural neighbour, but the TV-am building would have been publicised in the architectural press at exactly the right time to still have exerted an influence – conscious or otherwise – on the detailed design of Elm Village.

So, what are the characteristics of postmodernism, and does Elm Village share them? According to the Royal Institute of British Architects (RIBA) there are four main identifying features of a postmodernist building: classical motifs, bright colours, a variety of materials and playfulness.[32] Let us briefly consider each of these in turn and determine whether they can be found in Elm Village. There is no doubt whatsoever that Elm Village's architecture contains classical motifs in abundance, at both the urban level and at the scale of the individual house. What about the bright colours, usually so forcibly present in postmodern architecture? This is less obvious in Elm Village, as a visitor's immediate, first experience of the estate is definitely more monochrome: white render, buff brick and pre-cast concrete elements. But once first impressions are over, and when starting to examine the architecture more carefully, it soon becomes apparent that there are subtle flashes of colour present. Many of the flats had metal balconies which were painted red and blue – coloured metalwork was very characteristic of postmodernist architecture – not to mention the red brick banding along Rossendale Way (also reminiscent of Victorian polychromatic brickwork; see Chapter 7), so I think it is possible to say that there is sufficient colourful whimsy to fulfil this criterion. The third characteristic of postmodern architecture is the use of a variety of materials. Again, this is certainly true of Elm Village's architecture, with the architects' use of varying combinations of bricks (buffs and red), grey split facings, pre-cast concrete mouldings, exterior metalwork and glazed porches. So, this leaves us with RIBA's final criteria of 'playfulness', and this is where my thoughts on the scheme's postmodernist credentials falter a little,

LIVING IN HOUSES

as Elm Village was clearly a 'serious' scheme, with serious aspirations (high density, low cost and socially mixed); but I think there are some playful flourishes to be found. Patrick Hannay, writing of the scheme in the *Architects' Journal*, describes the 'extraordinary eclecticism' of the details and finishes as being '. . . sprinkled [with] familiar post-modern details – curvaceous stairs, implied pediments on balls over doors and trellis verandas'.[33] And in an article for *Building* magazine, Anthony Williams says of the decorative features of Elm Village: 'the embellishment is pure theatre'. On balance, therefore, I think a certain degree of 'playfulness' can be detected.

However, for me, the decisive factor as to whether Elm Village should be considered postmodernist or not lies in this fascinating appraisal by Terry Farrell of a number of prominent postmodernist architects of the period. He describes how they 'were all leaning towards the vernacular, looking at natural materials – bricks, timber etc. – and mixing them with varying degrees of Modernism for inventive new forms of visual expression, combined with community activism and awareness of popular taste'. If this is not a good description of what Peter Mishcon and Associates were trying to do at Elm Village, then I don't know what else is. And so, it has probably taken me over a quarter of a century to decide whether Elm Village is an example of postmodernism or not, and I have now come to the conclusion that it is. Although this reminds me of something I was once told by a librarian: the harder it is to decide which bookshelf (and hence book classification) a book belongs to, the less it probably matters; I am sure the current residents of Elm Village do not care for one moment if their homes are considered to be postmodernist or not. However, I suppose that the last word on this should really go to the architects. When I asked Peter Mishcon if Elm Village was an example of postmodernist architecture, he admitted: 'I don't think it was deliberate . . . looking back with hindsight . . . it ticks the boxes for postmodernism . . . but I can honestly say there wasn't a conscious effort [to be postmodern].'[34] This is echoed by one of the other architects of the scheme, Mike Brookes, who said: 'I don't think there was direct intent to be PoMo but we were obviously aware of the movement . . . Our main intent was to differentiate the "neighbourhoods" of the scheme and give each area a distinctive character.'[35]

ELM VILLAGE (1984)

The Influence and Inspiration of Elm Village's Modern Timber Construction

Structurally, the houses of Elm Village can be considered more the direct descendants of the house in Chapter 1, Yearnor Cottage, than any of the other houses in this book. This is because of their timber construction. If you recall, the construction of Yearnor Cottage consisted of a primary structure of wood with infill panels, probably first made of wattle and daub, and later replaced by bricks inserted between its wooden structure. Strangely, the Elm Village houses are not so dissimilar in their construction. They consist of a primary wooden structure made of rectangular, timber-frame panels. These panels were manufactured offsite and brought to site pre-fabricated. Because of problems regarding bringing cranes onto the site, the architect chose to use smaller panels that could be easily manhandled without mechanical assistance. The Elm Village timber panels consisted of two types: open timber panel frames (just as they sound, a simple rectangular, skeletal frame) and a closed panel, faced with plywood. The open panel frames were used internally and once they had been erected and made weathertight, insulation could be fitted into the stud cavity, where needed. The closed, ply-sheathed panel frames were used on the external walls and were designed to support the external cladding (mostly combinations of brick and render).

Although, as shown above, there is nothing new about houses having a timber structure, Elm Village was nonetheless a trailblazer due to the fact that it was the first timber-structured, large-scale housing estate to be built in the UK. Therefore, if I had to suggest any legacy or long-term influence of Elm Village, this probably has to be it. While timber-frame construction had always been more common in North America and Europe compared to the UK, Elm Village demonstrated that it was possible to use such technologies in the UK and at scale. Sadly, the legacy of Elm Village appears to be all but forgotten, and since researching this book I have come across more than one reference suggesting that the large-scale, commercial use of timber-frame methods in the housing industry did not arrive in the UK until the late 1990s.

A discussion of the legacy of timber-frame houses is impossible without also briefly mentioning the architect Walter Segal,[36] an

LIVING IN HOUSES

architect whom every student of architecture should learn about. Segal – a Swiss-German architect who moved to the UK in 1936 – pioneered a method of modular, timber-frame construction that employed a kit of standard building materials. This was known as the 'Segal Method', and could be erected by a self-builder with little or no prior construction experience. The London borough of Lewisham made some land available for a number of small-scale experiments with timber-framed, self-build houses, and Segal's first project started in 1979, taking approximately five years to complete, hence was contemporaneous with Elm Village. Phase Two of the Lewisham scheme began in 1984, the year that Elm Village was completed. Segal died, aged 78, in October 1985, just over a year after Elm Village was finished. In total, 27 houses were completed in the two Lewisham self-build schemes.[37] What is interesting is how synchronous were Segal's self-build projects in Lewisham and the construction of Elm Village in Camden, and how, together, they represent such different, yet in many ways highly complementary, approaches to timber-frame construction. One was high volume, rapid and utilised offsite fabrication methods; the other was small-scale, individualistic (hence, certainly not rapid) and low-skilled, but using standard modular components. Both, I would argue, were influential in their own ways.

Since Elm Village's demonstration of what was possible with commercial timber-frame construction and Walter Segal's self-build experiments, there has been a huge transformation in how we use wood, structurally, in house construction. The biggest change has been in how closed panel timber frames (still available, as are open panels) have evolved into a third type of panel – what we now call structural insulated panels (or SIPs for short). SIPs are still relatively new to British housing construction but are becoming more popular all the time. Today, most SIPs consist of a timber frame, faced on both sides with oriented strand board (OSB), a type of engineered wood similar to particle board. This forms a sandwich whose interior is pre-filled with insulation. In fact, it looks rather like an ice-cream sandwich (if you imagine that the insulation is the ice-cream and the OSB the biscuit). Another advantage of fusing the insulating core with the rigid panel facings is that the resultant panels are remarkably airtight, which further helps improve their insulating properties. SIPs did not really start being used in the UK until around the beginning of the millennium – nearly 20 years after Elm Village was designed and 15 years after it was built – but there is a clear line of descent that can be traced between the closed panel timber frames used in Elm Village and modern SIPs.

It is now possible to build large-scale structures that were never possible before, not only through modern timber technologies such as SIPs, but also using glulam beams (glued laminated timber) and cross-laminated timber (CLT) – the fastest growing type of structure timber – all of which can be manufactured offsite. Structural timber is a highly sustainable structural material: it is renewable (once a tree is cut down, you can grow another tree in its place), and it has a low carbon footprint (by using timber in construction, you are literally capturing carbon and storing it in your building). Modern timber structures – 'going back to the future' – certainly have the potential of being the future of the housing industry.

Personal Lessons Learnt for Architectural Practice

I suppose, as an architect, the primary personal lesson that I learnt through living in this house was about the benefits of timber construction. First, there is the insulation: the U-value of the exterior walls in Elm Village was $0.35W/m^2K$. The U-value is a measure of thermal conductivity, or how easy it is for heat (or conversely cold) to pass through any given material: the lower the U-value, the less its conductivity and the better its insulating properties. According to current building regulations, a U-value of $0.35W/m^2K$ for exterior walls is barely sufficient to meet today's higher standards,[38] but in the 1980s such a value represented an exceptional degree of insulation. Indeed, this value was so low that the architects struggled to specify an appropriately low-powered boiler[39] for the houses' heating systems that could match such well-insulated houses (they could not – the boilers ended up being overpowered).

My own recollection is that the house was extremely warm and cosy in the winter and, combined with the solar-heated water system

LIVING IN HOUSES

I installed, this meant that my fuel bills were extremely low. However, the other surprising aspect of the timber-frame construction – and I would never have believed this without having lived in and experienced a timber-framed house myself – was that the sound insulation between the houses was also extremely good. I do not recall ever hearing any noise from the houses on either side of ours in the terrace, and that is not something I can say about most of the houses I have lived in. In conclusion, were I to build a new house for myself, I would not hesitate to use modern methods of timber-frame construction.

Another lesson I would say that I have vicariously learnt from living in Elm Village is the importance of landscape design. This is interesting as it is something that is rarely taught in schools of architecture; indeed, it is usually considered something that an architect is either expected to 'pick up on the job' and/or to give no thought to, other than to subcontract it out to landscape architects. Given our current focus on mental health and wellbeing and the restorative effect of green spaces, I think that landscape design should be given more prominence in an architectural education.

Finally – and I hope this does not sound frivolous – remember the wall-to-wall 'bed' room I made? This stands out for me as having been so much fun that I would love to deliberately design such a feature into a new house (client willing, of course). I suppose the lesson this taught me is that size is not everything, and even the smallest of rooms can have its own charm if you only know where to look for it or how to design it.

Epilogue

I know that my husband hopes that our current house will be our last one, but I suspect that it will not. Soon our children will be leaving to go to university, and at some point my mother will no longer be living in the granny annexe. It is inevitable that by this stage our Orchard Place house will feel far too large for just two people and 'downsizing' would be the sensible course of action. At the same time, as an architect, I also feel that I have 'one more house' left in me. Therefore, I would very much hope, one day, to end this story by designing a small, sustainable (ideally zero-carbon) eco-home just for the two of us, as our retirement home.

Notes

1 Yearnor Cottage (1651)

1 W.G. Hoskins, 'The Rebuilding of Rural England, 1570–1640', *Past & Present*, vol.4, no.1 (1953), p.59.

2 As evidenced by a recently discovered date carved onto one of the beams.

3 Hoskins, 'Rebuilding of Rural England', p.50.

4 This is a broad generalisation (and there is some debate as to whether this distinction is even a binary one) which is that one came from Anglo-Saxon and the other from Norse and Danish traditions of building.

5 Hoskins, 'Rebuilding of Rural England', pp 44–59.

6 M.W. Barley, 'The Use of Upper Floors in Rural Houses', *Vernacular Architecture*, vol.22, no.1 (1991), pp 20–23.

7 R.B. Wood-Jones, *Traditional Domestic Architecture of the Banbury Region*, Manchester, Manchester University Press, 1963.

8 Compare this to the 4,378 people living on the Gloucester Grove Estate in Chapter 8.

9 This is an estimate based on an extrapolation between a recorded population of 217 in 1603 and 122 in 1676.

10 W.M. Williams, *The Sociology of an English Village: Gosforth*, London, Routledge, 2013, p.163.

11 According to the UK government's *English Housing Survey 2019–2020*, approximately 3 per cent of all current houses are from before 1850; there are no records for what small proportion of this 3 per cent also pre-date 1700.

12 Wood-Jones, *Traditional Domestic Architecture*, p.232.

13 ibid., p.139.

14 There are records of permanent brick works just to the north of St Mary's Road, Market Harborough from the late 18th to early 19th centuries.

15 A. McWhirr, 'Brickmaking in Leicestershire before 1710', *Transactions of the Leicestershire Archaeological and Historical Society*, vol.71 (1997), p.49.

16 Food miles are the distance food is transported from its place of production to the place of its consumption.

17 H. Hartman, 'Is This the Most Influential House in a Generation?', *Architects' Journal*, 30 January 2015. Retrieved from www.architectsjournal.co.uk/buildings/is-this-the-most-influential-house-in-a-generation.

18 Not all thatch is straw, of course; as with everything, there are regional variations, and typically thatch is made from either straw, water reed or wheat reed/wheat straw.

2 Priestpopple (c.1700)

1 In Marjorie Dallison's article on Priestpopple in the June 2000 edition of the *Hexham Historian* (see note 7 below), she says that: 'The antiquity of Priestpopple is confirmed by its appearance in the Inspeximus of 1298

NOTES

as "Prestpoffel" and in the 14th century Black Book of Hexham as "Prestpofyll" and it probably means simply "the priests' little piece of land" (Raine, 1864).'

2 Currently, it is a square opening with a horizontal lintel supporting the stonework above; however, in older photographs from around 1900 it clearly used to be a stone archway.

3 Pigot & Co., *Pigot & Co's Trade Directory for Northumberland*, 1834. Retrieved from https://communities.northumberland.gov. uk/005092FS.htm.

4 This is a John Hutchinson of Priestpopple. I would love to think that he might have been the stonemason who originally carved the stone column capital I discuss in Chapter 4.

5 These were the late John Chapman – a local historian and author of a number of books, some on Hexham, and also the 'The House Dater's Toolkit', published in 1998 – along with the late Colin Dallison, a respected local historian and author of a number of books about Hexham. This visit took place on 18 April 2011.

6 Source: a report written on the findings of the visit, provided by Roger Higgins.

7 M. Dallison, 'Life in a Hexham Street: Priestpopple, Cattle Market, Battle Hill', in A. Rossiter (ed.), *Hexham Historian*, Hexham Local History Society, vol.10 (2000), p.42.

8 Note that in one of the leases of Priestpopple, the ground floor is actually referred to as the 'cellar'.

9 B.R. Bennison, 'The Brewing Trade in North East England, 1869–1939', PhD thesis, University of Newcastle upon Tyne, Newcastle upon Tyne, 1992. Retrieved from https:// theses.ncl.ac.uk/jspui/bitstream/10443/199/1/ bennison92.pdf, p.15.

10 According to the Hexham Local History Society (HLHS), the County Mills building (a former flour mill and grain warehouse) – which is located on the opposite side of the road from the Priestpopple house – was built on the site of Armstrong's brewery in 1884. Retrieved from www. hexhamhistorian.org/historic-hexham/ test-your-hexham-building-knowledge/ answer-april-2019/.

11 First, William Armstrong (1822, 1827), then John Armstrong (1834), who was finally joined by Thomas Armstrong (1848, 1855). John Pearson was also followed by Thomas Pearson in the late 1860s.

12 In Bennison's description of Hexham Old Brewery, also a small brewery, he says that: 'The Old Brewery brewed twice a week, the two brewings giving a weekly output of 150 barrels.' Bennison, 'Brewing Trade in North East England', p.16.

13 On Wood's 1826 *Plan of Hexham*, the land on which the Priestpopple house lies appears to be owned by a 'Mrs Lee' (see Fig.4.2, p.80). I believe that this Mrs Lee could have been the illegitimate daughter of Sir Thomas Wentworth Blackett (of the Blackett Baronets of Newcastle-Upon-Tyne), born Sophia Wentworth Blackett in 1765. Her father died without issue and left a proportion of his estate to his three illegitimate daughters, a Mrs Beaumont (b. Diana Wentworth, the eldest), Mrs Lee, and Mrs Stackpole (b. Louisa Blackett Wentworth, the youngest). Blackett charged a significant proportion of his real estates in Northumberland and Durham upon trust for the use of Sophia Lee and her husband, William, as well as giving her £10,000 upon her marriage in 1792 (worth between £1,295,000 and £109,100,000

today: https://www.measuringworth.com/).
Wood's *Plan of Hexham* consequently contains
numerous parcels of land owned by Mrs Lee, of
which one is on Priestpopple. See https://www.
theblacketts.com/ and Stackpole v. Beaumont,
3 Ves. Jr. 89, 30 Eng. Rep. 909, 912 (1796).

14 '25 Years Ago', *Hexham Courant*, 8 January 1999.

15 Referred to in Ronnie Turnbull's obituary in
the *Hexham Courant*, 11 April 2014. Retrieved
from www.myfamilyannouncements.co.uk/
hexhamcourant/LeaveDonation/3444149.

16 Citizensadvice.org.uk, 'History of the Citizens
Advice Service', 2021. Retrieved from www.
citizensadvice.org.uk/about-us/about-us1/
history-of-the-citizens-advice-service/.

17 When Roger Higgins first moved in, this was
little more than a dark 'cellar' with restricted
head room and an earth floor. He removed
approximately two feet of earth, lay new stone
flags with underfloor heating, and brought in
more light via new, enlarged windows.

18 There had not been a proper staircase before
Roger Higgins' conversion: access between
the second and third floors had previously
been via a ladder.

19 According to English Heritage's 'Building
Stone Atlas of Northumberland', the 'Tyne
Formation sandstones have provided good
quality building stone in abundance, and
many small quarries have been opened to
work freestone. They were (and in some
cases still are) quarried at Little Bell Crags,
Cairnglastenhope Moor, Cop Crag (near
Byrness), West Woodburn, High Nick and
Milknock.'

20 According to Roger Higgins, 'The limewash
applied in several layers was a recipe
containing 50% lime putty to 50% water, with
[the] addition of 5% linseed oil.' R. Higgins,
personal communication, 7 June 2011.

21 See 'Conservation Areas'. Retrieved from
https://historicengland.org.uk/advice/hpg/has/
conservation-areas/.

22 ICOMOS, 'European Charter of the
Architectural Heritage', 1975. Retrieved from
www.icomos.org/en/charters-and-texts/179-
articles-en-francais/ressources/charters-
and-standards/170-european-charter-of-the-
architectural-heritage.

23 P. Burman and D. Rodwell, 'The Contribution
of the United Kingdom to European
Architectural Heritage Year 1975', *Monumenta*,
vol.3 (2015), p.266.

24 ibid., p.273.

25 'RIBA Climate Literacy Knowledge Schedule',
2021. Retrieved from https://www.architecture.
com/-/media/GatherContent/Mandatory-
competences/Additional-documents/
RIBA-Knowledge-Schedule-Climate-Literacy-
March-2021.pdf.

26 D. Latham, *Creative Reuse of Buildings: Volume
One*, London, Routledge, 2000.

27 'Astley Castle, Warwickshire' (n.d.). Retrieved
from www.architecture.com/awards-
and-competitions-landing-page/awards/
riba-stirling-prize-astley-castle-warwickshire.

3   Gower Street (1789)

1 Now known as John Tovell House; it was
subsequently named after a former Secretary
of UCL, in line with many other UCL student
residences.

2 'Gower Street', in J.R. Howard Roberts and
W.H. Godfrey (eds), *Survey of London: Volume
21: The Parish of St Pancras Part 3: Tottenham
Court Road and Neighbourhood*, London,
London County Council, 1949, pp 78–84.
Retrieved from British History Online,

NOTES

www.british-history.ac.uk/survey-london/vol21/pt3/pp78–84, last accessed 7 February 2021.

3 J. Summerson, *Georgian London*, Harmondsworth, Penguin Books, 1978, pp 127–8.

4 I say 'relative' peace in Europe; it is worth noting that, among other conflicts, the year that nos 93–97 Gower Street were constructed also happened to be the year that the French Revolution began. (It is a tangential but nevertheless interesting fact that Yearnor Cottage was built at the end of the English Civil War, whilst Gower Street was built at the start of the French one.)

5 Both drivers are clearly important: population growth without prosperity usually implies a housing shortage, while prosperity without population growth tends not to lead to new houses being built at volume.

6 This is probably just to avoid having an identity-less seven years that would otherwise be sandwiched awkwardly between the Georgian and Victorian eras.

7 In 2019, the company Anglian Home Improvements produced a quiz called 'Homes across the Decades'. Retrieved from www.anglianhome.co.uk/homes-across-the-decades/.

8 The land constituting modern-day Bloomsbury belonged to a number of different landowners, but by far the largest part was the Duke of Bedford's estate. The next largest landowner was the Foundling Hospital. See UCL's 'Bloomsbury Project' for maps and a full list of the different Bloomsbury estates. Retrieved from https://www.ucl.ac.uk/bloomsbury-project/index.htm.

9 Apparently pronounced 'lewson-gore', according to *Brewer's Britain and Ireland*. I personally think that Gower Street got off lightly by avoiding being called *Gore Street* (as did, incidentally, UCL, for whom being known as 'that Godless institution in Gore Street' would have made a disparaging moniker even worse).

10 This is taken from a diagrammatic representation of the major, original estates that constituted contemporary Bloomsbury and Fitzrovia in the Camden History Society's publication, 'Streets of Bloomsbury and Fitzrovia: A Survey of Streets, Buildings and Former Residents', published in 1997.

11 Summerson, *Georgian London*, p.40.

12 The dates for Francis Russell's Grand Tour are according to notes accompanying William Grimaldi's miniature of him, written by the Royal Collection Trust. Indeed, another painting of Francis Russell, by Joshua Reynolds, shows him surrounded by items he collected during his Grand Tour, including a book of classical etchings.

13 Howard Roberts and Godfrey, *Survey of London*.

14 The two most famous builders who were associated with the development of Bloomsbury were James Burton and, later, Thomas Cubitt. However, the first time either of them worked on the Bedford Estate was in 1800 (when James Burton constructed a row of houses on Russell Square) – in other words, after the Gower Street houses had already been built – and so, although we cannot say who were the builders, we can state emphatically who it was *not*.

15 Summerson, *Georgian London*, pp 127–8.

16 For example, from the entry on 'Gower Street' in Howard Roberts and Godfrey, *Survey of London*.

17 UCL's Bloomsbury Project is a research project funded by the Leverhulme Trust to investigate the development of 19th-century

Bloomsbury. Retrieved from www.ucl.ac.uk/bloomsbury-project.

18 UCL Bloomsbury Project (n.d.). Retrieved from www.ucl.ac.uk/bloomsbury-project/streets/gower_street.htm, last accessed 28 October 2021.

19 The Racket family papers form part of the National Archive and are currently held by the Dorset History Centre. It would be interesting to see if any of his letters describe what it was like living in Gower Street in the early 19th century.

20 Number 99, the neighbouring house, seems to have had a far more colourful history: for a time, it served as the offices of *The Spectator* newspaper, and in an article for the same newspaper on the history of number 99, Wilson Harris claims that it was once the site of a 'College of Life and Occult Sciences', later becoming the 'Order of the Golden Dawn' run by a notorious adventuress with a penchant for serial marriages (each followed rapidly by convenient widowhood).

21 This is for a large upper-class house; the medium, middle-class houses were typically 19 feet wide, and the smallest, lower-class flats were often 14 feet wide.

22 This was a well-known effect used in the building of Renaissance palazzos; for example, see Murray's description of the Palazzo Davanzati in his book on the architecture of the Italian Renaissance. The use of stucco on just the ground floor of some Georgian houses also mimics the use of rough, rusticated stonework on lower floors and increasingly smoother materials on the upper floors of Renaissance palazzos, which, again, helps accentuate this optical illusion of greater height.

23 According to Louw and Crayford: 'The only verifiable examples of this historically most

significant development are the six windows installed by Robert Hooke in the main block of the College of Physicians, London, in 1674.' See H. Louw and R. Crayford, 'A Constructional History of the Sash Window *c*. 1670–*c*. 1725 (Part 1)', Architectural History, vol.41 (1998), p.86

24 For a discussion of what people prefer compared to what is considered good taste, see H.J. Gans, *Popular Culture and High Culture: An Analysis and Evaluation of Taste*, New York, Basic Books, 1999.

25 A party wall is simply a wall that is, typically, owned jointly by both owners of the properties either side of the wall, and with the property boundary, again typically, running through the middle of the wall.

26 'Nos. 55 and 56, Great Queen Street', in W. Edward Riley and L. Gomme (eds), *Survey of London: Volume 5, St Giles-in-The-Fields, Pt II*, London, 1914, pp 42–58. Retrieved from British History Online, www.british-history.ac.uk/survey-london/vol5/pt2/pp42-58, last accessed 7 February 2021.

27 Summerson, *Georgian London*, p.34.

28 See The Keep (1957), Corner Green (1959), Hall II (1958), The Plantation (1962) and The Lane (1964).

29 See the interesting paper by H.C. Santos, M.E. Varnum and I. Grossmann, 'Global Increases in Individualism', *Psychological Science*, vol.28, no.9 (2017), pp 1228–39.

30 Belated apologies to the late David Dunster.

4 Orchard Place (1824)

1 This was even an education for me, as an architect: I did not know that asbestos could be used in so many different ways.

NOTES

2   Garth is the most delightful word which is derived from an Old Norse word *garðr* or *garthr*, meaning an enclosure. In Northumberland and Cumbria, it is still used to describe a walled garden; an *apple garth* was an orchard, a *barn garth* was an enclosed farm-yard and a *stack garth* was an enclosed space for storing stacks of hay.

3   Amongst other things, Charles Head was the driving force behind the building of Hexham Town Hall and Corn Exchange (now the Queen's Hall), one of Hexham's most significant buildings, and is further commemorated with a stained-glass window in Hexham Abbey.

4   This, as well as additional quotes in this section, are taken from a selection of legal documents and letters in my possession.

5   In Dallison's article on Priestpopple in the June 2000 edition of the *Hexham Historian*, she mentions that 'Solicitors were often associated with the formation of banks: Charles Head, William Carr and Hugh Friend all operated as bankers as well as attorneys.' M. Dallison, 'Life in a Hexham Street: Priestpopple, Cattle Market, Battle Hill', in A. Rossiter (ed.), *Hexham Historian*, Hexham Local History Society, vol.10 (2000), pp 35–52.

6   Its full title being R. Kerr, *The Gentleman's House; Or, How to Plan English Residences, from the Parsonage to the Palace; with Tables of Accommodation and Cost, and a Series of Selected Plans*, London, John Murray, 1865.

7   ibid., p.79.

8   In Andrew Biggs Wright, *An Essay Towards a History of Hexham in Three Parts: Illustrating its Ancient and its Present State, Civil and Ecclesiastical Economy, Antiquities and Statistics, with Descriptive Sketches of the Scenery and Natural History of the*

Neighbourhood, Alnwick, W. Davison, 1823, written the year before 1 Orchard Place was built, he observes that: 'it is well said that in the vale of Hexham "the harvests are the earliest, its trees have the richest foliage, and its landscape is the most diversified and interesting, of any in Northumberland"'.

9   Documents in my ownership.

10 According to R.R. Lawrence and T. Chris, *The Period House: Style, Detail and Decoration, 1774–1914*, London, Weidenfeld & Nicolson, 1996, at this time 'Building investment brought a return of four and a half to five per cent, which was usually a bit better than Government stock and one to two per cent less than more risky ventures like railways.'

11 I looked through John Dobson's records to see if there was any chance that 1 Orchard Place had also been an early building of his, but I could find no evidence to support this conjecture. Whoever was the architect of the Orchard Place houses remains, sadly, unknown.

12 It is also worth noting that Henry Bell had four children, in contrast to Charles Head's only child, and therefore this may have accounted for the need for additional space.

13 The word 'Eastgarth' can be seen carved on the frieze of the entablature.

14 J.M. Richards, *A Miniature History of the English House*, London, The Architectural Press, 1938, p.50.

15 The hayloft only covers a small portion of the coach house/stables. Interestingly, in John Stewart's book on the management of horses, he stressed the importance of light in stables. He suggests that: 'When side-windows cannot be conveniently introduced, a portion of the hay-loft must be sacrificed, and light obtained from the roof. This in

LIVING IN HOUSES

ordinary cases will not be greatly missed.' And so, this may be why the hayloft appears to only cover part of Orchard Place's coach house/stables. Finally, Stewart goes on to suggest that if all the stalls are on one side of the stable, then any side-windows should be located opposite them, which supports our reconstruction of the stables. J. Stewart, *The Stable Book; Being a Treatise on the Management of Horses, in Relation to Stabling, Grooming, Feeding, Watering and Working. Construction of Stables, Ventilation, Stable Appendages, Management of the Feet. Management of Diseases and Defective Horses*, New York, C.M. Saxton & Co., 1856.

16 John Stewart strongly advocates that 'For a pair of carriage-horses, the stable should have three stalls. The odd one is useful.'

17 According to the stonemason who carved the capital, the pegs, or dowels, are exterior grade stainless steel, 12 mm in diameter (approximately half an inch) and are bedded in a polyester resin. 'One dowel to the bottom bed and one to the top bed of the column (central)'; he also mentions that 'Originally the dowels would have been slate pegs or a simple oval shaped river pebble . . . the Victorians . . . used pig iron dowels which in time rust and damage the surrounding masonry.' (D. France, personal communication, 28 April 2021).

18 D. Arnold, *The Georgian Villa*, Stroud, Sutton Publishing, 1998, p.ix.

19 J.S. Ackerman, *The Villa: Form and Ideology of Country Houses*, Princeton, NJ, Princeton University Press, 1990.

20 C. Middleton, *Picturesque and Architectural Views for Cottages, Farm Houses, and Country Villas*, Farnborough, Gregg International Publishers, 1972, p.9.

21 Lawrence and Chris, *The Period House*, p.41.

22 J.C. Loudon, *An Encyclopaedia of Cottage, Farm, and Villa Architecture and Furniture, Etc.*, London, Longman, Orme, Brown, Green & Longmans, and sold by John Weale, 1839 [1833], p.763.

23 This might be better qualified as 'somewhat' democratised as it is still the case that, in Ackerman's words on the villa, a large suburban house is still a 'luxury commodity available only to persons of privilege', as at the moment younger generations are finding it increasingly difficult to own a home of any kind.

24 J. Summerson, 'The Idea of the Villa', *RSA Journal*, vol.107, no.5036 (1959), p.570.

25 Colin Rowe's essay on 'The Mathematics of the Ideal Villa', in his book of essays of the same name, compares not only Le Corbusier's Villa Savoye to Palladio's Villa Rotunda, but further examines the influence of Palladio's Villa Malcontenta on Le Corbusier's house at Garches. C. Rowe, *The Mathematics of the Ideal Villa and Other Essays*, Boston, MA, MIT Press, 1982.

5 Wharf Place (c.1902)

1 According to N. Monnery, *Safe as Houses? A Historical Analysis of Property Prices*, London, London Publishing Partnership, 2011.

2 Darton's *New Plan Of The Cities Of London & Westminster, & Borough Of Southwark*, 1817.

3 Apropos of nothing, Darton was a Quaker and an alumnus of the Quaker school, Ackworth School, in West Yorkshire (see his publication, 'Ackworth School catalogue: being a list of all the boys and girls educated at that institution, from its commencement in 1779, to the present period', published by Harvey

NOTES

and Darton, 1831) – two facts that, strangely enough, we share.

4 'Bethnal Green: Building and Social Conditions from 1837 to 1875', in T.F.T. Baker (ed.), *A History of the County of Middlesex: Volume 11, Stepney, Bethnal Green*, London, Victoria County History, 1998, pp 120–26. Retrieved from British History Online, www.british-history.ac.uk/vch/middx/vol11/pp120-126, last accessed 12 January 2021.

5 According to Mike Ellison's unpublished reference work, 'The Topography of Tower Hamlets', which has an entry for Wharf Road/Wharf Place.

6 G.H. Duckworth, 'Notebook: Police District 5 [Old Street, Finsbury and Shoreditch], District 6 [Hoxton and Haggerston], District 9 [Bethnal Green, North and South]', 1998, Reference BOOTH/B/352. Retrieved from https://booth.lse.ac.uk/notebooks/b352#?c=0&m=0&s=0&cv=25&z=-285.8808%2C-77.0033%2C6331.7617%2C3766.0066, last accessed 8 August 2021.

7 Retrieved from https://booth.lse.ac.uk/learn-more/what-were-the-poverty-maps, last accessed on 8 August 2021.

8 'Bethnal Green: Economic History', in Baker, *History of the County of Middlesex*, pp 168–90. Retrieved from British History Online, www.british-history.ac.uk/vch/middx/vol11/pp168-190, last accessed 12 January 2021.

9 Entry in *Phillips' Paper Trade Directory of the World, 1923*, London, S.C. Phillips. Retrieved from https://archive.org/details/phillipspapertra1923phil, last accessed 12 January 2021.

10 Also from Ellison, 'The Topography of Tower Hamlets'.

11 'London, England, City Directories, 1736–1943', London Metropolitan Archives.

12 'London County Council Bomb Damage Maps 1939–1945'. Retrieved from https://search.lma.gov.uk/scripts/mwimain.dll/144/LMA_OPAC/web_detail?SESSION SEARCH&exp=REFD+LCC~2FAR~2FTP~2FP~2F039~2F036#?c=0&m=0&s=0&cv=2&z=-0.0556%2C-0.058%2C1.1111%2C0.8441.

13 R. Lawrence, 'Police prepared to evacuate hundreds of sleeping families from their homes yesterday (Monday) as a blaze at a toy warehouse threatened to spread to three nearby gasometers', *Hackney Gazette*, 16 November 1982.

14 P. Wood, personal communication, 4 August 2021.

15 P. Wood, personal communication, 5 August 2021.

16 S. Zukin, *Loft Living: Culture and Capital in Urban Change*, New Brunswick, NJ, Rutgers University Press, 1989, p.1.

17 J. Sims, 'Design decade: 1980s', *Financial Times*, 17 May 2008. Retrieved from www.ft.com/content/83376ed4-2233-11dd-a50a-000077b07658.

18 I am sure that everyone reading this will be curious as to the origins of the name, 'Cat and Mutton'. The website, thestreetnames.com, puts forward a number of theories, of which the one I find most plausible is that it is a corruption of 'Cattle and Shoulder of Mutton', in reference to drovers passing over the bridge on their way to London to sell their animals at market. Still, it is a delightful name and I wish I had known of it when I lived there. thestreetnames.com (n.d.). 'Cat and mutton bridge'. Retrieved from https://thestreetnames.com/tag/cat-and-mutton-bridge/, last accessed 22 August 2021.

19 S. Parissien and Georgian Group, *The Georgian Group Guides No 8. Ironwork. A Brief Guide to*

LIVING IN HOUSES

Georgian Ironwork, London, Georgian Group, 1991.

20 Coincidentally, this also happened to be the site of a mixed-use housing scheme that I designed as an architecture student when at UCL.

21 See www.ahmm.co.uk/projects/residential/adelaide-wharf/.

22 See www.hawkinsbrown.com/projects/the-wenlock-building.

6 Bradwell Road (1902)

1 R.A. Croft and D.C. Mynard, *The Changing Landscape of Milton Keynes*, Monograph Series No. 5, Milton Keynes, Buckinghamshire Archaeological Society, 1993, p.113.

2 ibid., p.116.

3 The first edition (1885) of the Ordnance Survey map.

4 See http://clutch.open.ac.uk/schools/loughman99/pages/The%20Teachers%209.html.

5 P. Bodley, personal communication, 17 October 2022. Peggy clearly remembers Jess Cox running the post office during the war. See also http://clutch.open.ac.uk/schools/loughmid99/residents/peggys_fullstory.html for more memories of Loughton village courtesy of Peggy Bodley.

6 That is the equivalent of five quarry tiles for £1, converted into today's money and purchasing power.

7 M.J. Stratton, 'The Manufacture and Utilisation of Architectural Terracotta and Faience', PhD diss., Birmingham, Aston University, 1983.

8 ibid.

9 The architect specified these as follows: 'The arches to front elevation and entrances to be of a 9" pressed brick, all others 9" common red in 2 reds. Main 3 courses in cornice, 2 moulded and 1 plain over sculleries, in front 2 courses plain, back 1 course pressed bricks and 1 moulded and 1 plain as string course.'

10 Stratton, 'Manufacture and Utilisation'.

11 L.F. Pearson, *Tile Gazetteer: A Guide to British Tile and Architectural Ceramics Locations*, Tiles and Architectural Ceramics Society, Ilminster, Richard Dennis, 2005, pp 182, 472 (Appendix 1); and A. Cox, 'Brick and Tilemaking in the Nuneaton Area', British Brick Society, *Information*, vol.114 (2010), pp 11–23.

12 A. Sadler, 'Victorian Commemorative Plaques', *Leicestershire Historian*, vol.35 (1999), pp 1–2.

13 ibid., p.2.

14 For example, compare the commemoration plaque of this house with a larger plaque on the exterior of Quebec House, Leeds, known to be by J.C. Edwards; they are very similar, including the details of the 'fronds'.

15 J.C. Edwards, *Bricks, Tiles and Terra Cotta Catalogue of Patterns*, Ruabon, 1903.

16 The Victoria & Albert Museum in London holds amongst its industrial and commercial trade catalogues one for Stanley Brothers for 1903-4, but sadly not from the previous year, 1902.

17 J. Burnett, *A Social History of Housing, 1815–1985, Volume 228*, London, Methuen, 1986, p.250.

18 P. Lofthouse, 'The Development of English Semi-detached Dwellings during the Nineteenth Century', *Papers from the Institute of Archaeology*, vol.22 (2013), pp 83–98.

19 According to the government's English Housing Survey, 25.4 per cent of all houses are semi-detached, 18.4 per cent are mid-terrace, 17.9 per cent are medium/large terraced; 17.4 per cent are detached; 14.9 per cent are

NOTES

purpose-built low-rise flats, and 11.3 per cent are end of terrace. The remainder – 24.4 per – cent are small, terraced houses, bungalows, converted flats and purpose-built high-rise flats.

20 Ministry of Housing, Communities & Local Government (2021), *English Housing Survey 2019 to 2020: Headline Report*. Retrieved from www.gov.uk/government/statistics/english-housing-survey-2019-to-2020-headline-report, last accessed 11 October 2021.

21 My great aunt lived in one of these in Letchworth, and so I am fortunate enough to have been inside one of them.

22 The housing stock profile for Scotland and Northern Ireland is slightly different.

23 See www.hta.co.uk/project/officers-field-osprey-quay.

24 See www.studiopartington.co.uk/osbaldwick.

7 Haberdasher Street (1912)

1 A. Rayner, 'Gentrification's ground zero: the rise and fall of Hoxton Square', *The Guardian*, 14 March 2018. Retrieved from www.theguardian.com/cities/2018/mar/14/hoxton-square-london-shoreditch-aviva-gentrification-yba-damien-hirst#comment-113524183.

2 ibid.

3 See the page on 'Company History' at https://haberdashers.co.uk/company-history, as well as the two books by Ian Archer on their history: *The History of the Haberdashers' Company*, Chichester, Phillimore & Co., 1991; *The Haberdashers' Company in the Later Twentieth Century*, Chichester, Phillimore & Co., 2004.

4 The land in Hoxton had formed part of an estate bequeathed to the Haberdashers'

Company in 1690 by the silk merchant Robert Aske, and by 1940 the Hoxton estate comprised 21 acres (Archer, *Haberdashers' Company in the Later Twentieth Century*). Robert Aske's association with the Haberdashers' Company is currently not without some controversy due to the fact that he held £500 in shares in the Royal African Company which in turn was actively involved in the slave trade – see www.british-history.ac.uk/no-series/london-rulers/1660-89/pp14-21#h3-0039.

5 I. Watson, 'The First Generation of Flats', *Hackney History*, vol.11 (2005), pp 33–46.

6 C. Maunder Taylor, personal communication, 6 July 2021.

7 Watson, 'The First Generation of Flats',p.34.

8 In correspondence with John Fowler of Stock Page Stock, he tells how he 'was able to find details of a bank account being opened in 1825, so although I do believe the practice is older, the first documentary proof I had of its existence is 1825'.

9 Dates about when Henry William Stock and Robert Page joined Stock Page & Stock is based on census records and trade directories.

10 A. Brodie et al., British Architectural Library and Royal Institute of British Architects, *Directory of British Architects 1834–1914*, 2 vols, London, Continuum, 2001.

11 Stock Page & Stock's association with the Haberdashers' Company lasted for over 150 years, and Henry Stock (senior) was elected a Liveryman of the Haberdashers' Company (Archer, *Haberdashers' Company in the Later Twentieth Century*, p.57).

12 Unfortunately, at the time of writing this chapter, the archives of the Metropolitan Police were packed away, due to planned

building work, and so were inaccessible. It would, however, be fascinating to see what material about the Haberdasher Street flats is held by the Metropolitan Police.

13 'A Note on Lord Trenchard's Report and the Government White Paper', *The Police Journal*, vol.6, no.3 (1933), pp 295–307. Retrieved from https://doi.org/10.1177/0032258X3300600304.

14 C. Maunder Taylor, personal communication, 6 July 2021.

15 Archer, *Haberdashers' Company in the Later Twentieth Century*, p.28.

16 One reason why I might have so readily made this association was that when I was living in Haberdasher Street, I was working for the architect Norman Foster on his scheme for transforming St Pancras station in order to accommodate Eurostar, the international high-speed rail service. Within the boundary of our site was a block of flats known as the Stanley Buildings – this was an early prototype model dwelling designed by the architect Matthew Allen and based on Roberts' 1851 building. One of my tasks was to survey, draw and then build a 3D computer model of this building (along with all the other listed buildings in the curtilage of our site) as part of our large-scale site analysis and as a backdrop for our visual renderings. I was, therefore, extremely familiar with the Stanley Buildings and it was perhaps only natural that, on returning home from work, I would draw associations between the Haberdasher Street blocks and the Stanley Buildings, and by extension the model dwellings movement in general.

17 The 1851 model cottage was exhibited in Hyde Park. It was later dismantled and relocated to Kennington Park in South London, where it was rebuilt and still stands today.

18 Many of Dickens' publications written in the 1830s–40s describe, in vivid detail, the conditions of the London slum – for example, in *Oliver Twist*, first published in 1838. Equally, Mayhew wrote a number of articles on poverty and housing conditions for the *Morning Chronicle* in the 1840s. Emily Cuming suggests that there was a 'predominant sense that the domestic lives of the poor needed to be seen to be believed', and that the task of writers in the period was to use text to paint a vivid picture of these lives, such that they could be 'seen' by a wider portion of society. See E. Cuming, '"Home is home be it never so homely": Reading Mid-Victorian Slum Interiors', *Journal of Victorian Culture*, vol.18, no.3 (2013), pp 368–86.

19 The design is often misattributed to Prince Albert. He clearly had an interest in and influence on the design process as President of the Society for Improving the Condition of the Labouring Classes, but the design was undoubtedly by Henry Roberts.

20 According to the Royal Collection Trust – see www.rct.uk/collection/1077793/the-model-houses-for-families-built-in-connexion-with-the-great-exhibition-of.

21 P. Malpass, 'The Discontinuous History of Housing Associations in England', *Housing Studies*, vol.15, no.2 (2000), pp 195–212.

22 ibid.

23 If you want to compare the value of a £1,209,359 project in 1875, there are three choices. In 2019, the relative real cost of that project is £122,100,000; the labour cost of that project is £628,200,000; the economic cost of that project is £2,139,000,000. See www.measuringworth.com/.

24 A. Wohl, *The Eternal Slum*, London, Edward Arnold, 1977.

NOTES

25 The 'four per cent' here is a reference to the projected rate of return for the company's investors. Five per cent was the more usual, advertised rate of return, and this gave rise to what was known as 'five per cent philanthropy'. This was the idea that people could invest in a good cause – improved housing for workers – and still receive a return for their investment, albeit a slightly smaller one compared to the 7–10 per cent rate of other commercial investments, but a return nonetheless.

26 See www.ids.org.uk/about-us/the-history-of-ids/.

27 Malpass, 'Discontinuous History', p.202

28 S. Smith, 'Ditchwater', *Urbannarrative*, n.d. Retrieved from www.urbannarrative.com/.

29 For example, 'Colour was subject to fashion . . . Polychromy became a real possibility, even for small houses, after the middle of the nineteenth century.' R.R. Lawrence and T. Chris, *The Period House: Style, Detail & Decoration, 1774–1914*, London, Weidenfeld & Nicolson, 1996, p.147.

30 The tradition of the Grand Tour came to an end with the arrival of railway travel and mass tourism in the 1840s (Thomas Cook's first excursion was made in 1841; see www.storyofleicester.info/city-stories/thomas-cooks-leicester/).

31 J. Ruskin, *The Stones of Venice* (3 vols), 1851. Retrieved from www.lancaster.ac.uk/media/lancaster-university/content-assets/documents/ruskin/9-11StonesofVenice.pdf.

32 On this point, Ruskin (1851) says: 'Yet even in this separate art of colouring, as referred to architecture, it is very notable that the best tints are always those of natural stones. These can hardly be wrong; I think I never yet saw an offensive introduction of the natural colours of marble and precious stones, unless in small mosaics, and in one or two glaring instances of the resolute determination to produce something ugly at any cost.'

33 A. Chatterjee, 'Between Colour and Pattern: Ruskin's Ambivalent Theory of Constructional Polychromy', *Interstices: Journal of Architecture and Related Arts*, vol.18 (2017), pp 11–18.

34 G.E. Street, *Brick and Marble in the Middle Ages: Notes of Tours in the North of Italy*, 1855. Retrieved from www.gutenberg.org/files/46326/46326-h/46326-h.htm.

35 ibid.

36 I have read, with interest, multiple estate agents' descriptions of the flats being traditional – or period – *Victorian* properties.

37 LCC's first council housing scheme was the Boundary Street Estate, built just 600 metres – or a third of a mile – away from Haberdasher Street. There is no question that Robert Page would have been familiar with this scheme when he was designing Haberdasher Street.

38 R. Evans, 'Rookeries and Model Dwellings', in *Translations from Drawing to Building and Other Essays*, London, Architectural Association, 1996, pp 94-117; the word 'rookery' was a colloquial word for a slum.

8 The Gloucester Grove (1977) and North Peckham Estates

1 The former Bishop of Southwark, the Right Reverend Tom Butler, described the North Peckham Estate as one of the toughest in Europe; see S. Morris, 'Estate "one of toughest in Europe"', *The Guardian*, 30 November 2000. Retrieved from www.theguardian.com/uk/2000/nov/30/ukcrime.stevenmorris.

219

LIVING IN HOUSES

2 I am using storey here, instead of floor, to avoid any transatlantic confusion. In the UK, our flat spanned the sixth and seventh floors (as the ground floor is counted as floor zero). In the US, this would be the equivalent of the seventh and eighth floors (as the ground floor is the first floor in the USA).

3 If you draw a line due north from the former location of our old flat, you arrive at Foster + Partners' 30 St Mary Axe building ('The Gherkin'), passing through parts of Walworth, Bermondsey and Southwark on the way. Although the Gherkin and our flat never coexisted, had they done so, they would have been just over two miles apart, which is surprisingly close, given how 'segregated' and 'far away' from everything the estate always seemed to be.

4 J.H. Forshaw and P. Abercrombie, *County of London Plan*, London, Macmillan and Company, Ltd, 1943.

5 Albany Road/Bagshot Street, 17 December 1944, 17 dead (www.flyingbombsandrockets.com/V1_summary_se5.html); and Waite St at Trafalgar Avenue junction, 14 February 1945, 18 dead (www.flyingbombsandrockets.com/V1_summary_se15.html).

6 On the site of the entire 28-acre Gloucester Grove Estate, just 17 houses were damaged beyond repair, according to LCC Bomb Damage Maps 1939–1945. Retrieved from https://search.lma.gov.uk/scripts/mwimain.dll/144/LMA_OPAC/web_detail?SESSIONSEARCH&exp=REFD+LCC~2FAR~2FTP~2FP~2F039~2F036#?c=0&m=0&s=0&cv=2&z=-0.3102%2C-0.2514%2C1.6203%2C1.2309.

7 C. Barnett, *The Lost Victory: British Dreams, British Realities, 1945–1950*, London, Pan Macmillan, 1995, p.153.

8 P. Jones, 'The Place of Design in English High-rise Flats During the Post-war Period', unpublished working paper, 2000.

9 T. Tinker, personal communication, 15 June 2021.

10 See London Metropolitan Archives, GLC/MA/SC/03/1906 and GLC/MA/SC/03/1907. The time period for the compulsory purchase orders appears to have spanned 1961 to 1967, that is to say, six years.

11 The North Peckham Estate's design team worked under the direction of F.O. Hayes, the Borough Architect, and Hans Peter (Felix) Trenton, the Deputy Borough Architect. The Group Leader was W. (Bill) Solman and the architectural assistants were R. Goodyear, J. Ritter, G. Barlow and T. Tinker.

12 T. Tinker, personal communication, 15 June 2021.

13 According to Ruth Lang, in 1952–3 the LCC's Architects' Department had become the world's largest, with 1,577 staff including 350 professional architects and trainees. See R. Lang, 'Architects Take Command: The LCC Architects' Department', *Volume*, no.41 (2014), p.24.

14 B. Swallow, 'Campbell's Kingdom', *Building Design*, no.96 (7 April 1972), p.6; 'Former GLC Housing Architect Dies Aged 92', *Building*, 19 July 2002. Retrieved from www.building.co.uk/news/former-glc-housing-architect-dies-aged-92/1020146.article.

15 Caleb Femi lived in Winchcombe Court, one of the blocks adjacent to Withington Court. C. Croft, 'Caleb Femi sees poetry in life, death and the built environment', *RIBA Journal*, 8 June 2021. Retrieved from www.ribaj.com/products/caleb-femi-on-life-death-and-the-built-environment-north-peckham-estate.

NOTES

16 C. Femi, *Poor*, Harmondsworth, Penguin Books, 2020, p.8.

17 L. Hanley, *Estates: An Intimate History*, London, Granta Books, 2012, p.111.

18 'GLC Architect Sir Roger Walters Opts for Early Retirement', *Building*, vol.234, no.7029 (24 March 1978), p.12.

19 T. Zupančič, personal communication, 22 September 2021.

20 'The Cost of Mismanagement', *Architects' Journal*, vol.162, no.27 (2 July 1975), p.10.

21 Although in an article in *Building Design*, the original contract price is given as £9,245,000 in 1971. I have also seen the 'overspend' quoted as being both £7 million and £10 million, meaning the final costs could have been anywhere between £15.3 million and £19.2 million.

22 See www.measuringworth.com/: £16 million in 1975 is worth approximately £122,900,000 (the real cost of a project), or £199,000,000 (the labour cost of a project), or £293,800,000 (the economic cost of a project) in 2020 prices.

23 'GLC Orders Inquiry into £7m Rise in Cost of Homes Scheme', *Building Design*, no.232 (10 January 1975), p.24.

24 'Cost of Mismanagement', p.10.

25 Although, in fairness, I should add that Serge Lourie stated that: 'My recollection, which may be wrong, is that we were more interested in the systemic failure of the council to control the costs rather than blaming the job architect.' S. Lourie, personal communication, 27 September 2021.

26 In 1971, Roger Walters won a 'Good Design in Housing' award for Perronet House in the Elephant and Castle. The award credits both Roger Walters and another GLC architect, R. Jackson, presumably also the same architect of the Gloucester Grove Estate. Given that the two schemes share the same 'scissor flats'

layout, it is highly likely that Jackson was the architect of both.

27 'Scrutiny Panel, Gloucester Grove', London Metropolitan Archives, GLC/DG/AR/17/007.

28 The earliest design document I have been able to locate in the London Metropolitan Archives is from 1967 (this also being the final year of the compulsory purchase orders). Equally, in an article, 'Behind the Scenes at County Hall', *Building Design*, no.326 (1976), pp 14–15, it says that there was 'political pressure to get the job started after years of frustrating planning delays'.

29 'Behind the Scenes at County Hall', pp 14–15.

30 'Cost of Mismanagement', p.10.

31 Withington Court was designed for 288 bed spaces. Burton Overy had 289 residents in the 2001 census (the last census for which Burton Overy was returned as a separate village).

32 I produced a map to see if there was any relationship between the proximity of named blocks on the estate and the original positions of their namesake towns/villages in Gloucestershire (that is to say, were adjacent blocks on the estate also closer together in Gloucestershire?). There was no geographic relationship between the original towns/ villages and the block names.

33 Which is peculiar since, spatially, they were not courts (an open space surrounded by buildings) but slab blocks, and neither did groups of blocks form courtyard spaces between them.

34 As an aside, this is over eight times Dunbar's number, that is, the optimal number for a human social network, which is between 100 and 250, and typically judged to be around 150 people. See R.I.M. Dunbar, 'Neocortex Size as a Constraint on Group Size in Primates', *Journal of Human Evolution*, vol.22, no.6 (1992), pp 469–93. Indeed, nearly 40 per cent of the

LIVING IN HOUSES

individual blocks on the estate housed more than 150 people each.

35 The first residents moved in from 1973 onwards; it appears that people moved in when a block was completed, so there was a staggered occupation from 1973 at the earliest, to 1977 at the latest.

36 Croft, 'Caleb Femi sees poetry in life, death and the built environment'.

37 J. Boughton, 'The Five Estates, Peckham, Part I: 'Planning Is for People', 11 October 2016. Retrieved from https://municipal dreams.wordpress.com/2016/10/11/the-five-estates-peckham-part-one/.

38 *Housing Complaints, Award Winning Estate, Thames News*, film, Thames Television, UK, https://youtu.be/ucChoGo9oMg, 30 August 1983. I have been unable to verify what award the estate was meant to have won – it is possible that this is an early example of confusion between the Gloucester Grove Estate and the North Peckham Estate.

39 A. Coleman, S. Brown, L. Cottle, P. Marshall and C. Redknap, *Utopia on Trial: Vision and Reality in Planned Housing*, London, Hilary Shipman Ltd, 1985.

40 B. Hillier, 'City of Alice's Dreams', *Architects' Journal*, vol.9 (1986), pp 39–41.

41 At this point, I should declare my own bias: Professor Bill Hillier was my doctoral advisor. Furthermore, my husband was part of the team that conducted the subsequent 1993 Space Syntax study of the North Peckham Estate. I enrolled on UCL's Space Syntax master's course in 1994, so missed the North Peckham Estate study by a year.

42 See also B. Anson, 'Don't Shoot the Graffiti Man', *Architects' Journal*, vol.184, no.27 (1986), pp 16–17; B. Heaven, 'Comeback on Coleman', *Architects' Journal*, vol.184, no.36 (1986), pp 32–3;

P. Spicker, 'Poverty and Depressed Estates: A Critique of Utopia on Trial', *Housing Studies*, vol.2, no.4 (1987), pp 283–92; M. Jenks, 'Housing Problems and the Dangers of Certainty', in T. Necdet, T.A. Markus and T. Woolley (eds), *Rehumanizing Housing*, London, Butterworth & Co. Publishers, 1988, pp 53–60; and more recently, G. Towers, *Shelter Is Not Enough: Transforming Multi-storey Housing*, Bristol, Policy Press, 2000.

43 'Walkways to Go in Five Year Plan', News, *Architects' Journal*, vol.187, no.3 (20 January 1988), p.11.

44 R. Rothermel, 'Long-Term Solutions', Letters, *Architects' Journal*, vol.187, no.1 (6 January 1988), p.16.

45 'Coleman's Prescription', *Building Design*, no.801 (22 August 1986), p.5

46 J. Coles, 'Is there life in Peckham?', *The Spectator*, 3 July 1987.

47 There is an additional story from this period about how the Gloucester Grove and North Peckham Estates were designated a Housing Action Trust in 1988, but this was subsequently voted against by the residents in 1990. Sadly, I do not have sufficient room to discuss this, but there is a good discussion of it on John Boughton's 'Municipal Dreams' blog: https://municipaldreams.wordpress.com/2016/10/.

48 H. Harman, 'Renewable Energy Sources (Promotion)', *Hansard*, vol.92, 25 February 1986. Retrieved from https://hansard.parliament.uk/commons/1986-02-25/debates/f5f1f540-499d-4dc8-bbdc-440d91898e54/RenewableEnergySources(Promotion).

49 J. Fisher, 'Residential Domination at RIBA Regional Awards', *Building Design*, no.1236 (29 September 1995), p.6.

50 'RIBA Regional Awards', *Architects' Journal* (28 September 1995), pp 10–11.

NOTES

51 R. Booth, 'Damilola: Could Better Design Have Saved His Life?', *Architects' Journal*, vol.212, no.1 (7 December 2000), p.14.

52 There was a comment on the Facebook group 'who used to live on the gloucester grove estate in peckham' page which explained: 'Damiola [*sic*] lived upstairs from me at St Braivels [*sic*] Court. On the 1st floor.'

53 In 2008, Alice Coleman claimed that Damilola's death would not have occurred had her recommendations for change been implemented in full. See A. Coleman, 'Design Disadvantage in Southwark', *Dulwich Society Journal*, 2008. Retrieved from www.dulwichsociety.com/summer-2008/45-design-disadvantage-in-southwark, last accessed 3 October 2021.

54 *Damilola: The Boy Next Door*, directed by A. Francis Roy, film, Channel 4, UK, 28 October 2020.

55 See https://inews.co.uk/culture/yinka-bokinni-damilola-taylor-channel-4-documentary-north-peckham-estate-737397, last accessed 18 June 2021.

56 L. Glucksberg, '"The Blue Bit, that Was My Bedroom": Rubble, Displacement and Regeneration in Inner-City London', in P. Wall and P. Smets (eds), *Social Housing and Urban Renewal: A Cross-National Perspective*, Bingley, Emerald Publishing Limited, 2017, pp 69–103.

57 I would recommend reading both Glucksberg's chapter and Lees and Hubbard's journal article (see note 58 below) to understand more about this.

58 L. Lees and P. Hubbard, '"So, Don't You Want Us Here No More?" Slow Violence, Frustrated Hope, and Racialized Struggle on London's Council Estates', *Housing, Theory and Society* (2021), pp 1–18. Retrieved from https://doi.org/10.1080/14036096.2021.1959392.

59 From the very beginning, the Gloucester Grove Estate was known to be under-occupied, with single people frequently being placed in flats designed for families. Arguably some of the problems of the estate might be traced back to housing policies that led to such under-occupation and hence a disproportionate number of young, single residents on the estate.

60 'Cost of Mismanagement', p.10.

61 *Inquiry: The Great British Housing Disaster*, video, directed by A. Curtis, UK, 1984.

62 For example, the notorious Ronan Point disaster had already happened in 1968.

63 See https://nonstandardhouse.com/industrialised-non-traditional-house-list-by-system-name-england-wales/.

64 This figure of 1,100 dwellings using the GLE System was provided by Kenneth Campbell as part of his evidence given to the Scrutiny Panel and is held in the London Metropolitan Archives, GLC/DG/AR/17/007.

65 'Watch Out – There's an Artist About', *Building Design*, no.492 (18 April 1980), pp 34–7.

66 Tetris is an early computer game in which differently shaped blocks are stacked together with as few gaps as possible; the analogy with the scissor flats is quite apt since part of their aim was reducing 'dead' gaps of circulation space. Nintendo of America, *Tetris*, Redmond, WA, Nintendo of America, 1989.

67 Hanley, *Estates*, p.202.

68 Croft, 'Caleb Femi sees poetry in life, death and the built environment'.

9 Elm Village (1984)

1 Architects' salaries, and especially assistant architects' salaries, are lower than non-

architects tend to think they must be – they are generally about the same as a schoolteacher, which in London is not particularly high. See RIBA Jobs Salary Guide 2021 and https://getintoteaching.education.gov.uk/salaries-and-benefits).

2   Also helped by the exceptionally high U-values, for the time, of the house's external walls: they were 0.35 W/m^2K.

3   In fact, I might even go as far as to say that without the security and relatively low cost of living in Blakeney Close, I doubt I would have returned to study to do a PhD in the mid-1990s and my career would have been quite different.

4   Camden History Society, 'Newsletter of the Camden History Society', no.37, September 1976, p.4.

5   980 residents attended the meetings. The focus of their concerns is described in N. Cairns, 'Environmental Perception, Public Participation and Urban Planning in the London Borough of Camden', PhD diss., University of Glasgow, 1981.

6   See London Borough of Camden, *A Plan for Camden: Written Statement: Summary of Policies*, London Borough of Camden, Department of Planning and Communications, September 1976.

7   A timeline of the process for producing the 'Plan for Camden' is shown in Figure 10.2, 'Timetable of Events Leading to Camden's District Plan', in Cairns, 'Environmental Perception'.

8   B. Latham, 'Meeting the Challenge', *Camden New Journal*, 4 August 1984.

9   In 1997, the United Kingdom Housing Trust became absorbed into another housing association, the North British Housing Association, and in 1999 they merged with

the Bristol Churches Housing Association to become Places for People.

10 According to the architect Peter Mishcon, the initial brief was for housing on just one part of the site with a giant supermarket and associated car parking on the other part, but after UKHT won the bid, the brief changed. Peter Mishcon suggests that 'clearly there was some pushback by local residents and councillors and the hypermarket component fell by the wayside and private/market housing was substituted'. P. Mishcon, private correspondence, 29 July 2021.

11 United Kingdom Housing Trust Limited, Halifax Building Society and Nationwide Building Society, 'The Story of Elm Village', *Housing Review*, vol.34, no.2 (1985), pp 46–8.

12 The number of dwellings varies depending on the source, and the current Elm Village Tenants & Residents Association describes Elm Village as consisting of 150 dwellings (see www.evtra.org.uk/about/); however, 162 is the most accurate figure I can establish and therefore I assume that the Elm Village Tenants & Residents Association is not, for some reason, counting the 12 flats on the corner of St Pancras Way.

13 Source: Census 2001, Census 2011, Housing Flows Reconciliation, the Greater London Authority and Regional Assembly joint returns. Data from DCLG, Table 125.

14 G. Darley, 'Elm Village – a view of the future', *Financial Times*, 4 January 1985.

15 A decision clearly disliked by Patrick Hannay in his article for the *Architects' Journal* in which he questions 'the motivation for such variety' and hypothesised that it was possibly due to 'internal paranoia in the profession, exaggerated by a misconceived over-reaction to some earlier atrocities in social housing'.

NOTES

See P. Hannay, 'Private Gain, Public Loss', *Architects' Journal*, 3 October 1984.

16 The cost and specification for the soft landscaping were particularly unusual at the time, with £8,000 per acre spent on the planting. See A.T. Williams, 'Elm Village', *Building*, vol.247, no.47 (1984), p.40.

17 United Kingdom Housing Trust Limited, Halifax Building Society and Nationwide Building Society, 'The Story of Elm Village'.

18 Hannay, 'Private Gain, Public Loss'.

19 'Table 101: by tenure, United Kingdom (historical series)'. Retrieved from www.gov.uk/government/statistical-data-sets/live-tables-on-dwelling-stock-including-vacants.

20 Adapted from a table in United Kingdom Housing Trust Limited, Halifax Building Society and Nationwide Building Society, 'The Story of Elm Village'.

21 P. Malpass, 'The Uneven Development of "Social Rented Housing": Explaining the Historically Marginal Position of Housing Associations in Britain', *Housing Studies*, vol.16, no.2 (2001), pp 225–42.

22 P. Malpass, 'The Discontinuous History of Housing Associations in England', *Housing Studies*, vol.15, no.2 (2000), pp 195–212.

23 Department of Environment, *Housing: The Government's Proposals*, Cmd 214, London, HMSO, 1987.

24 P. Malpass, 'Housing Associations and Housing Policy in Britain since 1989', *Housing Studies*, vol.14, no.6 (1999), pp 881–93.

25 Malpass, 'Discontinuous History', pp 195–212.

26 New Journal Reporter, 'When the "hammer hands" put life into the Elm Village', *Camden New Journal*, 4 August 1984.

27 See www.evtra.org.uk/about/.

28 Anon., personal communication, 6 October 2021.

29 My entire house (both floors) in Elm Village was around 80 per cent of my master bedroom in my Priestpopple house.

30 And when Elm Village was built, its room sizes were even 10 per cent smaller than the Parker Morris room standards from the 1960s, according to Williams, 'Elm Village', p.39.

31 These figures are from a 2018 report by LABC Labs. Retrieved from www.labc.co.uk/news/what-average-house-size-uk?language_content_entity=cy. Unfortunately, data was only available on master bedroom sizes and did not cover all bedrooms, although the average number of bedrooms per house has also reduced from 3.58 bedrooms in the 1980s to 2.95 bedrooms in 2018.

32 See www.architecture.com/explore-architecture/postmodernism.

33 Hannay, 'Private Gain, Public Loss'.

34 P. Mishcon, personal communication, 3 August 2021.

35 M. Brookes, personal communication, 8 September 2021.

36 J. Broome, 'The Segal Method [Timber-frame Construction]', *Architects' Journal*, vol.184, no.35 (1986), pp 31–68.

37 See www.segalselfbuild.co.uk/projects/waltersway,lewis.html.

38 Currently, with improvements in offsite manufacturing of structural insulated panels, U-values of almost 0.10W/m^{2}K are achievable.

39 Williams, 'Elm Village', p.40.

Bibliography

Ackerman, J. 'The Villa as Paradigm', *Perspecta*, vol.22 (1986), pp 10–31.

Ackerman, J. *The Villa: Form and Ideology of Country Houses*, Princeton, NJ, Princeton University Press, 1990.

'A Note on Lord Trenchard's Report and the Government White Paper', *The Police Journal*, vol.6, no.3 (1933), pp 295–307. Retrieved from https://doi.org/10.1177/0032258X3300600304.

Anson, B. 'Don't Shoot the Graffiti Man', *Architects' Journal*, vol.184, no.27 (1986), pp 16–17.

Archer, I. *The Haberdashers' Company in the Later Twentieth Century*, Chichester, Phillimore & Co., 2004.

Archer, I. *The History of the Haberdashers' Company*, Chichester, Phillimore & Co., 1991.

Architecture.com. 'Astley Castle, Warwickshire'. Retrieved from www.architecture.com/awards-and-competitions-landing-page/awards/riba-stirling-prize/astley-castle-warwickshire.

Arnold, D. *The Georgian Villa*, Stroud, Sutton Publishing, 1998.

Ayto, J., I. Crofton and P. Cavill. *Brewer's Britain and Ireland: The History, Culture, Folklore and Etymology of 7500 Places in these Islands*, London, Weidenfeld & Nicholson, 2005.

Barley, M.W. 'The Use of Upper Floors in Rural Houses', *Vernacular Architecture*, vol.22, no.1 (1991), pp 20–23.

Barnett, C. *The Lost Victory: British Dreams, British Realities, 1945–1950*, London, Pan Macmillan, 1995.

Bates, A. 'Hexham's Leather Heritage', *Hexham Historian*, Hexham Local History Society, vol.22 (2012), pp 3–29.

'Behind the Scenes at County Hall', *Building Design*, no.326 (1976), pp 14–15.

Bennison, B.R. 'The Brewing Trade in North East England, 1869–1939', PhD thesis, University of Newcastle upon Tyne, Newcastle upon Tyne, 1992. Retrieved from https://theses.ncl.ac.uk/jspui/bitstream/10443/199/1/bennison92.pdf.

'Bethnal Green: Building and Social Conditions from 1876 to 1914', in T.F.T Baker (ed.), *A History of the County of Middlesex: Volume 11, Stepney, Bethnal Green*, London, Victoria County History, 1998, pp 126–32. Retrieved from British History Onine, www.british-history.ac.uk/vch/middx/vol11/pp126–132, last accessed 27 May 2021.

Booth, R. 'Damilola: Could Better Design Have Saved His Life?', *Architects' Journal*, vol.212, no.1 (7 December 2000), p.14.

Boughton, J. *Municipal Dreams: The Rise and Fall of Council Housing*, London, Verso Books, 2018.

British Brick Society. *The Story of Brick*, Sigglesthorne, Hull, British Brick Society, 1976 (repr. 2001).

Brittain-Catlin, T. *The Edwardians and their Houses: The New Life of Old England*, London, Lund Humphries, 2020.

Brodie, A. et al., British Architectural Library and Royal Institute of British Architects. *Directory of British Architects 1834–1914*, 2 vols, London, Continuum, 2001.

BIBLIOGRAPHY

Broome, J. 'The Segal Method [Timber-frame Construction]', *Architects' Journal*, vol.184, no.35 (1986), pp 31–68.

Burman, P., and D. Rodwell. 'The Contribution of the United Kingdom to European Architectural Heritage Year 1975', *Monumenta*, vol.3 (2015), pp 262–75.

Burnett, J. *A Social History of Housing, 1815–1985, Volume 228*, London, Methuen, 1986.

Burton Overy History Group. *Aspects of Burton Overy*, Market Harborough, Troubadour Publishing Ltd, 2000.

Cairns, N. 'Environmental Perception, Public Participation and Urban Planning in the London Borough of Camden', PhD diss., University of Glasgow, 1981.

Camden History Society, 'Newsletter of the Camden History Society', no.37, September 1976, p.4.

Carter, M. *The Archaeological Investigation of a Seventeenth-century Blacksmith Shop at Ferryland, Newfoundland*, PhD diss., Memorial University of Newfoundland, 1997.

Chadwick, E. *Report on the Sanitary Condition of the Labouring Population of Great Britain: Supplementary Report on the Results of Special Inquiry into the Practice of Interment in Towns (Vol. 2)*, London, HMSO, 1843.

Chatterjee, A. 'Between Colour and Pattern: Ruskin's Ambivalent Theory of Constructional Polychromy', *Interstices: Journal of Architecture and Related Arts*, vol.18 (2017), pp 11–18.

Citizensadvice.org.uk. 'History of the Citizens Advice Service', 2021. Retrieved from www. citizensadvice.org.uk/about-us/about-us1/ history-of-the-citizens-advice-service/.

City of London Livery Companies Commission. 'Report on the Charities of the Haberdashers' Company: Appendix', in *City of London Livery Companies Commission. Report; Volume 4.*

London, Eyre and Spottiswoode, 1884, pp 478–86. Retrieved from British History Online, www.british-history.ac.uk/livery-companies-commission/vol4/pp478–48, last accessed 26 May 2021.

Coleman, A. 'Design Disadvantage in Southwark', *Dulwich Society Journal*, 2008. Retrieved from www.dulwichsociety.com/summer-2008/45-design-disadvantage-in-southwark, last accessed 3 October 2021.

Coleman, A., S. Brown, L. Cottle, P. Marshall and C. Redknap. *Utopia on Trial: Vision and Reality in Planned Housing*, London, Hilary Shipman Ltd, 1985.

'Coleman's Prescription', *Building Design*, no.801, (22 August 1986), p.5.

Coles, J. 'Is there life in Peckham?', *The Spectator*, 3 July 1987.

Cowan, D., H. Carr and A. Wallace. '"Thank heavens for the lease": Histories of Shared Ownership', *Housing Studies*, vol.33, no.6 (2018), pp 855–75.

Cox, A. 'Brick and Tilemaking in the Nuneaton Area', British Brick Society, *Information*, vol.114 (2010), pp 11–23.

Croft, C. 'Caleb Femi sees poetry in life, death and the built environment', *RIBA Journal*, 8 June 2021. Retrieved from www.ribaj.com/products/ caleb-femi-on-life-death-and-the-built-environment-north-peckham-estate.

Croft, R.A., and D.C. Mynard. *The Changing Landscape of Milton Keynes*, Monograph Series No. 5, Milton Keynes, Buckinghamshire Archaeological Society, 1993.

Cromarty, H. *Shared Ownership (England): The Fourth Tenure?* Briefing Paper Number 08828, House of Commons Library, 12 November 2020.

Crowley, J.E. *The Invention of Comfort: Sensibilities and Design in Early Modern Britain and Early*

America, Baltimore, MD, Johns Hopkins University Press, 2003.

Cuming, E. '"Home is home be it never so homely": Reading Mid-Victorian Slum Interiors', *Journal of Victorian Culture*, vol.18, no.3 (2013), pp 368–86.

Curl, J.S. 'All Saints Margaret Street, London', *Architects' Journal*, vol.191, no.25 (1990), pp 36–55.

Curl, J.S. *The Life and Work of Henry Roberts, 1803–1876: The Evangelical Conscience and the Campaign for Model Housing and Healthy Nations*, Chichester, Phillimore & Co., 1983.

Dallison, M. 'Life in a Hexham Street: Priestpopple, Cattle Market, Battle Hill', in A. Rossiter (ed.), *Hexham Historian*, Hexham Local History Society, vol.10 (2000), pp 35–52.

Damilola: The Boy Next Door, directed by A. Francis-Roy, film, Channel 4, UK, 28 October 2020.

Darley, G. 'Elm Village – a view of the future', *Financial Times*, 4 January 1985.

Department of the Environment, *What Is Our Heritage? United Kingdom Achievements for European Architectural Heritage Year 1975: Photographs of Restorations and Improvements Done between 1972 and 1975*, London, HMSO, 1975.

Dunbar, R.I.M. 'Neocortex Size as a Constraint on Group Size in Primates', *Journal of Human Evolution*, vol.22, no.6 (1992), pp 469–93.

Edwards, J.C. *Bricks, Tiles and Terra Cotta Catalogue of Patterns*, Ruabon, 1903.

English Heritage. 'Strategic Stone Study: A Building Stone Atlas of Northumberland', 2012. Retrieved from www2.bgs.ac.uk/mineralsuk/download/EHCountyAtlases/Northumberland_Building_Stone_Atlas.pdf.

Evans, R. 'Rookeries and Model Dwellings', in *Translations from Drawing to Building and Other Essays*, London, Architectural Association, 1996, pp 94–117.

Farrell, T., and A.N. Furman. *Revisiting Postmodernism*, London, RIBA Publishing, 2019.

Femi, C. *Poor*, Harmondsworth, Penguin Books, 2020.

Fisher, J. 'Residential Domination at RIBA Regional Awards', *Building Design*, no.1236 (29 September 1995), p.6.

Flanders, J. *The Making of Home: The 500-year Story of How Our Houses Became Homes*, London, Atlantic Books Ltd, 2014.

'Former GLC Housing Architect Dies Aged 92', *Building*, 19 July 2002. Retrieved from www.building.co.uk/news/former-glc-housing-architect-dies-aged-92/1020146.article.

Forshaw, J.H., and P. Abercrombie. *County of London Plan*, London, Macmillan and Company Ltd, 1943.

Gans, H.J. *Popular Culture and High Culture: An Analysis and Evaluation of Taste*, New York, Basic Books, 1999.

Gatliff, C. 'On Improved Dwellings and Their Beneficial Effect on Health and Morals, with Suggestions for Their Extension', *Journal of the Statistical Society of London*, vol.38, no.1 (1875), pp 33–63.

Gerhold, D. 'London's Suburban Villas and Mansions, 1660–1830', *The London Journal*, vol.34, no.3 (2009), pp 233–63.

'GLC Architect Sir Roger Walters Opts for Early Retirement', *Building*, vol.234, no.7029 (24 March 1978), p.12.

'GLC Orders Inquiry into £7m Rise in Cost of Homes Scheme', *Building Design*, no.232 (10 January 1975), p.24.

Glucksberg, L. '"The Blue Bit, that Was My Bedroom": Rubble, Displacement and Regeneration in Inner-City London', in P. Wall and P. Smets (eds), *Social Housing and Urban Renewal: A Cross-National Perspective*, Bingley, Emerald Publishing Ltd, 2017, pp 69–103.

'Gower Street and its Reminiscences', *Temple Bar*, vol.97, no.386 (1893), pp 46–54.

Graham, T. 'Wattle and Daub', in M. Forsyth (ed.), *Materials and Skills for Historic Building Conservation*, Chichester, Wiley-Blackwell, 2008, pp 178–90.

Green, P.E., and V.R. Rao. 'Conjoint Measurement for Quantifying Judgmental Data', *Journal of Marketing Research*, vol.8 (1971), pp 355–63.

Hammond, P., and C. Hammond. *Life in an Eighteenth-Century Country House*, Stroud, Amberley Publishing, 2012.

Hanley, L. *Estates: An Intimate History*, London, Granta Books, 2012.

Hannay, P. 'Private Gain, Public Loss', *Architects' Journal*, 3 October 1984.

Harman, H. 'Renewable Energy Sources (Promotion)', *Hansard*, vol.92, 25 February 1986. Retrieved from https://hansard.parliament.uk/commons/1986-02-25/debates/f5f1f540-499d-4dc8-bbdc-440d91898e54/RenewableEnergySources(Promotion).

Harris, W. 'Gower Street and all that', *The Spectator*, 28 September 1951.

Hartman, H. 'Is This the Most Influential House in a Generation?', *Architects' Journal*, 30 January 2015. Retrieved from www.architectsjournal.co.uk/buildings/is-this-the-most-influential-house-in-a-generation.

Hayes, S., M. Jopling and R. Gul. 'What Have the Changes Made to Primary and Secondary Assessment Frameworks since 2014 Done to the "London Effect" in School Performance?', *London Review of Education*, vol.16, no.3 (2018), pp 491–506.

Heaven, B. 'Comeback on Coleman', *Architects' Journal*, vol.184, no.36 (1986), pp 32–3.

Hillier, B. 'City of Alice's Dreams', *Architects' Journal*, vol.9 (1986), pp 39–41.

Hoskins, W.G. 'The Rebuilding of Rural England, 1570–1640', *Past & Present*, vol.4, no.1 (1953), pp 44–59.

Housing Complaints, Award Winning Estate, *Thames News*, film, Thames Television, UK, https://youtu.be/ucChoG090Mg, 30 August 1983.

Howard Roberts, J.R., and W.H. Godfrey (eds). *Survey of London: Volume 21: The Parish of St Pancras Part 3: Tottenham Court Road and Neighbourhood*, London, London County Council, 1949.

Inquiry: The Great British Housing Disaster, video, directed by A. Curtis, UK, 1984.

International Council on Monuments and Sites (ICOMOS). 'European Charter of the Architectural Heritage', 1975. Retrieved from www.icomos.org/en/charters-and-texts/179-articles-en-francais/ressources/charters-and-standards/170-european-charter-of-the-architectural-heritage.

Jackson, N. 'Christ Church, Streatham, and the Rise of Constructional Polychromy', *Architectural History*, vol.43 (2000), pp 219–52.

Jenks, M. 'Housing Problems and the Dangers of Certainty', in T. Necdet, T.A. Markus and T. Woolley (eds), *Rehumanizing Housing*, London, Butterworth & Co. Publishers, 1988, pp 53–60.

Jensen, F. *The English Semi-Detached House: How and Why the Semi Became Britain's Most Popular House-Type*, Ellington, Ovolo Publishing Ltd, 2007.

Johnson, M.H. 'Rethinking the Great Rebuilding', *Oxford Journal of Archaeology*, vol.12, no.1 (1993), pp 117–25.

Jones, E., and C. Woodward. *A Guide to the Architecture of London*, London, Weidenfeld & Nicolson, 1992.

Jones, P. 'The Place of Design in English High-rise Flats During the Post-war Period', unpublished working paper, 2000.

Kerr, R. *The Gentleman's House: Or, How to Plan English Residences, from the Parsonage to the Palace; with Tables of Accommodation and Cost, and a Series of Selected Plans,* London, John Murray, 1865.

Lang, R. 'Architects Take Command: The LCC Architects' Department', *Volume*, no.41 (2014), p.24.

Latham, B. 'Meeting the Challenge', *Camden New Journal*, 4 August 1984.

Latham, D. *Creative Reuse of Buildings: Volume One*, London, Routledge, 2000.

Latham, D. *Creative Reuse of Buildings: Volume Two*, London, Routledge, 2000.

Lawrence, R. 'Police prepared to evacuate hundreds of sleeping families from their homes yesterday (Monday) as a blaze at a toy warehouse threatened to spread to three nearby gasometers', *Hackney Gazette*, 16 November 1982.

Lawrence, R.R., and T. Chris. *The Period House: Style, Detail and Decoration, 1774–1914*, London, Weidenfeld & Nicolson, 1996.

Lees, L., and P. Hubbard. '"So, Don't You Want Us Here No More?" Slow Violence, Frustrated Hope, and Racialized Struggle on London's Council Estates', *Housing, Theory and Society* (2021). Retrieved from https://doi.org/10.1080/14036096.2021.1959392.

Lofthouse, P. 'The Development of English Semi-Detached Dwellings during the Nineteenth Century', *Papers from the Institute of Archaeology*, vol.22 (2013), pp 83–98.

London Borough of Camden. *A Plan for Camden: The Environmental Code*, London Borough of Camden, Department of Planning and Communications, 1976.

London Borough of Camden. *A Plan for Camden: Written Statement: Summary of Policies*, London Borough of Camden, Department of Planning and Communications, September 1976.

London Borough of Camden. *A Plan for Camden: Written Statement: The Reason Why*, London Borough of Camden, Department of Planning and Communications, 1976.

Loudon, J.C. *An Encyclopaedia of Cottage, Farm, and Villa Architecture and Furniture, Etc.*, London, Longman, Orme, Brown, Green, & Longmans, and sold by John Weale, 1839 [1833].

Louw, H., and R. Crayford. 'A Constructional History of the Sash Window c. 1670–c. 1725 (Part 1)', *Architectural History*, vol.41 (1998), pp 82–130.

Louw, H., and R. Crayford. 'A Constructional History of the Sash Window, c. 1670–c. 1725 (Part 2)', *Architectural History*, vol.42 (1999), pp 173–239.

Louw, M., and S. Papanicolaou. *Buildings Reimagined: A Dialogue Between Old and New*, Melbourne, The Images Publishing Group, 2019.

Malpass, P. 'Histories of Social Housing: A Comparative Approach', in K. Scanlon, C. Whitehead and M. Fernández Arrigoitia (eds), *Social Housing in Europe*, Chichester, Wiley-Blackwell, 2014, pp 259–94.

Malpass, P. 'Housing Associations and Housing Policy in Britain since 1989', *Housing Studies*, vol.14, no.6 (1999), pp 881–93.

Malpass, P. 'The Discontinuous History of Housing Associations in England', *Housing Studies*, vol.15, no.2 (2000), pp 195–212.

Malpass, P. 'The Uneven Development of "Social Rented Housing": Explaining the Historically Marginal Position of Housing Associations in Britain', *Housing Studies*, vol.16, no.2 (2001), pp 225–42.

McNamara, M., and J. Hardi. *NRP Enterprise Centre – The Use of Local Timber Materials*, Norwich, University of East Anglia, Centre for the Built Environment, 2013.

McWhirr, A. 'Brickmaking in Leicestershire before 1710', *Transactions of the Leicestershire Archaeological and Historical Society*, vol.71 (1997), pp 37–59.

Middleton, C. *Picturesque and Architectural Views for Cottages, Farm Houses, and Country Villas*, Farnborough, Gregg International Publishers, 1972.

Ministry of Housing, Communities and Local Government (2021). *English Housing Survey 2019 to 2020: Headline Report*. Retrieved from www.gov.uk/government/statistics/english-housing-survey-2019-to-2020-headline-report, last accessed 11 October 2021.

Monnery, N. *Safe as Houses? A Historical Analysis of Property Prices*, London, London Publishing Partnership, 2011.

Morris, S. 'Estate "one of toughest in Europe"', *The Guardian*, 30 November 2000. Retrieved from www.theguardian.com/uk/2000/nov/30/ukcrime.stevenmorris.

Murray, P. *The Architecture of the Italian Renaissance*, London, Thames & Hudson, 1969.

Nenadic, S. 'Architect-Builders in London and Edinburgh, c.1750–1800, and the Market for Expertise', *The Historical Journal*, vol.55, no.3 (2012), pp 597–617.

New Journal Reporter. 'When the "hammer hands" put life into the Elm Village', *Camden New Journal*, 4 August 1984.

Parissien, S., and Georgian Group. *The Georgian Group Guides No 8. Ironwork. A Brief Guide to Georgian Ironwork*, London, Georgian Group, 1991.

Pearson, L.F. *British Breweries: An Architectural History*, London, Bloomsbury Publishing, 1999.

Pearson, L.F. *Built to Brew: The History and Heritage of the Brewery*, Swindon, English Heritage, 2014.

Pearson, L.F. *Tile Gazetteer: A Guide to British Tile and Architectural Ceramics Locations*, Tiles and Architectural Ceramics Society, Ilminster, Richard Dennis, 2005.

Petegorsky, D.W. 'Class Forces in the English Civil War', *Science & Society*, vol.6, no.2 (1942), pp 111–32.

Peter Mishcon and Associates. 'Architect's Report', *Building*, vol.247, no.47 (1984), pp 41–2.

Pigot & Co., *Pigot & Co's Trade Directory for Northumberland*, 1834. Retrieved from https://communities.northumberland.gov.uk/005092FS.htm.

Piveteau, E., and C. Wietzel. *Lofts: A Style of Living*, Sutton, Silverback Books, 2004.

Platt, C. *The Great Rebuildings of Tudor and Stuart England: Revolutions in Architectural Taste*, London, Routledge, 2013.

Raine, J. *The Priory of Hexham, its Title Deeds, Black book, etc.*, Durham [Eng.] Pub. for the Society by Andrews and Co., 1864.

Rayner, A. 'Gentrification's ground zero: the rise and fall of Hoxton Square', *The Guardian*, 14 March 2018. Retrieved from www.theguardian.com/cities/2018/mar/14/hoxton-square-london-shoreditch-aviva-gentrification-yba-damien-hirst#comment-113524183.

Reeves, P. *Affordable and Social Housing: Policy and Practice*, London, Routledge, 2013.

'RIBA Regional Awards', *Architects' Journal* (28 September 1995), pp 10–11.

Richards, J.M. *A Miniature History of the English House*, London, The Architectural Press, 1938.

Riley, W.E. and L. Gomme (eds). *Survey of London: Volume 5, St Giles-in-The-Fields, Pt II*, London, 1914, pp 42–58. Retrieved from British History

Online, www.british-history.ac.uk/survey-london/vol5/pt2/pp42-58.

Roberts, H. *The Dwellings of the Labouring Classes, Their Arrangement and Construction; Illustrated by a Reference to the Model Houses of the Society for Improving the Condition of the Labouring Classes, with Other Buildings Recently Erected: and an Appendix Containing H.R.H. Prince Albert's Exhibition Model Houses, Hyde Park, 1851; the Model Cottages &c. Built by the Windsor Royal Society: With Plans and Elevations of Dwellings Adapted to Towns, as well as to Agricultural and Manufacturing Districts*, London, Society for Improving the Condition of Labouring Classes, 1851.

Rothermel, R. 'Long-Term Solutions', Letters, *Architects' Journal*, vol.187, no.1 (6 January 1988), p.16.

Rowe, C. *The Mathematics of the Ideal Villa and Other Essays*, Boston, MA, MIT Press, 1982.

Ruskin, J. *The Seven Lamps of Architecture*, 1849. Retrieved from www.lancaster.ac.uk/media/lancaster-university/content-assets/documents/ruskin/8SevenLampsof Architecture.pdf.

Ruskin, J. *The Stones of Venice* (3 vols), 1851. Retrieved from www.lancaster.ac.uk/media/lancaster-university/content-assets/documents/ruskin/9-11StonesofVenice.pdf.

Sadler, A. 'Victorian Commemorative Plaques', *Leicestershire Historian*, vol.35 (1999), pp 1–2.

Santos, H.C., M.E. Varnum and I. Grossmann. 'Global Increases in Individualism', *Psychological Science*, vol.28, no.9 (2017), 1228–39.

Service, A. *Edwardian Architecture: A Handbook to Building Design in Britain: 1890–1914*, Oxford, Oxford University Press, 1977.

Sims, J. 'Design Decade: 1980s', *Financial Times*, 17 May 2008.

Smith, J.T. 'The Evolution of the English Peasant House to the Late Seventeenth Century: The Evidence of Buildings', *Journal of the British Archaeological Association*, vol.33, no.1 (1970), pp 122–47.

Smith, S. 'Ditchwater', *Urbannarrative*, n.d. Retrieved from www.urbannarrative.com/DITCHWATER.

Spicker, P. 'Poverty and Depressed Estates: A Critique of Utopia on Trial', *Housing Studies*, vol.2, no.4 (1987), pp 283–92.

Stewart, J. *The Stable Book; Being a Treatise on the Management of Horses, in Relation to Stabling, Grooming, Feeding, Watering and Working. Construction of Stables, Ventilation, Stable Appendages, Management of the Feet. Management of Diseases and Defective Horses*, New York, C.M. Saxton & Co., 1856.

Stobart, J. '"So agreeable and suitable a place": The Character, Use and Provisioning of a Late Eighteenth-Century Suburban Villa', *Journal for Eighteenth-Century Studies*, vol.39, no.1 (2016), pp 89–102.

Stratton, M.J. 'The Manufacture and Utilisation of Architectural Terracotta and Faience', PhD diss., Birmingham, Aston University, 1983.

Street, G.E. *Brick and Marble in the Middle Ages: Notes of Tours in the North of Italy*, 1855. Retrieved from www.gutenberg.org/files/46326/46326-h/46326-h.htm.

Summerson, J. *Georgian London*, Harmondsworth, Penguin Books, 1978.

Summerson, J. 'The Idea of the Villa', *RSA Journal*, vol.107, no.5036 (1959), p.570.

Swallow, B. 'Campbell's Kingdom', *Building Design*, no.96 (7 April 1972), p.6.

Tarn, J.N. *Five Percent Philanthropy: An Account of Housing in Urban Areas between 1840 and 1914*, Cambridge, Cambridge University Press, 1973.

BIBLIOGRAPHY

Tarn, J.N. 'The Improved Industrial Dwellings Company', *Transactions of the London and Middlesex Archaeological Society*, vol.22 (1968), pp 43–59.

'The Cost of Mismanagement', *Architects' Journal*, vol.162 (2 July 1975).

thestreetnames (n.d.). 'Cat and Mutton Bridge'. Retrieved from https://thestreetnames.com/tag/cat-and-mutton-bridge/, last accessed 22 August 2021.

Till, J., and S. Wigglesworth. 'The Straw House and Quilted Office, 9–10 Stock Orchard Street, Islington, London', *Architectural Design*, vol.76, no.6 (2006), p.27.

Towers, G. *Shelter Is Not Enough: Transforming Multi-storey Housing*, Bristol, Policy Press, 2000.

UCL Bloomsbury Project (n.d.). Retrieved from www.ucl.ac.uk/bloomsbury-project/streets/gower_street.htm, last accessed 28 October 2021.

United Kingdom Housing Trust Limited, Halifax Building Society and Nationwide Building Society. 'The Story of Elm Village', *Housing Review*, vol.34, no.2 (1985), pp 46–8.

Uttley, A. *A Traveller in Time*, London, Faber & Faber, 1939.

'Walkways to Go in Five Year Plan', News, *Architects' Journal*, vol.187, no.3 (1988), p.11.

'Watch Out – There's an Artist About', *Building Design*, no.492 (18 April 1980), pp 34–7.

Watson, I. 'The First Generation of Flats', *Hackney History*, vol.11 (2005), pp 33–46.

Watt, K.A. 'Nineteenth Century Brickmaking Innovations in Britain: Building and Technological Change', PhD diss., University of York, 1990.

Williams, A.T. 'Elm Village', *Building*, vol.247, no.47 (1984), p.40.

Williams, W.M. *The Sociology of an English Village: Gosforth*, London, Routledge, 2013.

Wilson, P. *The Modern Timber House in the UK: New Paradigms and Technologies*, Edinburgh, Arcamedia Ltd, 2017.

Wohl, A. *The Eternal Slum*, London, Edward Arnold, 1977.

Woodford, F.P. (ed.). *Streets of Bloomsbury and Fitzrovia: A Survey of Streets, Buildings and Former Residents in a Part of Camden*, London, Camden History Society, 1997.

Wood-Jones, R.B. *Traditional Domestic Architecture of the Banbury Region*, Manchester, Manchester University Press, 1963.

Wright, A.B. *An Essay Towards a History of Hexham in Three Parts: Illustrating its Ancient and its Present State, Civil and Ecclesiastical Economy, Antiquities and Statistics, with Descriptive Sketches of the Scenery and Natural History of the Neighbourhood*, Alnwick, W. Davison, 1823.

Yorke, T. *Georgian and Regency Houses Explained*, England's Living History, Newbury, Countryside Books, 2007.

Zukin, S. *Loft Living: Culture and Capital in Urban Change*, New Brunswick, NJ, Rutgers University Press, 1989.

Index

Note: *italic* page numbers indicate figures; numbers containing n. refer to notes.

Acts of Parliament
  Civic Amenities Act (1967) 54
  Housing Acts (1961 and 1980)
    193, 194
  Landlord and Tenant Act
    (1985) 144
  London Building Act (1894)
    128
  Metropolitan Police Act
    (1933) 144
  New Towns Act (1946) 126
Adelaide Wharf 116, *117*
Allford Hall Monaghan Morris
  116, *117*
architectural awards
  Building Magazine's Housing
    Project of The Year 116
  Housing Centre Trust
    Golden Jubilee Award 189
  RIBA House of the Year 92
  Stirling Prize 56, 74
architectural styles
  Brutalist 10, 12, 174
  classical 63, 88, 90, 96, *200*,
    201
  Edwardian 10, 12, 115, 121–2,
    124, 127, 130, 132, 133–5,
    142, 151
  Georgian 10, 12, 59, 62–7,
    68–70, 91, 96, 130, 184–5,
    200

medieval 18–20, 29, 121, 122,
  142, 150, 167
neo-classical 72, 137, 184,
  200
postmodern 12, 115, 184–5,
  200–202
Regency 10, 12, 63, 83–7, *85*,
  90–92, 96, 114, 135
Victorian 12, 15, 63, 82, 93,
  124, 127, 130, 132, 134, 140,
  142, 145, 146, 150, 151, 153
Architype 35
Astley Castle 56

Beddington Zero Energy
  Development 73–4
blacksmith 15, 22–4, 43
block
  scissor *see* scissor flat
  slab 160, 167, 221 n.33
  spine 166–7
  stair/stair tower 170, *176–7*,
    164
Bloomsbury
  streets 65, 66, *66*, 70, 73
  see also Georgian London;
    Russell family; University
    College London
bomb damage 103, 106, 107, 162,
  220 n.6
  see also maps

Boughton, John 10, 169, 222 n.47
brick/s
  cladding 13, 117, 179, 203
  colour of 74–5, 130, 147,
    150–51, 179, 201
  infill panel 19, 28, 30, *31*, 32
  manufacture of 30, 208 n.14
  nogging 30, *31*, 32
  shaped/moulded 131–2, *131*,
    216 n.9
  soot-blackened 62, 75
  stock 13, *60*, 74–5, 111, 150, 179
  string course 122, *123*, 131, *131*
  transportation of 32
builders
  contractors/sub-contractors
    12, 62, 65–6, 130, 179
  speculative *see* speculative
    development
building
  boom 19, 62–4, 72
  problems
    asbestos 78, 92–3, 212 n.1
    dampness 15, 56–7, 77–8
    fire 33, 56, 70, 106–8, *107*,
      114–15, 170
    movement/subsidence 77, 78
    rot 77, 78
    woodworm 77, 78
  specifications 62, 127, *128*,
    130, 132, 225 n.16

234

INDEX

Burgess Park 157, 160, 161, 162, *166*, 167, 174, *175*
Burton Overy 15, 22, 24, 30, 167, 221 n.31

Campbell, Kenneth John 12, 165, 223 n.64
canal
  basin
    Limehouse 100, *117*
    Paddington 100, *117*, 115
    Wenlock 116
  boats 96
  bridges *98–9*, *102*, 109, 215 n.18
  Grand Surrey 161–2
  Regent's 95, 96, 97, *98–9*, 100, 106, *110*, 111, 115–17, *118*, 119, 201
  warehouses *see* industrial/ utilitarian buildings
  wharves 100, 101, 116, 117, 161
ceilings 21, 96, 97, 109
charitable organisations 142, 143, 145, 194
chimney/fireplace 17, 20–21, 32, 59, *60*, 77, 78, 83, 93, 124, 127, 128, 130, 137
class
  artisan 10, 11
  middle 23, 24, 67, 92, 125, 134, 152, 212 n.21
  structure 23–4
  upper 63, 70, 90, 91
  working/labouring 19, 23, 108, 125, 143, 145, 152
coach
  house 70, 79, *84*, *86*, 87, 93, 213–14 n.15

stables *see* industrial/ utilitarian buildings
Coach and Horses Inn, Hexham 44, *44*, 45, 48, *50*
Coleman, Alice 169–70, 223 n.53
concrete 13, 87, 179, 201, 223 n.64
cottage
  thatched 23, 32–4
  see also fibre-based building materials
council houses 10, 147, 152, 180, 193
Cube, the 116, *117*

Darton, William 100, 214–15 n.3
Darwen & Company, J.S. 103, 107
decanting, the process of 171
decorative features
  arch *40*, 54, *60*, 79, 147, *148*, *200*, 209 n.2
  column 88, *89*, 114, *200*, 214 n.17
  corbel *200*
  cornice 71, 83, 131, 132, 216 n.9
  entablature 72, *81*, 213 n.13
  finial 122, *123*, 124, 131, *131*
  frieze *81*, 213 n.13
  moulding/s 13, 59, *60*, 77, 122, *123*, 131, *131*, 216 n.9
  pediment 72, *200*
  pilaster 72, 200, *200*
density 74, 117, 152, 188–9, 202
Dobson, John 82, 213 n.11
door
  French windows 96, 125, 127
  front 15, 28, 45, 51, 72, 125, 127, 128, 137, *148*, 172
  porch 122, 124, 127, *128*
  secret 39

trap 39, 41, 48, *50*
wicket 39, 43
Duckworth, George H. 100–102

earth
  -based building materials
    clay 32, 36
    daub *see* wattle and daub
    dung 36, 19
    see also terracotta
  floors 210 n.17
East End Dwellings Company 146
Edward VII
  coronation of 125, 131, *131*, 132
  period *see* periods, historic
  semi-detached house *see* residential buildings
Edwards, J.C. 133, 216 n.14
Elm Village Tenants & Residents Association 195, 224 n.12
European Architectural Heritage Year (1975) 54–5

Farrell, Terry 115, 116, 200, 201, 202
  postmodernism *see* architectural styles
  see also TV-am building
Femi, Caleb 164, 168, 181, 220 n.15
fibre-based building materials
  hemp 36
  reinforcement, as 88
  straw 34–5, 36
  thatch/ed
    fire-risk 16
    insurance 33, 34
    roof 15, 19, *28*, 30, 36
    walls 35–6

235

LIVING IN HOUSES

fire
event 56, 70, 106–7, 107
fireplace *see* chimney/
fireplace
protection against 114–15
risk of 33, 170
First World War 12, 124, 125, 142,
146, 151, 152, 194
former residents of the
Gloucester Grove Estate 164
Four Per Cent Industrial
Dwellings Company 146,
219 n.25
frontage 32, 65, 68, 70

garden village *see* New Town
Movement
gasometers 106, 109, *117, 118,*
119
Georgian 12, 59, 62, 68, 69, 72–3,
91, 96, 130, 200
growth *see* building boom
London 62–7, 72, 184, 185
neo- 72, 137, 184, 185, 200,
200
glass
stained/coloured *123,* 124,
127, 135, 213 n.3
GLC *see* Greater London
Council
GLC Department of
Architecture and Civic
Design 12, 165, 223 n.64
Gleeson, M.J. 179, 223 n.64
Gower
Leveson-Gower, Gertrude
64–5
Street 62, 64–5, *66,* 70
Street houses *61,* 65, 67, *68*
see also Bloomsbury

Grand Tour 63, 65, 90, 150,
211 n.12, 219 n.30
Great Fire of London (1666) 70
Great Rebuilding, the 19–22,
24, 62
Greater London Council 12,
164–6, 167, 172, 174, 179, 180,
221 n.26
Grimshaw, Nicholas 73, 115

Haberdashers' (Livery)
Company *see* Worshipful
Company of Haberdashers
142–5, 152
Hanley, Lynsey 164, 180
Harman, Harriet 170
Head, Charles 79, 82, 83, 92,
213 n.3, 213 n.5, 213 n.12
heating or lack of
central heating 205
cold in winter 15, 17
underfloor 54, 210 n.17
woodburning stove 17, 51,
87
see also insulation
heritage
building listing 56, 73, 119,
149
conservation areas 54
restoration 55, 78, *89,* 93
scheduled ancient
monument 79, 122
see also European
Architectural Heritage
Year (1975)
Hexham Old Brewery 45,
209 n.12
Hillier, Bill 169, 222 n.41
Hoskins, William George 19–20,
21, 23

house price crash (1989) 95,
106, 107
housing associations 13, 117,
183, 186, 189, 192, 193, 194–5
Hoxton 140, 142, 145, 154, 217 n.4

indoor space
attic 22, 67, 70
basement/semi-basement
51, 57, 59, 62, 67, 69, 70, 79,
83, 87, 109
bathroom 43, 45, 51, 87, 111,
130, 137, 149, 174
bedroom 17, 21, 36, 39, *41,* 41,
43, 51, 53, 59, 78, 111, 134, 137,
148, 149, 153, 172, 174, 198
cellar/wine cellar 48, 70, 87,
209 n.8, 210 n.17
coach house 70, 79, *84, 86,*
87, 93, 213–14 n.15
corridor/passage 22, 29, 148,
160, 172, 174, *175*
dining room 17, 83, 93, 128
entrance hall/hallway 28, 51,
83, 109, 111, 127, 128, 172–3,
197
hayloft *86,* 87, 213–14 n.15
kitchen 21, 22, 29, 51, 57,
59, 69, *69,* 70, 83, 87, 109,
111, 127, 130, 137, 149, 161,
173–4, 197, 21
landing 29, 53, 148, 174, 180
library/study 69, 83
living room/sitting room 17,
41, 43, 45, 51, 96, *97,* 109,
111, 119, 122, 125, 128, 130,
137, 149, 161, 173, 174, 197
pantry/buttery 22, 26, 29, 70
parlour 21, 22, 28, 83, 127–8,
135

236

INDEX

porch 122, 124, 127, *128*

scullery 70, 87, 130

store/storage room 15, 17, 22, 29, 49, 51, 111, 161, 197, 198

industrial/utilitarian buildings

barn 20, 55, 79, 213 n.2

brewery 44–5, 48, 108, 209 n.10, 209 n.12

bridge *98*, *102*, 109, 111, 121, 215 n.18

factory 95, 96, 102, 103, 106–7, 114, 117

mill 101, 209 n.10

stables/mews 17, 26, 29, 55, 59, 70, 87, 184, 213–14 n.15

warehouse 10, 11, 49, 54, 55, 95, 96, *98–9*, 100, 101, 102–3, 106–8, 114–15, 115–17, 209 n.10

workshop 29, *42*, 43, 45, 49, 51

institutional/civic buildings

museum 64, 130, 133

railway station 55, 119, 121, 127, 137, 184, 186

school 125, 131, 166

insulation

properties 34, 35, 36, 70, 93, 203, 204–5, 205–6

sound 54, 206

U-value of 205, 224 n.2, 225 n.38

investment/rate of return 213 n.10, 219 n.25

iron

cast 51, 111, 114, 119, 124, 127, 128, 137, 149

fireplace 128, 137

railings *60*, 69, 111, 137, 149, 154

structural 111–14

window fasteners 122, 124

wrought/decorative 111, 122

Jackson, R. 12, 166, 221 n.26

Jones, Inigo 90, 96

Joseph Rowntree Trusts 134, 135

King's Cross gasholders

apartments 117, 119

labouring classes *see* Class

lath and plaster 13, 19, 88–90, *89*

Latham, Derek 54, 55

LCC *see* London County Council

Le Corbusier 92, 214 n.25

loft/s

artists 108

culture 115

history of 108–9

yuppies 109

see also industrial/utilitarian buildings; Zukin, Sharon

London Borough of

Camden 185–6, 189, 195

Lewisham 204

Southwark 157, 160, 162, 169, 171

London County Council 65, 103, 152, 164, 165, 174, 219 n.37, 220 n.13

long house vs the hall 20–22

Lourie, Serge 165, 221 n.25

Malpass, Peter 145, 146, 194, 195

maps

Cary's New And Accurate Plan Of London And Westminster, 1795 66, *66*

London County Council

Bomb Damage Maps 1939–1945 103–6, 220 n.6

map of London 1817, by William Darton 100, 214 n.3

Ordnance Survey 44, *44*, 45, 82, *187*

plan of Hexham 1826, by John Wood 44, 79, *80*, 209 n.13

William Booth's 100–102

Maunder Taylor, Christopher 143, 144

mercantile buildings

shop/retail 49, 77, 125

warehouse 49, 95, 96, 100, 101, 102–8, 114–15, 115–19

metal

iron *see* iron

steel-frame 13, 111, 114–15, 117

window shutters 43, 45

Metropolitan Police 140, 143–4, *144*, 152

Milton Keynes 121, 122, 125–6, 134, 183

Mishcon, Peter 12, 185, 186, 189, 200, 202, 224 n.10

mixed development 65, 74, 135

Model Dwelling Movement 145–7, *148*, 150, 152

New Town Movement 121, 122, 125–7

North Peckham Estate 157, 162, 166, 219 n.1, 222 n.38, 222 n.41

Oatley, James William 12, 165, 166

office/s 35, 77, 83

LIVING IN HOUSES

outdoor space
  airy 69, 70
  alley 45, 53
  balcony 51, 96, 111, 119, 173–4
  courtyard 39, *40*, 43, 45, 51, 70, 87, 143, 149, 154, 221 n.33
  field 30, 67, 121
  garden 15, 17, 26, 29, 41, 51, 53, 67, 70, 78, 83, 101, 117, 121, 125, 127, 134, 154, 161, *163*, 167, 170, 174, 183, 184, 197
  garth 79, *81*, 213 n.2
  park 157, 160, 161, 162, 167, 174, 218 n.17
  play area 167, 174, 180
  prospect of 79, *80*, 91, 122
  restorative effects of 154, 206
  square 64, 65, 211 n.14
  terrace/roof terrace 137, 148, 149, 154, *155*, 167, 174
  with planting 154, *155*, 184, 192, 225 n.16, *190*
ownership *see* tenure

Page, Robert 12, 143, 146, 152, 217 n.9, 219 n.37
Palladio, Andrea 90, 214 n.25
paper 103, 114
Peabody Trust 117, 146
periods, historic
  Edwardian 12, 115, *123*, 124, 127, 130, 132, 133–4, 142, 151
  Elizabethan 17, 21
  First World War 12, 124, 125, 142, 146, 151, 152, 194
  Georgian 12, 59, 62, 68, 69, 72–3, 91, 96, 130, 200
  medieval 18, 19, 20, 29, 121, 122, 142, 150, 167

Second World War 10, 12, 126, 162, 193, 194
  Tudor 21, 63, 82
  Victorian 12, 15, 63, 82, 93, 124, 127, 130, 134, 140, 142, 145, 146, 150, 151, 153, 162, 194, 201, 218 n.18, 219 n.36
Perronet House 174, 221 n.26
plaque, commemorative *123*, 124, 125, 131, *131*, 132–3, 216 n.14
plinth 28, *28*, 79
Pollard Thomas Edwards 117, *117*, 171
polychromy 150, 219 n.29
postmodernism
  examples of 12, 115, 184–5, 200–202
  see also Farrell, Terry
Prince Regent *see* Georgian
proportion 20, 69, 71, 72, 77, 90, 96, 97, 111, 137, 197, *197*

Quitman, Harold 144

Red Star Wharf 102–3, 106, 107, 114
Regency
  plan 83, *85*
  villa 90–91
  see also Georgian
residential buildings
  castle 56
  detached house 72, 81–2, 91, 92, 216–17 n.19
  flat/apartment 78, 95–7, 102, 106, 107, 108, 109–11, 114, 115, 135, 137, 140, 142, 143–5, 146, 147, 148–9, 150, 151, 152, 154, 157, 160–61,

169, 170, 171, 172, 173 174, 180, 189, 192, 216–17 n.19
  palace 69, 114, 212 n.22
  semi-detached house 121, 125, *126*, 127, 133–5, 161, 216–17 n.19
  studio flat 137
  terraced house 142, 161, 197, 216–17 n.19
  villa 90–91
retrofit 55–6
Roberts, Henry 145, 146, 147, *148*, 150, 218 n.19
roof
  bargeboards *123*, 124
  finials 122, *123*, 124, 131, *131*
  flat/terrace *see* outdoor space 137, 148, 149, 154, *155*, 167, 174
  mansard 109
  ridge tiles 122, 124, 131
  saw-tooth 117
Rothermel, Rolf 170
Royal Institute of British Architects 55, 56, 92, 171, 201
Ruskin, John 150, 219 n.32
Russell family 64–5, 211 n.12

Sadler, Arthur 132
scissor flat 161, 164, 174, *175*, 180, 221 n.26, 223 n.66
Second World War 10, 12, 126, 162, 193, 194
Segal, Walter 203–4
Society for Improving the Condition of the Labouring Classes 145, 218 n.19
sound *see* insulation, sound
speculative development 64–5, 82, 143

238

INDEX

stair/steps
  ladder 29, 210 n.18
  landing 29, 51–3, 148, 174
  ramp 39, 48
  steps 28, 51, 53, 69, 70
Stanley Brothers 132–3, *133*,
    216 n.16
Stewart, John 87, 213–14 n.15,
    214 n.16
Stock, Henry 143, 217 n.11
Stock, Henry William 143, 217 n.9
Stock Page & Stock 12, 143, 144,
    217 n.9, 217 n.11
stone
  ashlar 13, 53, 81
  breathability *see* moisture in
  limestone/lime 36, 53, 57, 88,
    93, 210 n.20
  marble 78, 83, 93, 151, 219 n.32
  moisture in 56–7
  sandstone 13, 53, 81, 210 n.19
Straw Bale House 35
Summerson, John 62, 63, 65, 66,
    73, 92
sustainability
  carbon 205, 207
  designing for 34, 36, 37, 55,
    73, 74, 135, 205, 207
  solar energy 185, 205

Taylor, Damilola 160, 171, 223 n.53
tenure
  owner-occupied 13, 95, 144,
    154, 192
  private rented 13, 19, 144, 172
  rented from housing
    association 13, 183, 189,
    192, 194, 195
  rented from local authorities
    13, 172

terracotta
  decorative 13, 130, 131, 132–3
  plaques *123*, 124, 125, 131, *131*,
    132–3, 216 n.14
  Ruabon 133
  string course 122, *123*, 131,
    131, 216 n.9
tiles 93, 124, 130, 131, 171
timber
  cross-laminated timber
    (CRT) 117, 205
  frame 203, 204
  panels 19, 30, 32, 35, 203,
    204
  structure 19, 30, 35, 117, 203,
    205
Tinker, Tim 162, 164, 220 n.11
trade directories 43, 48, 103,
    217 n.9
Trellick Tower 164, 174
TV-am building 201, 115, 116

UK Housing Trust 186, 189, 192,
    195, 224 n.10
University College London
    59, 67, 183, 210 n.1, 211 n.8,
    211 n.9, 211 n.17, 222 n.41
Unwin, Raymond 134

ventilation 34, 57
  see also stone, moisture in
vernacular 12, 18–22, 34, 36, 53,
    54, 55, 116, 202
Victoria, Queen 12, 15, 63, 82,
    93, 124, 127, 130, 132, 134, 140,
    142, 145, 146, 150, 151, 153 162,
    194, 201, 218 n.18, 219 n.36
  see also periods, historic
villa
  idea of the 90–91

suburb 91, 92
Villa Savoye 92, 214 n.25

wall/s
  finishes 28, 35, 53, 57, 62, 150,
    201, 203, 210 n.20
  gable 20, 21, 78, 82, 124
  parapet 70, 71, 82, 149
  party walls 72, 212 n.25
  thickness of 43, 53, 54
Walters, Sir Roger 165, 174,
    221 n.26
warehouse conversions 54, 55,
    95, 96, 115–19
Watson, Isobel 142, 143
wattle and daub 13, 28, 30, 32,
    35, 36, 88, 203
Wigglesworth, Gordon M. 34, 35
window/s
  bay *123*, 124, 128
  casement 71, *123*, 124, 127, 135
  fanlight 71
  fasteners 122, 124
  fixed glazing 71
  French 96, 125, 127
  horizontal sliding sash 30, 71
  recessing of 70–71, 128
  sash 30, 71–2, 77, 78, 200, *200*,
    212 n.23
  shutters 43, 45, 51
  stained-glass *123*, 124, 127,
    135, 213 n.3
Wohl, Anthony 146, 152
Wood-Jones, Raymond 22–3, 26, 29
Worshipful Company of
    Haberdashers 142, 143, 144,
    145, 152, 217 n.3, 217 n.4,
    217 n.11

Zukin, Sharon 108

Illustration Credits

1.1 Igor Olszewski; 1.2 Arnold Beardsmore; 1.3 Unknown; 1.4, 1.5, 1.6, 1.7, 1.8, 1.9, 1.10, 1.11 Ruth Dalton; 2.1 Igor Olszewski; 2.2, 2.3, 2.4, 2.5 Ruth Dalton; 2.6 © Crown Copyright. Ordnance Survey, *c.*1863–5; 2.7 Ruth Dalton; 2.8 Roger Higgins; 2.9, 2.10 Ruth Dalton; 3.1 Igor Olszewski; 3.2 Ruth Dalton; 3.3 Photo © Andy Stone; 3.4, 3.5 Ruth Dalton; 3.6 © The British Library Board; 3.7 Ruth Dalton; 3.8 Photo © Andy Stone; 4.1 Igor Olszewski; 4.2 Ruth Dalton and Northumberland Archives; 4.3, 4.4, 4.5, 4.6 Ruth Dalton; 4.7 Richards, 1938; 4.8 Ruth Dalton and Northumberland Archives; 4.9 Ruth Dalton; 4.10 Ruth Dalton and Northumberland Archives; 5.1 Igor Olszewski; 5.2 Ruth Dalton; 5.3 Photo © Andy Stone; 5.4 George Duckworth, in the public domain; 5.5 Image © London Metropolitan Archives (City of London); 5.6 Ruth Dalton; 5.7 Photo: Harry Austin; 5.8 Ruth Dalton; 5.9 Photo © Andy Stone; 5.10 Ruth Dalton; 5.11 Photo © Andy Stone; 6.1 Igor Olszewski; 6.2 Unknown; 6.3 Ruth Dalton; 6.4 Unknown; 6.5 Ruth Dalton; 6.6 Unknown architect; 6.7, 6.8 Ruth Dalton; 6.9 Unknown; 7.1 Igor Olszewski; 7.2 Photo © Andy Stone; 7.3, 7.4, 7.5, 7.6 Ruth Dalton; 7.7 Photo © Andy Stone; 7.8 Grace (Mengwei) Guo; 8.1 Igor Olszewski; 8.2, 8.3 Photo © Andy Stone; 8.4 Ruth Dalton; 8.5 Ruth Dalton and Emad Alyedreessy; 8.6 Unknown; 8.7, 8.8 Ruth Dalton; 9.1 Igor Olszewski; 9.2 Ruth Dalton; 9.3 Peter Mishcon; 9.4 Digimap © Crown Copyright. Ordnance Survey, *c.*1890; 9.5 Courtesy of the architect, Peter Mishcon; 9.6 Photo © Andy Stone; 9.7, 9.8, 9.9, 9.10 Ruth Dalton.